Westminster Press Books
by
Suzanne de Dietrich

God's Unfolding Purpose,
A Guide to the Study of the Bible

The Witnessing Community,
The Biblical Record of God's Purpose

GOD'S UNFOLDING PURPOSE

GOD'S UNFOLDING PURPOSE

A Guide to the Study of the Bible

by

SUZANNE DE LDIETRICH

Translated by Robert McAfee Brown
from the French, *Le Dessein de Dieu*

Philadelphia
THE WESTMINSTER PRESS

Translation of *Le Dessein de Dieu. Itinéraire Biblique*. Delachaux & Niestlé, Neuchatel, Switzerland, 1957

LIBRARY OF CONGRESS CATALOG CARD NO. 60–6169

PRINTED IN THE UNITED STATES OF AMERICA

CONTENTS

N OT only do we understand God only through Jesus Christ, but we understand ourselves only through Jesus Christ. We understand life and death only through Jesus Christ. Apart from Jesus Christ, what we know is neither our life nor our death, neither God nor ourselves.

Thus, without Scripture, which has Jesus Christ as its sole concern, we understand nothing, and we see nothing but obscurity and confusion in the nature of God and in our own nature.

— Pascal, *Pensées*, #547.

INTRODUCTION
By the Translator

Since its original publication in 1943, Suzanne de Dietrich's *Le Dessein de Dieu* has had a long and useful life in Europe (the present translation is made from the sixth edition). It has been used by hundreds of study groups, seminarians, and laymen, and has thus provided an untold number of people with a new way of understanding the Bible. The book itself grew out of many years of experience on the part of the author in leading Bible study groups, and many Americans who have studied at the Ecumenical Institute at Bossey, on Lake Geneva, have had the privilege of sharing in these.

I

There are at least two distinct ways in which this book can be profitably used by American readers. One group of readers will find it a helpful way of reacquainting themselves with the over-all sweep of the Biblical drama and the high lights of the Biblical story. They will see in a fresh way " how it all fits together," where the psalms make their entrance into Jewish history, why Moses is so important, what significance the exile has, why the deliverance at the Red Sea has such lasting influence, and so forth. This will all be clear gain, and the book will be one that he who runs as he reads can still use profitably.

But by far the greater value of the book will be for the person who decides to use it for what it is clearly intended to be, " a guide to the *study of the Bible*." The reader who will, so to speak, hold Mlle. de Dietrich's book in one hand and a Bible in the other, and who in this case will let his left hand know what his right hand is doing, will find the Bible coming alive for him in an astonishing way. For one of the real riches of Mlle. de Dietrich's book is the wealth of Scriptural references that she has included. There is scarcely a statement made that does not include one, and sometimes half a dozen, references to the Bible itself, so that the reader can continually get " back to the source," and not only read about the Bible but begin with a new depth to read the Bible itself. To use her book in this way, looking up the Biblical references as they appear, will not be to make one's way through it in an evening, or a week, or even a month. But it will be to go through the experience of gaining a familiarity with the Bible itself that will be richly rewarding. Thus her book will become a guidebook, charting out a course through the hundreds of confusing chapters and verses that overwhelm the initiate to Biblical studies when he first glances at the pages of Holy Scripture.

II

To the person who uses the book in this second and more basic way, a number of interesting things may happen. He will almost certainly get a new slant on the Biblical material, no matter how familiar its main outlines may have been to him. For the method of Biblical interpretation employed by Mlle. de Dietrich is one that, although fairly common on the European Continent, is not nearly so widespread in the English-speaking world. This method can be described as " Christological interpretation." On the assumption that the Bible is speaking about one God throughout, and that this God has revealed himself definitively in Jesus Christ, the whole of the Biblical drama has therefore to be seen as the continuous activity of that same God. It is the " God and Father of our Lord Jesus Christ " who was at work in Eden, Egypt, and Sinai, even though he was not so recognized by Adam, Pharaoh, and Moses. Exponents of this method of interpretation sometimes slip into mechanical and unlikely attempts to " read Christ into the Old Testament," and Mlle. de Dietrich has avoided these extremes. But she has, at the same time, opened up the pages of the Old Testament in a way that will come as a surprise to many American readers, and enable them (even when they may not agree with the particular interpretation) to see in a new way the whole scope of the activity of the one God, from Creation through to the ultimate fulfillment of his purposes.

In the course of studying the Bible from this perspective, the reader will be enabled to see its unity in a fresh way. Mlle. de Dietrich, as the notes in the back of the book make clear, accepts and profits from the results of Biblical scholarship and criticism, and recognizes the diversity of authors and historical situations that produced the contents of the Biblical canon. And the persons for whom this diversity is sometimes bewildering and confusing can be helped by her to see wherein lies the common witness of the various books, as they endeavor, from their various historical vantage points, to render an account of the way in which the Living God has been at work. In the process of establishing this unity of theme and concern, Mlle. de Dietrich will acquaint the American reader with many parts of the Bible that he does not frequently turn to — in particular, such forbidding books as The Letter to the Hebrews, The Revelation to John, The Book of Daniel, and others. The reader will likewise have helpful light shed on many portions of the Bible that may not previ-

ously have meant much to him, such as the baffling story
of the ascension, the significance of those genealogies in
Matthew and Luke about which all that is usually known
is that they don't agree, the importance of such initially
strange terms as "first fruits," and the central Biblical
stress on the doctrine of election, which the author, to her
credit, does not dodge uncomfortably but discusses forth-
rightly and helpfully in half a dozen different places.

III

Having said these things about the book itself, the translator craves the indulgence of a few words about the translation. Translating *Le Dessein de Dieu* has been an exciting and exasperating, a thrilling and depressing, business.
In the midst of almost line-by-line reminders of my inade-
quacies for the job at hand, I have been sustained by the
knowledge that this is an important book so well done that
even a less than adequate translation could not completely
stifle it, and by the realization that I was getting a re-
education myself by living so closely with it. I have also
been sustained, to my daily if not hourly comfort, by some
words from Ronald Knox's *Trials of a Translator* (Sheed &
Ward, Inc., 1949). Monsignor Knox makes three comments that I reproduce here, since they have been my
guiding lights throughout the work on this book:

> The translator's business is to recondition, as often as
> not, whole sentences, so as to allow for the characteristic
> emphasis of his own language. . . . You cannot coin an
> exact English equivalent for a French word, as you
> might coin an exact English equivalent for a French
> coin. . . . The translator, let me suggest in passing, must
> never be frightened of the word "paraphrase"; it is a
> bogy of the half-educated. As I have already tried to
> point out, it is almost impossible to translate a *sentence*
> without paraphrasing. (Pp. 11, 13, 14.)

I hereby record that I have *not* been "frightened of the
word 'paraphrase.'" It has saved my life, and, I hope,

Mlle. de Dietrich's book. The procedure that I followed was, first, to make as accurate a translation of the French text itself as I was able, and then to go through the full manuscript in a fairly radical manner, trying to say in reasonably good English what Mlle. de Dietrich had said in very good French. I have not hesitated, therefore, to combine sentences and to chop up sentences; to divide paragraphs and to eliminate paragraphs; to introduce connecting words, phrases, and even sentences, that do not appear in the original, whenever it appeared that to do so would render the over-all sense of the French more faithfully in English. I have, in what may seem a quite cavalier fashion, introduced subheadings, taken material from the French footnotes and elevated it to the English text wherever it seemed to me that such a procedure would help an English-speaking reader, and substituted references to English works instead of French works wherever this was practicable.

All this means that a meticulous scholar, comparing a given sentence of mine with a given sentence of the original, might feel that he had caught me out of bounds — even 'way out of bounds. This is a hazard I am prepared to bear cheerfully, if, as I hope, the translation *as a whole* has caught the point and tone of the original book, and has not done any over-all injustices to the major themes Mlle. de Dietrich was trying to establish in it.

I add, most gratefully, that she has read the entire manuscript in English, and that she has helped me, far beyond the call of duty, to make better sense in English of what she meant in French than I could possibly have done by myself. She has also used this occasion to make changes of her own in the English text where she wanted to say something differently in 1959 from the way she had originally said it in 1943. I wish also to record my appreciation to Professor George Landes, of Union Theological Seminary, for help on some of the data contained in the notes, and to Sara Terrien for help in translating a few idioms (about

175, if truth be told) that gave me continued trouble. Needless to say, no one but myself bears any responsibility for the final form of the translation.

The time that I have spent in close contact with this book not only has increased my admiration for the comprehensiveness of Mlle. de Dietrich's scholarship but has also brought me, as I hope these pages will bring the reader, into a new understanding of the depth and relevance and contemporaneity of the Bible, and the way in which it sets forth, both to our comfort and to our warning, " God's unfolding purpose " for all mankind.

ROBERT McAFEE BROWN

PREFACE

Many people hesitate before the Bible in much the same way that they hesitate at the edge of a dense forest. Where is the best place to enter it? How shall they find their way through it? After that, most of them are content to stay on a number of well-worn paths. They return from their explorations with a bunch of texts — always the same ones — which they quite haphazardly combine just like flowers in a greenhouse.

We must be careful not to say that such expeditions are a waste of time. A single word truly received from the mouth of God can utterly transform a human life. But it is no less true that very often, as the saying goes, " you can't see the forest for the trees." The very accumulation of texts may prevent us from seeing the fundamental unity of the Biblical message.

The following pages will try to emphasize this unity. They do not pretend to do more than mark out a trail that the reader can follow through the forest of texts, and in order to accomplish even this a good deal of territory on either side of the trail must remain unexplored. The recurring motif for our study is provided by God himself. This recurring motif is *God's will to save mankind and the world.* This will has been at work since the world began, and it will continue to be operative throughout history until it has reached its final goal and God is all in all.

God Speaks and Acts

God speaks *in history.* For this reason, historical criticism, which puts each text in its proper historical context, has a legitimate place in all serious Biblical study. We know today that the editing of the books of the Bible, in the form in which we now have them, took at least a thousand years, and that some of them contain oral or written sources that are even older. We also know that the witness of the sacred writers was completed, revised, and elaborated over the course of several centuries. We are in the presence of the corporate witness of a believing community, the Israel of the Old Covenant and the church of the New Covenant. No matter how important the problem of " sources " may be for those who wish to understand the development of Hebraic thought across the centuries, this problem is only of indirect concern to faith. It is the Scriptures as they stand in their final form that the Jewish community (for the Old Testament) and the Christian church (for both Testaments) have acknowledged as " canonical," that is, as authoritative in matters of faith. Our faith is based upon the corporate witness of the church of the old and new covenants. This witness has remarkable *unity in spite of its diversity.* And all through its history, the church has recognized that the Holy Spirit has been responsible for this basic unity of the Biblical witness. This is what the church means when it declares that Holy Scripture is " the Word of God " for those who hear it and receive it in faith. The same Holy Spirit who inspired the prophets and apostles and made them witnesses to Christ confirms their witness in our hearts. Only he can transform this Book so that it becomes more than just another page — no matter how exciting — in the history of religions, and becomes instead a message from the Living God which is addressed to us, and on which our very salvation depends (Isa. 55:10-11; I Peter 1:10-12; Heb. 4:12-13; II Tim. 3:14-17).

In the present volume we are seeking to describe the history of salvation as the Biblical writers understood it. Our real question is, What truth does this book, this chapter, this verse, mean to convey about God and his will for men? We shall not try to deal with all the linguistic, historical, and literary problems with which the Bible confronts us, but this does not mean that we underestimate their importance. We shall, however, leave such study to more specialized works.[1] For even when we have analyzed the sources of all the books of the Bible, or found the points of contact between the Hebraic tradition and the Babylonian or Egyptian or Persian traditions, we will find that the mystery of the Bible has not been resolved. This kind of research is important, but it can never explain either the unique role that the Bible has played throughout the centuries or the authority that emanates from it. To understand the secret of the Bible, we must turn to the Bible itself. What does it claim to be, and what is it trying to reveal to us?

We do not find the Bible claiming to be a book of philosophy or science or history. It does not speak to us *of* God, but *in the name of* God. And this God, as Pascal put it, is the Living God, " the God of Abraham, Isaac, and Jacob, not the God of the philosophers and scholars." He speaks in history, and wherever he speaks he speaks by what he does. Each of his words is an act. For this reason we can refer interchangeably to the Bible as the Word of God or as *the Book of the acts of God.*

God speaks at the beginning of time, and this Word creates the world. God speaks in history and this Word forges the destiny of nations. But most of all, God speaks in and through his Son, and this " Word made flesh " is the definitive revelation of God to man, for it is *the* Word which clarifies all the other words that God has spoken across space and time.

The Mystery of the Bible and the Mystery of Love

The Bible is a difficult book to understand precisely because it is a book that is both human and divine, both " Word of God " and " words of men." It is written by men whose perspectives are bound by special historical circumstances and by the language in which they write. In this sense the Bible is simply a slice of human history. But throughout this human history another history unfolds: the history that God himself writes on men's hearts, the history of what *he does* for us, through us, and in spite of us. This history is the history of salvation, the history of a battle that God wages with men, for men, and against men.

The Bible is a magnificently and tragically human book. In it we meet men of flesh and blood, with all their loves and hates and passions and vices — and sometimes these passions even seem to be typical of God himself! If we are only looking for a code of ethics in the Bible, we will miss the point completely, for its patriarchs are consummate liars, and its prophets and psalmists are sometimes fearful preachers of hatred. No, from beginning to end, the Bible is something quite other than a " book of edification," as that term is usually understood. Rather, it shows us the unfolding of a drama, which brings God and man face to face, and in which, if we can dare to speak in such a fashion, God makes up the rules. The Bible shows us that history is a never-ending battle between a God who calls and men who resist his call.

And at the center of this history stands a cross. This cross is the great paradox of the Bible and of all human history, for it shows us that God, in order to save the world, chose a way of doing so that meant being nailed to a cross. From the first page of Genesis to the last page of Revelation,

everything that happens points toward this cross, and likewise everything arises from it. Ever since it was firmly fixed
in the center of the world, the world has been understandable only in terms of it and by means of it. The cross is
the place where the battle between God and man reaches
its climax. It is the place where God's all-powerful love
wins the decisive victory over evil and death, the place
where God is willing, apparently, to lose the contest in
order that he may truly win it.

The mystery of the cross is the focal point of a mystery
that we find throughout the Bible, for God is nowhere
more visible and nowhere more hidden than he is at Golgotha: " My God, my God, why hast thou forsaken me? "
(Mark 15:34) is uttered there.

Suppose we were unacquainted with the story of Jesus,
and someone told us that God had devised a way to send
his Son to men to convert them to himself. We would
probably picture this Son coming in such dazzling splendor
and glory that everyone would be irresistibly drawn to
him. But the mystery of Jesus is just this, that he looked so
much like other men that the crowds were able to pass him
by without knowing who he was — and those who did
know who he was found him such an embarrassing nui-
sance that they had only one thought, which was to get rid
of him as quickly and effectively as they could.

Or suppose that we knew nothing of the Bible, and were
told that God had revealed himself to men through a book
in which those who had seen and heard him bore witness to
him. We would probably imagine a book of such over-
whelming and invincible logic that it could convince any-
body who would read it. And instead, what do we find?
We find that the Bible is a very human book, full of ob-
scurities and contradictions. Luther went so far as to compare the Old Testament to the swaddling clothes in which
the baby Jesus was wrapped. God chose to reveal himself
through the frailty of human words, just as he chose the

humble poverty of the manger for his Son.

The mystery of the divine love is a mystery of humiliation. God undertakes to lift his creatures to himself by first of all stooping down to them — he speaks their language; he shares their flesh. God gives himself to men in the Bible in the same way that he gives himself to men in his Son. Men can make anything they please of this Book — they can analyze it away or dismiss it as nonsense by the simple process of denying the spirit and retaining only the letter. They have, in fact, done this sort of thing to their hearts' content. But to those whose eyes God has opened, the darkness becomes light. And the Bible becomes " the mighty acts of God in Christ," in whom all the distresses of men and all the enigmas of history are resolved.

The Three Decisive Moments

The Biblical story of salvation is placed between two visions that constitute the prologue and the epilogue to the human drama. They are the vision of Paradise lost and the vision of the City of God. They are like two open windows to eternity, for they show us the revelation of what would have been possible if man had not cut himself off from God, and the revelation of what shall be when the redemptive work of the Lord is finished and a reconciled humanity is joyful in God's joy.

These two visions in Genesis and Revelation are the two beacons that cast light upon the whole sweep of human history that lies between them. Now history has meaning and direction, for its final word is God's decisive victory. Everything in history points toward this victory, which is accomplished by the sacrifice and resurrection of Jesus Christ.

The mighty work of God throughout the centuries is made up of three essential moments, or " times," as they can also be called, and each of the three major portions of this book will be devoted to one of them.

1. The Bible shows us how God, in his free grace, *chooses a people* whom he uses as his instrument and witness among all other peoples. This people, Israel, becomes the bearer of God's promises and judgments, the " sign " of the salvation to come, the proclaimer of the Messiah.

2. The second significant moment is the *incarnation,* the coming of Jesus Christ to earth, when " the time is fulfilled." By his life and by his sacrifice on the cross, Jesus conquers the demonic powers, and brings to fulfillment the judgments and promises of the Old Testament. He is *the Man* — the Second Adam, the origin of a new humanity, a new people. This " new people " comprises the church.

3. By his resurrection and ascension, Jesus Christ is proclaimed Lord of heaven and earth. His sovereignty, although real, is not yet clearly visible and will be so only at the end of time, when he shall come again to judge the world and deliver up all things to his Father. This time of waiting, which separates us from the final fulfillment, is *the time of God's patience, the time of the church,* the time that God gives us in order that we may proclaim his salvation to the ends of the earth.

The Necessity of Choice

We are living in this latter time, " the time of the church." The apostolic age believed in the imminent return of the Lord; but II Peter reminds us that in God's sight a thousand years are as a single day (II Peter 3:8). Ever since the resurrection and Pentecost, humanity has been living in " the last times," which are times of mission, times of summons and times of judgment. For every generation of men there is a final decision to be made — for or against the Christ of God. " I have set before you life and death. . . . Choose." (Deut. 30:19.)

There are certain periods in history when these words have to be understood more drastically than in other periods, times when death takes off its mask in such a way that a whole civilization can be destroyed at one blow, times when what happens from day to day cannot fail to remind us, brutally and inexorably, that we live in a world under sentence of death.

At present we are in the midst of one of these periods. The chaos of our existence, the chaos of the historical period in which we are living, simply emphasizes the disorder of a creation that has gotten separated from its Creator, of a humanity that has revolted against its Lord, and that, confronted with the options of life and death, has chosen death. Our earth appears to have been handed over to some demonic power, and humanly speaking, we are tempted to say that the battle is a hopeless one.

The Bible knows all about this demonic power, for Jesus Christ did battle with it on the cross. But because he met it head on and conquered it there, the Bible also knows that the power of Satan, no matter how loudly it may claim the victory, is only apparent. In Jesus Christ, Satan has been conquered once and for all — and Satan knows it! The Christian who lives with this kind of faith in his Savior already has the pledge of victory. He has nothing to fear from either death or hell, for he knows that nothing can separate him from his Lord. And this is the victory that it is his task to proclaim to the world.

" The light shines in the darkness, and the darkness has not overcome it." (John 1:5.) From Genesis to Revelation, nothing else matters but this struggle between light and darkness. This struggle represents the history of all mankind, but it is also our *own* history, the history of each one of us.

The Bible is the crossroads where God encounters us in Jesus Christ and confronts each of us with the necessity of an ultimate choice — am I for him or against him?

PROLOGUE

THE BEGINNING OF TIME

HE drove out the man; and at
the east of the garden of Eden
he placed the cherubim, and a
flaming sword which turned every
way, to guard the way to the tree of
life. — Gen. 3:24.

PROLOGUE

THE BEGINNING OF TIME

Chapter I

THE CREATION AND THE FALL
(Genesis, chs. 1 to 11)

Summary

The word " genesis " means " origin " or " beginning." The first eleven chapters of the book of Genesis tell us about the origins of the world and of man, and how evil and death made their way into the world. All this is before the real history of the people of God begins.

1. The Creative Word (Gen., chs. 1; 2)
   a. The Bible tells us that everything that has existed since the beginning exists and is sustained only by the all-powerful Word of God:

   " God said . . ." (Gen. 1:3, 6, 9, etc.)

   " He spoke and it came to be;
       he commanded, and it stood forth."
   (Ps. 33:9; cf. Ps. 104; 148; Job, ch. 38.)

   " In the beginning was the Word." (John 1:1; cf. Heb. 11:3.)

   b. Only the New Testament discloses the mystery of the creative Word to us: it is in Jesus Christ, the Word made flesh, that the goal and the ultimate meaning of creation are revealed to us (John 1:1-18; Col. 1:15-20; Heb. 1:1-4).

2. Man (Gen. 1:26-31; 2:7-25; 5:1-2)
   a. The Bible points out that man has a double origin: he is created from the dust of the earth (Gen. 2:7), and created also in the image of God:

" God created man in his own image, in the image of God he created him; male and female he created them." (Gen. 1:27.)

" We are indeed his offspring." (Acts 17:28.)

God entrusts man with the care of his creation (Gen. 1:28-30; 2:15-19) .

The thing that sets man apart from all the other creatures consists in the fact that God speaks to man and man responds to him, and furthermore, that man has freedom either to submit to God's command or to rebel against it.

b. We can no longer know who this man in Paradise really was who was made " in the image of God." Only in Jesus Christ, " the image of the invisible God," the Second Adam (" Ad-ham " means " man " in Hebrew) , is the real meaning of our life revealed to us (Col. 1:15; I Cor. 15:47-49; II Cor. 3:18; Rom. 8:29) .

3. THE FALL (Gen., ch. 3)

The world that we know is not the good world that God fashioned, but a world of sin and death, a world cut off from God.

a. Man's basic revolt consists in his doubting the goodness of God and going beyond his creaturely limits by setting himself up as the master of good and evil (Gen. 3:1-5) . A triple judgment is the consequence (Gen. 3:14-19) , and man involves the whole of creation in his fall.

b. Jesus Christ, the Second Adam, goes in the opposite direction from the first Adam, by his voluntary humiliation and his obedience even unto death (Phil. 2:5-11; Rom. 5:12-19) . In this way he redeems the whole creation and gives it access once more to the Tree of Life (Rev. 22:1-5; Col. 1:19-20; I Cor. 15:20-28) .

4. THE REIGN OF DEATH AND THE FIRST SIGNS OF GRACE (Gen., chs. 4 to 11)

a. From this time on, man is in the clutches of demonic forces (Gen. 4:3-24; 6:1-7, 11) . But God limits the consequences of sin by continual interventions of his grace (Gen. 4:1-4; 5:24; 6:8-22) .

   b. God establishes a covenant of grace with Noah in which
      he promises to maintain man's existence (Gen. 9:1-17).
   c. The story of the Tower of Babel shows us how mankind,
      wishing to deify itself, goes down in confusion and divi-
      sion. The New Testament's reply to the story of the
      Tower of Babel is the miracle of Pentecost (Acts, ch. 2)
      and the vision of the New City (Rev., chs. 21; 22).

Genesis is the first of the five books of the Law.[2] Actually, the English word " law " does not quite do justice to
the meaning of the Hebrew word *torah*. The latter originally meant an oracle handed down by the priest; this
oracle was understood as expressing the will of God.

The five books of the law show us what God's will for
his people really is. They all contain legislation, but they
contain a good deal more than simply legislation. Genesis,
for example, tells us about God's will for this world and
deals with *the ultimate destiny of the world and the ultimate destiny of man*. Genesis tells us about the beginnings
of man and the beginnings of sin. It makes clear that in
spite of the calamity of the Fall, God's will for man's salvation remains steadfast. The genealogies listed in Genesis
are a way of showing that in this world of death God preserves a succession of persons until he is ready to raise up a
people to be the instrument of his salvation, a people who
will constitute a new succession of grace stretching from
Abraham to Jesus Christ.

Genesis therefore has a twofold beginning: the beginning of world history (chs. 1 to 11) and the beginning of
salvation-history, in the story of the chosen people (chs. 12
to 50).

The story of mankind, which culminates in the cross
and is completed by the renewal of all things in Christ, is
sketched out for us in these opening eleven chapters. They
are therefore basic for an understanding of the Bible as a
whole.

1. THE CREATIVE WORD: " God said . . ."

The very first words of the Bible are of utmost significance: " In the beginning God created the heavens and the
earth " (Gen. 1:1).

God is an everlasting God:

Before the mountains were brought forth,
   or ever thou hadst formed the earth and the world,
   from everlasting to everlasting thou art God.
                                        (Ps. 90:2.)

But our human minds are incapable of understanding
this God who exists before time itself. For finite creatures
like ourselves, the " beginning " is the moment when God
established the created world as a reality apart from and
other than himself. And in reflecting on this fact, we learn
something of the degree of our creatureliness, for we are
unable to think of God as he is " in himself." We can only
think of him as he is in relationship to us, that is, in whatever he decides to reveal of himself *to us,* by his word and
his works.

God Creates by His Word

" God *said,* ' Let there be light '; and there was light."
(Gen. 1:3.) " God said . . ." " God said . . ." This deliberate repetition, which recurs in each succeeding para-
graph of the first chapter of Genesis, emphasizes the fact
that the material world is not an emanation from God, as
the pantheists assert, nor coexistent with God, as the philo-
sophical dualists assert. On the contrary, it is *a creation of
his word.* " He spoke, and it came to be; he commanded,
and it stood forth." (Ps. 33:9.) God created the world and
he is Master and Lord of that world. Precisely because he
created it by a free act of his sovereign will, he can destroy
it or save it as he pleases. This is why, in the darkest hours
of Israel's history, prophets and psalmists raise their voices
in utter confidence to the Creator of heaven and earth.

Doubt concerning the creative sovereignty of God goes hand in hand with doubt concerning the salvation of the world. This world is God's world, brought into being by the breath of his mouth. For this reason, the last word about the world belongs to God and only to God. It is because he is the creator of the world that he is in full control of history, in spite of all appearances to the contrary. Such was the assurance of the prophets. (Isa. 40:12-26; Jer. 10:12-16; etc.). Such is the assurance of the Christian. (Rom. 11:36.)

Materialists of every age believe only in what they can "see for themselves." To them, mind is nothing but an emanation from matter: it is the gray matter of the brain that produces thought. The Bible acknowledges that the sovereignty of the invisible God over the visible world, of mind over matter, is a *revealed* truth, i.e., an affirmation of faith: "By faith we understand that the world was created by the word of God, so that what is seen was made out of things which do not appear" (Heb. 11:3). The Biblical revelation in its entirety is inextricably bound up with this axiom of faith. The form of this world passes away, but God is from everlasting to everlasting. "Heaven and earth will pass away," Jesus proclaims, "but my words will not pass away." (Matt. 24:35.)

In Hindu thought, and in some forms of Greek thought, the world is endless repetition: the wheel of history keeps going round and round in just the same way as the wheel of the seasons keeps going round and round, and in this cycle civilizations are born and die.

The Biblical revelation, on the other hand, tells us that this world has a meaning and goal and destiny, namely, that it is created by God for his glorification. Biblical history is thus unique: it moves from the first creation to the new creation in Christ (Rev. 21:1), and its center is the drama of the incarnation. This is why the first pages of the Bible can be understood only in the light of the last pages.

Genesis and Revelation are the beacons that cast light on
all that comes between. Together they make up the prologue and the epilogue of the drama of Calvary — which
is the history of our redemption.

" The Word Made Flesh " Is the Creative Word

Furthermore, it is in the last pages of the Bible that the
mystery of the creative Word is revealed to us. This Word,
by which God creates, judges, and saves the world is his
Son. The name of the witness who is " Faithful and True "
is the Word of God. (Rev. 19:11-16.) The prologue to
John's Gospel begins with these well-known words which
are a direct echo of the first lines of Genesis:

> In the beginning was the Word, and the Word was
> with God, and the Word was God. He was in the begin-
> ning with God; all things were made through him, and
> without him was not anything made that was made. In
> him was life, and the life was the light of men. . . . He
> was in the world, and the world was made through him,
> yet the world knew him not. (John 1:1-4, 10.)

It is this Word, by whom the world was created, who was
made flesh in Jesus of Nazareth. He " dwelt among us,"
and " we have beheld his glory." (John 1:14.) Jesus Christ
is the " true light of men," of whom the light that lightens
the visible world is no more than a parable. Jesus Christ is
God's face turned toward this world. The life-giving principle that has ruled the world from the very beginning, the
source of all light and all life, is none other than the love
of the Father revealed through the Son.

Paul develops the same idea when he writes that God
" chose us in [Christ] before the foundation of the
world . . . destined us in love to be his sons through
Jesus Christ " (Eph. 1:4-5).

> In him all things were created, in heaven and on earth,
> visible and invisible, whether thrones or dominions or

principalities or authorities — all things were created through him and for him. He is before all things, and in him all things hold together. (Col. 1:16-17.)

And The Letter to the Hebrews makes the same affirmation:

In many and various ways God spoke of old to our fathers by the prophets; but in these last days he has spoken to us by a Son, whom he appointed the heir of all things, *through whom also he created the world.* He reflects the glory of God and bears the very stamp of his nature, *upholding the universe by his word of power.* (Heb. 1:1-3, italics added.)

These words help us to understand the strange statement of Jesus, " Before Abraham was, I am " (John 8:58) .

The Son, invisible yet present, acts in the world from the very beginning, and leads it toward its destination: " My Father is working still, and I am working " (John 5:17) . He is the living Word who creates and sustains the world. He is the " secret and hidden " wisdom of whom Paul speaks (I Cor. 2:6-9) , present since time began:

The Lord created me at the beginning of his work,
    the first of his acts of old. . . .
I was beside him, like a master workman;
and I was daily his delight,
    rejoicing before him always.
                       (Prov. 8:22, 30.)

The eternal Word that God speaks to the world is in reality his Son; and all the words that God has spoken since the world began are gathered up in the mystery of this single Word. In him alone is the meaning and secret of creation revealed to us. The mystery of creation is a mystery springing from the depths of love. The creative will of God is a will motivated by love. It creates an object to love, and wishes to be loved in return.

And the instrument of this love is the Holy Spirit. Genesis says no more than that " the Spirit of God was moving over the face of the waters " (Gen. 1:2) . But from the first page of the Bible to the last, the Spirit is working. He watches over the chaos of the first creation. He is the witness, the proclaimer, of the second creation. (Acts 1:4-8; 2:16-21; Rom. 8:14-16; cf. John 3:5-6; Rev. 22:17.)

Actually, in spite of its grandeur and poetic beauty, we cannot understand the first page of Genesis unless we read it in the light of Christ and the Holy Spirit, unless we see it from the perspective of our election in Christ, from this " new creation " which is promised to us at the end of time. This is the real and glorious counterpart to the world of Genesis, which is a world created for life, to be sure, but a world that very shortly thereafter becomes involved in sin and death because of the unfaithfulness of its creatures.

2. MAN

God forsakes his divine solitude and establishes a world that is like a vast parable of his creative love. This world is run according to law: night follows day, day follows night, and every creature is appointed to fulfill a certain purpose and occupy a special place in the divine plan.

The " Image of God " in Man

But then God creates man. And he separates this creature, made of the dust of the earth, from all other creatures. He breathes into him the breath of life (Gen. 2:7) ; he creates him in his own image and after his own likeness (Gen. 1:26-27; 5:1; cf. Acts 17:28) . Man is unique in that God speaks to him and he responds to God. God delegates some of his powers to man by making him king of creation. (Gen. 1:26-30.) He brings all the animals of the earth to him so that he can give them names.[3] Man watches them all march by, and finds no creature who looks like him, until God confronts him with his true counterpart,

" bone of his bones and flesh of his flesh," namely, woman
(Gen. 2:19-23).

Notice that according to Gen. 1:27, it is the human
couple whom God created in his own image. Literally,
" God created man in his own image, in the image of God
he created him; male and female he created them." [4] God
is love. The Trinity is not explicit in Genesis, but we have
already seen that the triune God is implicitly present there.
God is, in his very nature, the one who gives himself. Thus
a solitary individual cannot really reflect the God of love.
Only a human couple, in the kind of unity that the family
represents, can reflect something of what God is really
like. Nothing could emphasize more clearly how wonderful it is to be a human being than the favor that God confers on man and woman, of being able to give themselves
fully to each other, as he gave himself to them, and of being able, by means of this mutual giving, to create new
life. Later on we find Paul taking up the same theme:
" Husbands, love your wives, as Christ loved the church
and gave himself up for her " (Eph. 5:25). Here again, the
Genesis story in its brevity does no more than establish the
basis for a reality whose full significance and import can
only be seen in the light of the gospel.

Jesus Christ, the True Man

Today we have no way of knowing what this man of
Paradise, " man in the image of God," was really like. The
mystery of our calling and of our destiny as men is ob-
scured by our sin. To know who " man " really is, we have
to turn toward the only Man worthy of the name who has
ever lived — the One of whom Pilate prophetically said,
" Here is *the man!* " (John 19:5). He is " the image of
the invisible God " (Col. 1:15), the One in whom our true
destiny as sons is revealed and restored to us (Rom. 8:14-
16). We see " with unveiled face, beholding the glory of
the Lord," and we are " being changed into his likeness

from one degree of glory to another; for this comes from the Lord who is the Spirit" (II Cor. 3:18). What was an ideal possibility for Adam becomes an actual reality for us, because of what Jesus Christ has done.

What has taken place in the interval between Adam and Jesus Christ? The drama of our freedom has been enacted. For the thing that makes us uniquely human is that, unlike the other creatures, we are able to say both " yes " and " no " to God. Man does not do the will of his Creator by necessity. The stars in the sky follow their prescribed orbits, the animals of the field obey their instincts, but man has this unique and frightening ability — he can refuse to be obedient to his Creator. For God does not want slaves, but sons.

God lets man have all the fruit of the Garden of Eden and all the produce of the earth. He imposes on man only one small limitation: he shall not eat of the fruit of the tree of the knowledge of good and evil. To know " good and evil " in the Hebrew language means to know " all things." There is a " knowledge " that belongs to God alone.

What does this symbolic tree represent? It indicates the dividing line between creature and Creator. It calls men to depend in utter trust upon God. To be all-knowing would mean to be God. The whole Bible states firmly that man can know God only inasmuch as it pleases God to reveal himself to man. Does this mean that the longing for knowledge is wrong? Not at all. But it will be bestowed on us in God's own time — when we shall have attained full manhood in Christ. (I Cor. 13:9-12.)

3. The Fall

The world that we know today is no longer the " good " world described in the first chapter of Genesis, but rather a world in which sin and suffering and death have gotten the upper hand.

The Pride of Man and Its Consequences

The account of the Fall in Gen., ch. 3, is one of the most extraordinary pages in the Bible. Furthermore, it has given rise to varying kinds of interpretations. Some commentators have interpreted it literally and have asked very seriously what language the serpent spoke, while others have reduced it to a myth describing the awakening of the sexual instinct. In reality, what the account reveals to us is the whole tragedy of our situation as men created for life and placed under sentence of death. The real temptation to which Adam and Eve succumb is the Promethean temptation — the temptation to go beyond their creaturely limits and set themselves up as God's equals. It is obvious that this initial revolt, this deifying of the creature, has immediate consequences in the relationship of Adam and Eve with each other. In fact, when the creature ceases to be governed by the will of the Creator, *all* his relationships turn out to be false, and everything becomes chaotic. From this point of view the Genesis account has extraordinary psychological profundity, and its imagery is so full of meaning that every single word counts. The whole drama of human existence is summed up in these few lines. We must now examine them more carefully.

The story of the Fall is not an attempt to explain the origin of evil, for it does not tell us where the serpent came from. It is important to realize that the serpent is a creature, and not an eternal principle coexistent with God. God permits man to be tempted by the serpent, but a time will come when the Savior of the world, born to one of Eve's descendants, will be the one to bruise the serpent's head (Gen. 3:5). This is a way of saying that the reign of evil will not last indefinitely (cf. I Cor. 15:24-26; Rev. 12:7-12).

The thing that the Genesis story emphasizes is the reality of sin and its consequences. Right away the serpent

insinuated a doubt into Eve's heart: " Did God [*really*]
say . . . ? " (This is like the doubt insinuated with the
words " *If* you are the Son of God . . ." in the story of
Jesus' temptation in the wilderness, as reported in Matt.
4:3-6.) A deadly chink is opened up in the creature's love
for his creator. And into this chink a little wedge is thrust
in the form of the assertion: " You will not die. For God
knows that when you eat [the fruit] your eyes will be
opened, and you will be like God, knowing good and evil "
(Gen. 3:4-5) .

The ongoing temptation, man's basic and really demonic temptation, is *to play the part of God*. We are immediately reminded of the grandiose delusions of the
princes of this world, drunk with pride and thirsty for
power, which Ezekiel describes so tellingly. (Cf. Ezek. 28:
1-10.) The person who plays the part of God makes himself into the center of his universe, whether that universe
be large or small; he seeks his own glory rather than the
glory of God, he wants to " run his own life " instead of
recognizing it as a gift from the hands of God. In briefest
terms, he wants to be his own master rather than God's
servant; he wants to dominate rather than to serve.

The first consequence of Adam and Eve's disastrous mistake is that they lose the initial innocence of their relationship: they see that they are naked. The second consequence
is that they flee from their Creator. The consequence of
sin is that man cannot endure to be known by God or to
be seen by God as he really is. Henceforth, he dreads the
God whom he was created to love, and he flees before his
face. For the Light of God that gives joy to the righteous
becomes a consuming fire to the sinner: " Thou shalt not
see me and live " (Ex. 33:20) .

But the separation is not only between man and God.
It extends to all human relationships as well, with the result that human beings pretend to be something other than
they really are. They cannot even bear the thought of let-

ting people see their true selves, for they are ashamed to
disclose the nakedness of what they really are in body,
heart, and mind. This is why humanity goes on living a
lie, and why men hide not only from one another but from
themselves as well. Henceforth, it will take the power of
God's grace to stop this evasion and to force men to look at
themselves as they really are. This is the only possible starting point for a true return to God.

God punishes the man and the woman. But even this
punishment, like all God's punishments, has within it an
intimation of grace, a possibility of salvation. For it is the
kind of experience that can lead the man and the woman
to a true knowledge of themselves, if only they will let
themselves be led.

God establishes the relationship of the human couple on
a new foundation. He humbles the woman by subjugating
her to the man. He humbles the man by forcing him to
struggle with a creation that has likewise become rebellious, because of what he has done, and that resists his attempts to control it. Thus, God subjects the man and the
woman to a discipline of suffering appropriate to each.
They are not deprived of the joy of sexual relationship,
the joy of having children, or the joy of work. But these
things become theirs only at the price of struggle and suffering. From now on there will be pain and heartache cor
nected with everything the man and the woman do. Thos
who accept this situation will discover that it can be transformed into a blessing.

As a way of showing the man and the woman that his
steadfast love reaches out to them even in the distress of
their new situation, God provides them with clothes. He
gives them " garments of skin " (Gen. 3:21).

Next, God drives them out of a paradise that is no more;
for life apart from communion with God would be worse
than death. And if humanity is to recover communion
with God, it must go through death and come to know the

miracle of resurrection. It can be saved only by being
" born anew " (John 3:3).

The Humiliation of Jesus Christ and Its Consequences

We will find that the New Testament refers to Jesus
Christ as the Second Adam. The first Adam brought about
his own downfall by taking the forbidden fruit, by going
beyond the established limits of his creaturehood, and by
desiring to play the part of God. Jesus Christ, the Son of
God, voluntarily takes upon himself the limitations of
humanity in becoming a man among men, and by his
obedience even unto death he reopens for men the way of
free and joyful obedience, the way to the Tree of Life
(Phil. 2:5-11; Rev. 22:1-2).

4. THE REIGN OF DEATH AND THE FIRST SIGNS OF GRACE
(Gen., chs. 4 to 11)

Man, driven out of Paradise, is in the clutches of demonic forces. Cain and his descendants exemplify man's
revolt against God with its bitter fruits of jealousy, hatred,
and murder. (Gen. 4:1-20.) The very difficult sixth chapter of Genesis, with its account of mankind's corruption,
emphasizes once more the sin of a humanity that trans-
gresses its limits and draws down upon itself the judgment
of God. These chapters show in a devastatingly clear way
that the fruit of sin is *death*.

But in this extremely dark picture there are some rays
of light. For even in a situation like this, God makes plain
that he is the God of grace. Even on the murderer Cain
he puts a mark (Gen. 4:15) so that whoever meets him
will not kill him or his descendants (Gen. 4:17-24).

Over against Cain the Bible puts Abel, who finds grace
in the sight of the Lord; over against the descendants of
Cain it puts the descendants of Seth, and of at least two of
these descendants it is said that they " walked with God "
(Gen. 5:24; 6:9; cf. Heb. 11:4-7).

Noah and the Covenant of Grace

Noah's ark, tossed and cast about by the waves of the flood, is a sign of the salvation still to come, through a church likewise uprooted by the sin of the world (I Peter 3:20). Perhaps, since all varieties of animals are included in the ark, we can already see a precursor of a new creation. God makes a covenant with Noah in which he promises not to destroy humanity. It is a covenant not only with Noah, the believer, but through Noah a covenant with the whole creation. God gives the management of the world back to man, but man is henceforth a master who is feared by the other creatures and who is allowed to kill animals for food. (The creatures of Paradise ate only herbs; cf. Gen. 1:29-30.) But he may not kill his own kind. Instead, the unity of the human race is solemnly affirmed, and murder is condemned:

> For your lifeblood I will surely require a reckoning; of every beast I will require it and of man; of every man's brother I will require the life of man. Whoever sheds the blood of man, by man shall his blood be shed; for God made man in his own image. (Gen. 9:5-6.)

God's covenant with Noah is his promise to all humanity that he will uphold and sustain man's life. But it also serves as a commandment to which all humanity must pledge itself. It is significant that this commandment has reference to *respect for life*.

The Tower of Babel

Genesis, ch. 11, shows us that up to this time all men were speaking the same language. But this unity which they possess only serves to separate them farther from God. They want to "make a name for themselves" (cf. Gen. 11:4) and climb up to heaven. What they did was apparently to build a huge temple. This is simply the temptation of Gen., ch. 3, recast in collective terms: human *so-ciety* deifies itself this time. God retaliates from on high by creating a confusion of languages, as a result of which men cannot understand one another any more, and the nations set themselves against one another.

We shall see in the New Testament that the Tower of Babel finds its true resolution in the miracle of Pentecost. Only the Holy Spirit can re-establish the broken unity. All human attempts to create unity among mankind remain doomed to defeat, as long as man's pride has not been broken, for man's ambition throughout history is devoted to this same sin, the desire to " make a name for himself." That is why, for groups as well as for individuals, there is only *one name* by which they can be saved (cf. Acts 4:12). Throughout the whole of Biblical history, Babylon (Babel) is the symbol of a pride that deifies itself, and of the kind of political power that tries to achieve the material and spiritual domination of the world. This is why the book of Revelation concludes with the vision of the final destruction of Babylon, symbolic of all the evil at large in the world (Rev., ch. 18), and with the vision of a New City, which comes not from below but from on high: " The glory of God is its light, and its lamp is the Lamb. By its light shall the nations walk; and the kings of the earth shall bring their glory into it " (Rev. 21:23-24).

PART
ONE

THE UNFOLDING OF TIME

The Period from Abraham to Jesus Christ

IF only one man had written a book of prophecies concerning Jesus Christ, dealing both with the time and the manner of his coming, and Jesus Christ had come just as these prophecies said he would, such a fact would carry infinite weight.

But there is much more to it than this. For we find a succession of men, spread out over four thousand years, who come, constantly and without variation, one after the other, and predict this same advent. A whole nation announces this — a nation which lives over four thousand years in order to make a united witness to the assurance which it has concerning this advent, and from which it cannot be diverted,

Pascal, *Pensées*, No. 709 (*Continued*)

no matter what dangers and persecutions lie in wait for it. This is something quite different.

— Pascal, *Pensées*, No. 709.

*The History of the Chosen People
from Abraham to Jesus Christ*

We shall make no attempt to retrace the whole history of Israel in this brief outline. Instead, we shall concentrate on five major events in Israel's history, devoting a chapter to each of these events:

1. The calling of the chosen people, in the person of *Abraham.* The figure of Abraham assumes symbolic importance for the entire history of salvation. The wonderful promise of election is passed on to all his descendants.

2. *The covenant at Sinai.* Through Moses, God removes Israel from slavery in Egypt, and by a solemn covenant binds himself to this people whom he has come to save. He gives them the law.

3. *The establishment of Israel in the Promised Land.* This represents both the literal and symbolic fulfillment of the promises made to Abraham and Moses. The reign of David is the high point in Israel's life as a nation. The throne and the Temple are the two tangible signs of God's presence in the midst of his people.

4. *The exile.* Because of their disobedience, the people of God are the recipients of his judgment. The preaching of the prophets is most clearly heard at this time. The exile represents a temporary exclusion from the Promised Land,

and during this period Israel has neither king nor temple. As was the case when Israel was in the wilderness, it can only wait for salvation from God alone.

5. Only a " *remnant* " from Israel returns to the Promised Land. The nation dwindles away into a religious community that lives in the hope of a Messiah whose coming will usher in the Kingdom of God.

The Bible divides this history of the chosen people into three equal periods: the first goes from Abraham to David, the second from David to the Babylonian deportation, and the third from the deportation to Jesus Christ (Matt. 1:17).

This division illumines the special significance that is given to the Davidic monarchy as a " sign " of the Kingdom to come. In fact, the duration of the Davidic monarchy coincides with the period when Israel is actually in possession of the Promised Land. The period that precedes it (from Abraham to David) is a journey by faith toward the Promised Land. And the period that follows it is likewise a journey by faith, but no longer understood in temporal terms, for this time God chooses a remnant who learns from the experience of suffering to wait for the Kingdom that is not here below. Thus God prepares the way for the coming of his Son, and thus the times unfold until the appointed time, fixed by God himself, which Scripture describes with the words " the time is fulfilled " (Mark 1:15; cf. Eph. 1:10) .

CHAPTER II

THE PROMISE

The Patriarchs
Abraham, Father of Believers
(Genesis, chs. 12 to 50)

SUMMARY

Chapters 12 to 50 of Genesis tell us about the beginnings of "salvation-history," or the history of the patriarchs. Chapters 12 to 26 tell about the promise made to Abraham and his son Isaac, while chapters 27 to 50 deal with the struggles undergone by Jacob and his sons, who are the inheritors of this promise.[5]

1. THE LIVING GOD: "GOD OF ABRAHAM, ISAAC, AND JACOB"
   a. God reveals himself to the patriarchs as the *Living God:* "God of Abraham, Isaac, and Jacob, not the God of the philosophers and scholars." The sovereign freedom of the Living God is revealed in the graciousness of his summons to men, the steadfast character of his promises, and the absoluteness of his demands.
   b. The God of Jesus Christ is none other than the "God of Abraham, Isaac, and Jacob," the God of Israel, the Living God (Gen. 15:7; 32:9, 28; Ex. 3:15; Deut. 34:4; I Kings 18:36-37; Acts 3:13).

2. COMMAND AND PROMISE
   a. The free election of God is expressed both in a command ("Go!") and in a promise ("I will bless you . . ."). In order to become the instrument of the salvation of all men, Abraham must leave his family, his homeland, and

47

his gods, and live by faith alone in the promises that are
made to him (Gen. 12:1-3; Heb. 11:8-16).

b. Abraham has two sons: Ishmael, a natural son, and Isaac,
the child of grace, on whom the promises rest. Isaac, offered up, returned and restored a second time " in a kind
of resurrection " (cf. Heb. 11:19), is a foretelling of the
true son in whom all the promises made to Abraham will
one day be fulfilled (Matt. 1:1; Gal. 3:16; John 8:56).

3. THE COVENANT

a. Melchizedek blesses Abraham in the name of the Most
High (Gen. 14:17-20; cf. Heb. 7:1-10).

b. God binds himself to Abraham and his descendants by an
" everlasting covenant " (Gen., chs. 15; 17:7) whose consequences nothing can destroy (Gal. 3:17; Rom. 11:28-
29). But this covenant always remains a covenant of
grace based on God's free election (Isa. 41:8-14).

4. ABRAHAM, FATHER OF BELIEVERS

a. The " fathers " are not saints. They are fallible men like
us. What distinguishes them is that they have *faith* in
God's promises and live under his judgment. Their encounter with the Living God is a battle (Gen. 15:12; ch.
22; 32:24-30) from which they emerge broken but triumphant.

b. The true descendants of Abraham are not those of flesh
and blood, but those of faith (Matt. 3:7-10; 8:10-12; John
8:33-40; Rom. 4:3, 16-25; Gal. 3:6-9; James 2:18-23).

1. THE LIVING GOD: " GOD OF ABRAHAM, ISAAC, AND JACOB "

Something most unusual happened to Pascal on the
night of his conversion, when he was led to write these
simple words in his *Memorial:* " God of Abraham, Isaac,
and Jacob, not the God of the philosophers and scholars."
To believe in a First Principle who ruled the universe
would have been relatively easy for a mathematician and
philosopher like Pascal. But what happened was that the
Living God entered into Pascal's life and conquered his

pride and his reason. And the God whom he acknowledged as *his* God is the same God who, thousands of
years earlier, had overpowered the leader of a nomad
tribe so that he might transform that tribe into his own
people.

This God of the Bible does strange things! He removes
Abram from the advanced civilization of Chaldea and
leads him through the wilderness into the unknown, to a
land where he will never have anything but a tomb. He
promises offspring to Abram, but he waits until Abram is
a hundred years old, and Sarah his wife is ninety, before
he gives them a child, concerning whom Sarah says, " Every one who hears will laugh over me " (Gen. 21:6) . When
this child, Isaac, has grown up, God, with all the cruelty
of a Phoenician Moloch, demands that his father sacrifice
him. And Isaac's heir is Jacob, a liar and impostor, whom
God prefers to his brother Esau, without giving us the
slightest reason why.

Such is the " God of Abraham, Isaac, and Jacob " before whom Pascal renounced all his human wisdom! Why?
Because this God revealed himself also to Pascal as a consuming " Fire "; because this is the God whom Jesus Christ
confessed and declared to be his Father; because just at the
place where our human good sense sees only a stumbling
block, faith shows us something quite different. It shows
us a God who is concerned about men; who does not think
it beneath his dignity to come down into the ordinary
reality of their daily existence; who chooses them right
where they are, even in Ur of the Chaldees. Graciously
and miraculously, he makes the impossible possible, reveals himself to men, speaks to them, calls them and saves
them — all of this in spite of what they are! He is a God
who, from Abraham to Jesus Christ, remains everlastingly
the same, which is to say that he remains everlastingly
faithful in his promises.

God takes a nobody, Abram, removes him from his country, his tribe, and his gods, strengthens his faith by stern tests, and out of Abram produces Abraham, the father of believers. This act is the first link in the long succession of divine interventions that we call "salvation-history." At each end of the chain stands a hill. The two hills are near to one another geographically; they are Mt. Moriah and Golgotha. Moriah is the Rock of sacrifice, while Golgotha held the wood of the cross. Before both of them our human wisdom is reduced to naught. According to Jewish tradition, the hill of Moriah is the same one on which the Temple of Jerusalem was later built (II Chron. 3:1). Even today the tourist who goes to the "Dome of the Rock" in Jerusalem is shown the rock on which Abraham prepared to sacrifice Isaac. While the tradition is probably legendary, it preserves an important symbolic truth.

2. COMMAND AND PROMISE

God's first word to Abraham is a command: "Go from your country and your kindred and your father's house to the land that I will show you" (Gen. 12:1).

This man is not alone: he has a wife, servants, property, and he is not young. He has no children. But God speaks and the man "goes," and goes for good. He leaves the security of the city of Ur. We now know that in 2000 B.C. Ur was a rich city in an advanced civilization. And yet Abraham leaves. To do what? To go to an unknown land that God promises to his descendants (and he doesn't even have any children!), a land where he himself will never have anything but a tomb. He leaves to lead a wandering life, in which he will become acquainted with poverty (Gen. 12:10) and war (Gen. 14:13-14). Why does he leave? Simply because that is what God tells him to do.

Abraham, and "the People" Who Will Succeed Him

When God speaks, the first response must always be "to leave." "Leaving" re-echoes from one end of the Bible to the other. " No one who puts his hand to the plow and looks back is fit for the kingdom of God." (Luke 9:62.) This "leaving" is what we are afraid of; this is why we do not listen very carefully to what God says to us.

Abraham does not say whether he was afraid or not. He simply obeys. And the great adventure of the people of faith begins with him and will be completed only in eternity.

Abraham sets out armed with the promise of God. This promise is breath-taking: " I will make of you a great nation. . . . In you all the families of the earth will be blessed " (Gen. 12:2-3, margin). But he had to wait twenty years before there was even a hint that this would come to pass.

Has Israel really become " a great nation "? Not if we measure its earthly fate in comparison to the powerful nations of the world. Aside from brief periods of relative glory, has it not been the nation that has been most trodden upon? Nor, again, is it a great nation if we compare the natural endowments of the Hebrew people to those of other ancient civilizations, such as Egypt or Greece. Israel's greatness is something quite different; Israel receives it from God and from God alone. Israel's greatness consists in the fact that it is *the people to whom God speaks* and *by whom God speaks to the rest of the world*. It is the witness and proclaimer of salvation. There is no place for another kind of greatness, besides this one. And from the very beginning, God himself makes plain that Israel's vocation extends far beyond its own destiny and is meant to be a source of blessing to all nations.

The natural descendants promised to Abraham are henceforth only the visible sign of those far more numerous descendants whom the true heir of Abraham, Jesus Christ, will beget in times to come, and who are Israel according to faith, namely, the church. These descendants, as numerous as the stars of the sky (cf. Gen. 15:5), are

the multitude "which no man could number," referred
to in the visions in Revelation (Rev. 7:9).

Ishmael and Isaac

Abraham has two sons, Ishmael and Isaac: Ishmael, the
child by nature, and Isaac, the child by faith. We must
observe in passing that while the natural child is symbolically rejected outside the Promised Land (Gen., chs. 16;
21:8-21), God certainly does not abandon him. His very
name is an indication of this, for Ishmael means "God
hears" (Gen. 16:7-14; 21:17-21; 25:12-18). Ishmael's own
fate is likewise the bearer of a promise, that the pagans
will finally re-enter the covenant of grace!

Isaac's birth, on the other hand, can be explained only
by the special miraculous activity of God. It reminds us
that in salvation-history, everything is a gift, everything is
grace, and nothing "just happens." God "remembers"
Sarah (Gen. 21:2), as he "remembers" Rebecca and
Rachel (Gen. 25:21-23; 30:22), and Hannah (I Sam. 1:19)
and Elizabeth (Luke 1:25). In each case, the bearing of
a son is interpreted as due to the sheer grace of God. There
are several instances in Scripture of sterile women who in
their distress believe that their prayers have been answered
by the direct intervention of God. In the Semitic world,
sterility is the worst dishonor that can befall a woman.
Motherhood is the greatest gift that God can bestow upon
her. The very name "Eve" means "mother of all living"
(Gen. 3:20). It is significant that this ordeal of sterility
should be imposed precisely on those women whose sons
are predestined to play major roles in the history of salvation: Sarah, Rebecca, Rachel, Hannah, and Elizabeth. The
faith of the mother is very important in the history of salvation; this faith is put to the test. The child promised by
God contrary to all hope and all human expectation is
truly a child of grace. Nothing is "natural" in the history
of salvation; everything is the free gift of God. That is why

Paul sees in the history of Hagar and Sarah a symbol of the two covenants and sets the Israel according to the flesh in opposition to the Israel of the promise (Gal. 4:21-31).

Abraham and Sarah have to wait twenty years for the fulfillment of the promise God had made to them. Finally the child is born. At last Abraham receives a clear sign of God's faithfulness.

And then, in a single command, God takes everything away from him. There is not a page in the whole Old Testament more poignant than the twenty-second chapter of Genesis: "Take your son, your only son Isaac, whom you love, and go to the land of Moriah, and offer him there as a burnt offering" (Gen. 22:2). *Your only son Isaac, whom you love!* This is one father speaking to another father, someone who is quite aware that he is making a costly demand. What is the origin of this shocking commandment? What can this annihilation of all the previously given promises possibly mean? Must we not agree with Chrysostom when he exclaims, "Here God contradicts God, faith contradicts faith, the commandment contradicts the promise." Luther writes: "God openly contradicts himself. The human reason staggers in the face of this, and only faith is able to make the leap and rely on God's sole promise. . . . Abraham has understood the article of faith which proclaims the resurrection of the dead, for he realizes that his descendants will be reborn from these ashes." Indeed, Abraham needs tremendous faith to survive such a test, for more is involved here than simply a single human life, precious as that is. What is involved here is the faithfulness of God, the hope of the believer, and even the salvation of the world.

Abraham obeys. To be sure, he obeys without understanding. But he still obeys. He walks for three days and the astonished child walks beside him. (We will see in the New Testament that Jesus also walks "three days" toward Jerusalem.) But although God stays the hand of Abraham at the fatal moment, later on God himself will experience the deepest suffering to which a father can be subjected, and will give his only Son for the salvation of the world. The very thing that God asks of Abraham, as a test of his faith, is something God himself is willing to endure.

"My son," says Abraham prophetically, "God will provide himself the lamb for a burnt offering." (Gen. 22:8.) This lamb will be an only Son — not Abraham's, but God's. And all the sacrifices offered until his coming will only point to and prefigure the one true offering, and they will receive their authentic meaning only in the light of it.

Isaac is restored to Abraham by a "prefiguring of the resurrection" (cf. Heb. 11:19). His son is given to him a second time. As Wilhelm Vischer has said: "The word of promise called him out of nothing into life, and only the word which raises the dead sustains his life. The patriarch, the story relates, still possesses his son only in faith." [6]

Has any man entered as deeply into the agony of God's own heart as Abraham, the believer? But because he trusted God, he also came to know more than agony. He came to know the certainty and joy of the deliverance of which his son Isaac and the Land of Canaan were only a foretaste. He saw and greeted the promised city "from afar." He dwelt as "a stranger and exile on the earth," just as will be the case with his people and also with the church. (Heb. 11:9, 13-14; cf. I Peter 2:11.) "Your father Abraham rejoiced that he was to see my day; he saw it and was glad." (John 8:56.)

3. THE COVENANT

The Blessing by Melchizedek

God promised Abraham his blessing. In Gen., ch. 14, it is mysteriously given to him by an unknown person who appears on the Biblical scene only to disappear as suddenly as he came, Melchizedek, "priest of God Most High." The name of this priest-king means "king of righteousness," and Salem, from which he comes, means

" peace," and possibly designates Jerusalem. Melchizedek blesses Abraham and gives him, significantly, bread and wine as a sign of the covenant. Psalm 110, which sings of the glory of the coming Messiah, proclaims that he will be a priest forever (and note that neither David nor his successors had been priests " after the order of Melchizedek "). Furthermore, in The Letter to the Hebrews, Melchizedek is identified as a symbol of the Great High Priest, Jesus Christ (Heb. 6:13 to 7:3).

Genesis, ch. 15, describes an even stranger episode. God establishes a legal covenant with Abraham. According to ancient custom, the two parties to the agreement had to pass between animals that had been cut in two. This meant that they were willing to be torn apart themselves, like the victims, if they broke their agreement. Some birds of prey, symbols of evil powers, try to swoop down on the divided animals. Abraham drives them away. He is encompassed by " deep darkness " and is filled with dread. God reveals to him the suffering through which his descendants will have to go. Then God himself passes between the divided animals in the form of a flame.

This dread, which Abraham experiences in the presence of God and in anticipation of the covenant he is about to ratify, is something that others chosen by God have likewise felt. This was true of Jacob, in his strange wrestling with God as he was about to enter the Promised Land (Gen. 32:24-32), of Moses at the time when he began his mission (Ex. 4:24-26), and it was especially true of Jesus in Gethsemane. These are the kinds of desperate conflicts in which the elect, who carry the burden of human sin, recognize that they are rejected and go through a death from which only the steadfast love of God can remove them. God reveals himself as he who " kills and brings to life " (I Sam. 2:6), and in this battle it is the one conquered by God who is the true conqueror.

The Everlasting Covenant a Covenant of Grace

It is *God alone* who is the guarantor of the covenant. His honor is pledged. And although Abraham's descendants break the covenant, God himself in Jesus Christ comes and offers himself in place of the defaulting partner, and pays the price of his faithlessness. We can even say that it is the shadow of the cross that envelops Abraham during his night of anxiety.

God gives Abraham a visible sign of his covenant: circumcision. But true believers in Israel will later understand that the circumcision of the flesh is meaningless unless it implies and involves the true circumcision, the circumcision of the heart (Jer. 4:4; Rom. 2:25-29). Circumcision is a visible sign of an invisible grace: " So shall my covenant be in your flesh an everlasting covenant " (Gen. 17:13). Jesus, circumcized on the eighth day, stresses the old covenant only for the purpose of substituting for it a new covenant sealed with his blood, of which the sign is " baptism in his death " (cf. Rom. 6:3).

One further point should be noted. Foreigners can become part of the people of God by circumcision. (Gen. 17:12-14.) From its very beginnings (and even before having this name which is not given to it until much later, cf. Gen. 32:28), Israel is not a community because of its race and blood, but a community because of its *faith,* and its unity is sealed by the rite of circumcision.

4. ABRAHAM, FATHER OF BELIEVERS

We have seen God test Abraham's faith by the initial command that Abraham leave his home: " He went out, not knowing where he was to go " (Heb. 11:8); then by the long years of waiting for the fulfillment of the promises; and finally by the ultimate test of the sacrifice of Isaac. To round out the picture we ought also to show Abraham as the intercessor pleading with God on behalf of the guilty cities of Sodom and Gomorrah (Gen., ch. 18).

Having Faith in God's Promises

In a single verse, the Bible sums up what makes Abraham important: " He believed the Lord; and he reckoned it to him as *righteousness* " (Gen. 15:6).[7] It is because of his faith in God that Abraham becomes the archetype for true belief. " And he was called the friend of God," the Bible tells us. (James 2:23.) *To believe means to trust the God who revealed himself to Abraham, Isaac, and Jacob, to take him at his word. It means to obey his commandments and to be convinced that his promises are absolutely sure.*

Jacob, that " child prodigy " of the Old Testament (even though he is also an impostor and liar) , likewise takes the Word of God and his promises very seriously. In the most desperate circumstances he clings to them and refuses to let them go: " O God of my father Abraham and God of my father Isaac, O Lord who didst say to me, ' Return.' . . . Thou didst say, ' I will do you good ' " (Gen. 32:9, 12) . The invincible weapon of prayer is found in those three words, " Thou didst say." Later on, Jacob says, " I will not let you go, unless you bless me." (Gen. 32:26.) And at the conclusion of his wrestling with God, Jacob receives the name of " Israel " (which means " he who strives with God ") , for as his opponent says, " You have striven with God and with men, and have prevailed " (Gen. 32:28) .

This is the most astonishing thing that has ever been said to a man or to a people! The full meaning of Israel's vocation is encompassed in this name. And when faithless Israel fails in its task, God, who is always faithful to himself, raises up One who, incarnating all Israel in his own person, attacks heaven, hell, and all mankind, and emerges the victor. He is the One who, invisible but present from the very beginning, sustains the faith of Abraham at Moriah, of Jacob at the ford of the Jabbok, of Joseph in his captivity in Egypt — this Joseph who is sold into captivity by his brothers and who gets his revenge on them by saving them.

Abraham's True Descendants

Now perhaps we can understand why the patriarchs play such an important role in the thought of the New Testament. They are faith's first witnesses to the Living God. And their witness stands against those very ones who refer to them most frequently, but are their sons only according to the flesh and not according to the spirit:

> I tell you, many will come from east and west and sit at table with Abraham, Isaac, and Jacob in the kingdom of heaven, while the sons of the kingdom will be thrown into the outer darkness. (Matt. 8:11-12.)

The "sons of the kingdom" referred to here are the circumcized of the Old Covenant and the baptized of the New Covenant who are Israelites only according to the flesh or Christians only in name; they are all those who are not the genuine sons of Abraham *according to faith.*

Only the "sons of Abraham" enter into the Kingdom. Whether we like it or not, the greatest promise that is made to us is that we shall meet him at the banquet in the heavenly Kingdom.

CHAPTER III

THE COVENANT AT SINAI

The Deliverance from Egypt
Moses, the Mediator Between God
and His People

(Exodus, Leviticus, Numbers, Deuteronomy)

SUMMARY

Israel's exile in Egypt is said to have lasted four hundred years. (Gen. 15:13.) The trials that God inflicted on the chosen people were long and harsh. However, throughout the rest of Israel's history, the deliverance from Egyptian bondage remains the most important sign of God's faithfulness and steadfast love, the foundation of the covenant established with him (Ex. 20:1-2; Hos. 11:1; Ps. 135:8-9; 136:10-16; etc.).

As the very word indicates, Exodus is the story of Israel's "going out" from Egypt toward the Promised Land, followed by the beginning of its life in the wilderness and the establishment of the law. The account of life in the wilderness is continued in the book of Numbers, while Deuteronomy and Leviticus resume and expand the teaching concerning the law of God.[8]

1. THE GOD OF THE PATRIARCHS REVEALS HIMSELF TO MOSES (Ex., chs. 1 to 4)
   a. God "remembers" his covenant and watches over his own (Ex. 1:17, 20; 2:1-10, 23-25).
   b. Moses identifies himself with his own enslaved people, but he must wait until God is ready to act (Ex. 2:11-22;

cf. Acts 7:20-29; Heb. 11:24-26) .

c. God reveals himself to Moses as the Holy, the Almighty, the God of Abraham, Isaac, and Jacob, the Savior (Ex., chs. 3; 4) . He reveals his name to Moses (Ex. 3:13-15) .

2. GOD SAVES HIS PEOPLE " WITH A STRONG HAND AND AN OUT-STRETCHED ARM " (Ex., chs. 5 to 18)

a. God shows that his power is present in the midst of his judgments by delivering his people from Egyptian bondage. Israel escapes judgment only by the special grace of God: the blood of the paschal lamb deters the destroyer's arm. The Feast of the Passover commemorates this " passing over " by the Lord (Ex. 12:1-28; 13:1-16; Deut. 16:1-8) . God makes a way for his people to cross the sea (Ex., chs. 14; 15) and feeds them in the wilderness (Ex. 15:22 to 16:36) .

b. Israel is a redeemed people and belongs to the One who brought it from bondage to liberty, from death to life (Ex. 20:2-3; Num. 15:41; cf. Ps. 81:1-11; 105; 114; Hos. 11:1) . But only those who trust God's promises enter the Promised Land (Num. 14:20-38) .

c. In these historic events, the New Testament sees an indication of the salvation to come and of the Last Judgment. This is why, in the book of Revelation, the elect sing the song of Moses and the song of the Lamb at the same time (Rev. 15:2-4) . The New Testament sees in Jesus Christ the true paschal lamb given for the salvation of the world (John 1:29; I Cor. 5:7; I Peter 1:17-21) , and in the crossing of the Red Sea a symbol of baptism into his death (I Cor. 10:1-5) . He is the true bread come down from heaven (John, ch. 6) , the spring of living water that will never go dry (John 4:7-14; 7:37) .

3. THE COVENANT AT SINAI (Ex., chs. 19; 24; 32 to 34)

a. God makes Israel " his people " and his witness to all other peoples (Ex. 19:1-6) . Israel is the church of the Old Covenant, but it is also a " nation." This means that its history has a dual character: it is different from that of all other nations, and yet it takes place within the give-and-take of the history of all other nations.

b. God is holy and he sets out the boundaries that his people cannot overstep without being destroyed by his holiness (Ex. 19:7-25; ch. 24). The covenant is solemnly ratified with all the people; God reveals his law to them, and its establishment is sealed by the sprinkling of blood (Ex. 24:3-8).

c. Moses, God's spokesman to the people and the people's intercessor to God, establisher of the covenant (Ex., chs. 3; 4; 17:4, 8-16; 19; 24; 33; 34), is admitted by special favor into the presence of the Almighty (Ex. 24:2, 15-18; 33:11; 34:34-35). In his special role he is occasionally, but only occasionally — for he remains a man and a sinner (Ex. 33:20; 40:34-35; cf. II Cor. 3:13, Num. 20:12; Deut. 3:23-28; cf. Ps. 99:6-9) — like a forerunner of the sole mediator to come, Jesus Christ (cf. Heb. 3:1-6; 9:11-24).

4. THE PLACE OF THE LAW IN GOD'S UNFOLDING PURPOSE OF SALVATION (Ex., chs. 20 to 40; Deut., chs. 5 to 10; 28 to 30)

a. The law is the charter that God gives his people after having saved them from death. It is " the guardian of the freedom we have received, the boundary of our existence as children of God " (R. de Pury). It shows us God's will for this world, a will whose transgression brings about destruction and death (Deut. 8:1; 10:12-21; 30:6, 11-20).

b. The law of God is given to us in the Ten Commandments (Ex. 20:2-17; cf. Deut. 5:6-21), and summarized in the two commandments to love God and our neighbor (Deut. 6:5; Lev. 19:18), concerning which Jesus said, " Do this, and you will live " (Luke 10:25-28).

c. The Ten Commandments are the basis of all that God decrees. The civil and cultic laws that follow them are concrete applications to the circumstances of the times; they show that the divine will encompasses all human relationships and the whole of man's social life. The Bible knows nothing of a " secular realm " that is not under divine control.

d. The law, given as a gift of grace, becomes our *condemnation* when it is broken (Deut. 28:15; 30:15; Rom. 3:19-24; ch. 7). The New Testament sees the law as a " school-

master " who shows us our actual situation and leads us
to Jesus Christ, in whom alone the condemnation of the
law can be overcome (Gal. 3:21-29; Rom. 5:6-21; 7:7-25) .

e. The gospel does not abolish the commandments; rather,
it produces in us the obedience of faith, which is the joyful response to the grace received in Christ by the power
of the Holy Spirit (Rom. 8:1-17; ch. 12; Gal. 5:13-23;
Matt., ch. 5) .

Only the laws dealing with sacrifice are abolished, for
they were merely " the shadow of things to come " and
have found their definitive fulfillment in Jesus Christ
(Heb., chs. 8 to 10) .

1. THE GOD OF THE PATRIARCHS REVEALS HIMSELF
TO MOSES
(Ex., chs. 1 to 4)

He for whom " a thousand years [are] as one day " (II
Peter 3:8; cf. Ps. 90:4) has a different conception of time
from ours. For after having spoken to Abraham, Isaac, Jacob, and Joseph, God remains silent for four hundred years
(Gen. 15:13; cf. Acts 7:6) ! Has he forgotten his covenant?
Has he forgotten his promise? Everything would lead us to
think so.

God " Remembers " His People

Jacob's descendants are settled in Egypt (Gen. 50:22 to
Ex. 1:1-7) . A new dynasty of Pharaohs comes to power and
Israel experiences persecution for the first time in its history. The Pharaoh tries to get rid of this troublesome and
prolific group of people, and uses every possible means of
doing so (Ex. 1:8-14) . One of the characteristics of pagan
despotism is its lack of regard for human life, and this reveals its demonic character, for this is a violation of the fundamental law of creation (Gen. 9:5-7) . Furthermore —
and this again is characteristic — the policies of the Pharaoh are full of contradictions: he despises the Israelites, but
he can't get along without their man power: " they built
for Pharaoh store cities " (Ex. 1:11) . Similarly, he tries to

destroy them, but he won't let them leave the country.

And then, quietly at first, but gradually more clearly and openly, God intervenes:

> And the people of Israel groaned under their bondage, and cried out for help, and their cry under bondage came up to God. And God heard their groaning, and God remembered his covenant with Abraham, with Isaac, and with Jacob. And God saw the people of Israel, and God knew their condition. (Ex. 2:23-25.)

God mocks the Pharaoh's plans. First of all, he blesses the midwives who disobey the despot because they are afraid of what God will do. Then he rescues a tiny baby from the waters of the Nile, the baby who will be Israel's savior, and, in a masterpiece of irony, has him brought up by the Pharaoh himself (Ex., ch. 2). " That," said Luther, " was really tweaking the Pharaoh's nose. The daughter of the great king is obliged to be the servant of the Lord! "

God chooses the weak things of the world to confound the strong. Moses in his basket of bulrushes and Jesus in his manger — the one rescued from the jaws of the Pharaoh, the other from the jaws of Herod — are both ways in which the omnipotence of God expresses itself through the weakness of men. Pharaoh and Herod each embody the evil forces in the world that seek to destroy God's plan of salvation at its very source.

The little basket, coated with bitumen and pitch just as Noah's ark had been coated (Ex. 2:3; cf. Gen. 6:14), carries the whole future of God's people within it. " Assuredly," Calvin writes, " he drew out Moses, who was to be the future redeemer of his people, as from the grave, in order that he might prove that the beginning of the safety of his church was like a creation out of nothing." [9]

Moses Identifies Himself with His People

When Moses grows up, he leaves the Pharaoh's palace in order to identify himself with his enslaved people. In the same way, as we shall see, Jesus Christ, son of the King of Kings, leaves his Father's home in order to identify himself with lost humanity and become a man among men.

> By faith Moses, when he was grown up, refused to be called the son of Pharaoh's daughter, choosing rather to share ill-treatment with the people of God than to enjoy the fleeting pleasures of sin. He considered abuse suffered for the Christ greater wealth than the treasures of Egypt, for he looked to the reward. (Heb. 11:24-26.)

The " leaving all," which was so important in the story of Abraham, reappears here in the story of Moses.

But Moses does not know how to wait until God is ready to act. He takes the people's cause into his own hands. As a result, he gets into trouble. He makes a bad mistake and has to flee (Ex. 2:11-22). Then God takes forty years pre-ᵗparing Moses and testing him (Acts 7:29-30),[10] before showing Moses who He is, and starting to make use of him.

God Reveals Himself in the Burning Bush

God reveals himself to Moses in the form of a burning bush that is not consumed. He thus indicates the distance between himself and his creatures. The closeness between God and man that existed in Paradise has been destroyed forever: God says, " Do not come near . . ." (Ex. 3:5).

Fire is a symbol of divine holiness. (Cf. Gen. 15:17; Ex. 19:18; Deut. 4:12, 36; 5:5; II Sam. 22:9.) The bush is not consumed because God is eternally the same, a consuming fire who is not himself consumed. But in the midst of the flames, God *speaks*. He speaks to Moses as he had spoken to the patriarchs. He reveals himself once more as the faithful God. He " remembers " his covenant with Abraham, Isaac, and Jacob, and solemnly reaffirms that his plan of salvation will continue to unfold.

Moses asks God his *name*. We have seen the importance of the name in Semitic thought. According to ancient belief, to know God's name was to possess magical powers, it almost meant to have control of him. But no one can have control of God.

God gives Moses an enigmatic reply. Various attempts have been made to translate the four consonants YHWH that stand for the name of God: " I AM," or " I AM WHO I AM." And since Hebraic writing does not use vowels, and since postexilic Judaism avoids pronouncing the name of God, there is uncertainty even today about the pronunciation of the tetragrammaton YHWH (Yahweh, Jehovah). There is the same uncertainty about the origin of the name. The translators give us a variety of renderings. It is noted by A. Lods that the Hebraic way of putting it is the way that is used when precision is not desired: " I am that I am." " The essential nature of the God of Israel is and must remain inscrutable." [11] Wilhelm Vischer translates impartially, " I am that I am," or more simply, " I am I." Vischer continues: " The utterance is made in the Hebrew imperfect which expresses an incompleted action, so that it might be equally well translated, ' I shall exist as I shall exist.' " [12] James Moffatt translates, " I-will-be-what-I-will-be," and the Chicago translation (Theophile J. Meek) goes, " I am who I am." For God is the *eternally living God,* the *eternally acting God.* He is the One who, without ever changing, has been working for man's salvation from the very beginning.

God describes himself as *he who is.* But he remains the hidden God, whom man knows only to the extent that God chooses to reveal himself to man. The mystery surrounding God's name will be removed only in Jesus Christ, the Word made flesh: " No one has ever seen God; the only Son, who is in the bosom of the Father, he has made him known " (John 1:18; cf. ch. 14:8-9; Rom. 8:15).

All that Moses needs to know is that *God will be with him* as he was with the patriarchs. God is, and will remain throughout all the ages, the God of Abraham, Isaac, and

Jacob (Ex. 3:13-15), the One who guides and guards his own people throughout all their stormy history.

2. GOD SAVES HIS PEOPLE "WITH A STRONG HAND AND AN OUTSTRETCHED ARM" (Ex., chs. 5 to 18)

God Delivers His People from the Egyptians

God reveals himself as the Living God of Israel by *an act of deliverance*. The contest between Moses and the Pharaoh is much more than it appears to be on the surface. It is really a decisive battle between the God of Israel and the gods of Egypt (represented by the magicians, cf. Ex. 7:22; 8:7, 18-19).

We must see "the finger of God" (Ex. 8:19) at work in these judgments on Egypt. Demonic powers can imitate the works of God, but only within certain limits; and if they are to be overthrown, this limit must be reached and exceeded.

Whenever God interferes in history, the forces working against him enter into a coalition, for the world revolts against the claim of the divine upon it. In this case, the Pharaoh embodies all the demonic forces of resistance. Evil must display all its power so that the judgment upon it can be more significant and God's glory shine forth to greater effect. Furthermore, the Bible interprets God's judgment upon Egypt as more than a simple historical event; it is also a kind of anticipation of the Last Judgment, and Israel's deliverance becomes a pointer to the final resurrection. Israel escapes judgment only by the special intervention of God: the blood of the paschal lamb, marking the lintel of the doors, deters the hand of the angel of death. This is the meaning of the great Feast of the Passover, which as the word suggests means "passing over," and refers to the Lord's "passing over" the houses of the Israelites on the night of judgment. In its celebration of this

feast, Israel always commemorates the escape from Egypt
(Ex. 12:1-28; 13:1-16) :

> And you shall tell your son on that day, " It is because
> of what the Lord did for me when I came out of Egypt."
> And it shall be to you as a sign on your hand and as a
> memorial between your eyes. (Ex. 13:8-9.)

The Passover is eaten standing up, for from this time on
Israel is an eternal pilgrim en route to the Promised Land.
By this gesture, Israel remembers that it is forever an alien
and exile on earth (cf. I Peter 2:11).

Actually, of course, only a handful of Israelites left Egypt
and crossed the Red Sea. But in Biblical thought, the part
represents the whole, and in the solidarity of faith, all share
in the gifts conferred on the few. This is why every Israelite celebrates the Passover " in memory of what the Lord
did *for me*." In dealing with the deliverance of the people
of Israel, the Babylonian Talmud puts it this way:

> This is why we are told to render thanks, to extol, to
> praise, to glorify, to exalt, to honor, to magnify him who
> has wrought this miracle for our fathers and *for us all,*
> who has brought *us* out of bondage into freedom, out of
> suffering into joy, out of mourning into rejoicing, out of
> darkness into his wondrous light, out of slavery into de-
> liverance. . . . Allelulia!

In the same way, Paul says, " Our fathers were *all* under
the cloud, and *all* passed through the sea, and *all* were baptized into Moses in the cloud and in the sea, and *all* ate the
same supernatural food and *all* drank the same supernatural drink." (I Cor. 10:1-2, italics added.)

All of this is a vivid reminder that in Hebraic thought
the part stands for the whole. The offering of the first fruits
of the harvest, for example, signifies the entire harvest. In
the one person of Abraham, all believing Israel is introduced to the benefits of the promise. In the same way, by
removing a handful of Israelites from slavery in Egypt and

leading them to the Promised Land, God makes his grace known to all Israel. This is why every Israelite can rejoice in the benefits conferred upon his fathers just as though they had been conferred upon him personally. In this solidarity of faith every Israelite, at whatever point in history he lives, must celebrate the deliverance granted to his fathers as *his own* deliverance, and see in it the guarantee of *his own* passage from bondage to freedom, from death to life.

It is in the light of this truth about solidarity that Jesus is later able to take the sin of his people upon himself and Paul is able to say that in Christ we have *all* died and have *all* been raised from the dead.

The Meaning of Deliverance and the Problem of " Rejection "

For us, as Christians, this event is the pointer toward an even more wonderful deliverance. This concrete act, written into the very pages of history itself, is an indication of God's eternal faithfulness, and of his final victory over all the powers of evil and death.

These are the terms in which we must understand the rather savage cry of praise and triumph of Miriam the prophetess:

> Sing to the Lord, for he has triumphed gloriously;
> the horse and his rider he has thrown into the sea.
> (Ex. 15:21.)

In the same way we must understand the magnificent song of Moses in Ex., ch. 15, which echoes through heaven itself in the book of Revelation (cf. Rev. 15:3-4). These are also the terms in which we must hear the paradoxical refrain of Ps. 136:

> O give thanks to the Lord, for he is good,
> for his steadfast love endures for ever. . . .
> to him who smote the first-born of Egypt,

> for his steadfast love endures for ever;
> and brought Israel out from among them,
> for his steadfast love endures for ever;
> with a strong hand and an outstretched arm,
> for his steadfast love endures for ever.
>
> (Ps. 136:1, 10-12.)

Here the historical event is understood as a sign, an anticipation of God's final victory, when he will bring all his enemies under his feet.

But what about those who are cast out? What about this
Pharaoh whose heart God " hardens "? What about these
pagan peoples who are destroyed without mercy?

All of this remains encompassed by the mystery of God.
But we may remember that there is a promise of redemption for Egypt in the Bible itself:

> In that day there will be a highway from Egypt to As-
> syria, and the Assyrian will come into Egypt, and the
> Egyptian into Assyria, and the Egyptians will worship
> with the Assyrians.
> In that day Israel will be the third with Egypt and As-
> syria, a blessing in the midst of the earth, whom the Lord
> of hosts has blessed, saying, " Blessed be Egypt my people,
> and Assyria the work of my hands, and Israel my heri-
> tage." (Isa. 19:23-25.)

On nearly every page the Bible insistently reminds us
that God will not be mocked and that the result of revolt
against him is death. This is why " natural man " is condemned and why the chosen are rescued from death only
by a miracle of grace. And when the Bible contrasts Abel
and Cain, Isaac and Ishmael, Jacob and Esau, Moses and
Pharaoh, its purpose is to remind us, by these examples,
of the state of our own sin, and of the fact that grace is a
sheer gift. But there is nothing in the Bible that allows us
to say that the rejection of a Cain or an Ishmael or a Pharaoh is final. As we have seen repeatedly, certain promises

are also given to them. And if, in the Old Testament, the ranks of the elect and the ranks of the rejected are contrasted, *in Jesus Christ the two ranks converge. He takes upon himself the curse of all the rejected ones in history and by doing this he opens up for them a gateway to salvation. In him we are all, by faith, both condemned and pardoned.* The chosen of the Old Testament are already in his orbit of light, visible signs of the deliverance to come. The others are still in the darkness. Where they will be when the final splendor of God's light bursts forth, only he can say or know. But the election of Israel as God's instrument of salvation no more signifies the final rejection of the pagans than the election of the pagans under the New Covenant means the final rejection of Israel (Rom. 11:25-26). If we are to understand the judgments of the Old Testament and the meaning of the part played by Israel, we must never lose sight of the *instrumental* character of its election. Israel is chosen to be the means by which others may be saved.[13]

We must never forget that the reality of freedom is still at the very heart of election. God's gift may be accepted or rejected. The times of testing in the wilderness, when God showed how patient he could be and taught his people to live by his grace alone, make clear that many Israelites simply scorned God's steadfast love when it was offered to them. It is this fact which gives particular significance to the story of the golden calf, and later to the welcome given to the first group of spies returning from the Land of Canaan. Only those who trust the promises of God enter into the Promised Land. (Num. 14:20-38.)

The Exodus as a " Sign " of Salvation to Come

The exodus is a historic event of the greatest importance for anyone who wants to understand the meaning of Israel's history, and all those who have responsibility for Israel's destiny keep referring to it again and again. It is at the exodus that God reveals himself to Israel as the God who rescues and sets free, and it is from the time of the exodus that Israel dates its existence as a nation, as the " people of God."

But in the total perspective of God's plan of salvation, this event has an even greater significance. It is a " sign " of the salvation to come — and the word " sign " in this connection means an event that already contains within itself something of the reality to which it is pointing. It is because Jesus Christ will later give his life for the salvation of the world, because he will be the *true* paschal lamb (John 1:29; I Cor. 5:7; I Peter 1:17-21), that the blood of the lamb spilled by the Israelites on the lintels of their doors has the power to protect them from the judgment of the angel of death. Without knowing it, Israel already lives under the sign of the promised grace. It is " as seeing him who is invisible " (Heb. 11:27) that Moses shows the people a way across the Red Sea. His faith and obedience disclose to Israel the actual route to the Promised Land, just as the faith and obedience of Jesus Christ disclose to Christians the way to the Kingdom of God. Israel goes through a kind of death and resurrection. This is why Paul sees the crossing of the Red Sea as a true baptism (I Cor. 10:2; cf. Rom. 6:2-4). And because in men's lives the only truly sustaining thing is bread come down from heaven (John, ch. 6), and the spring of living water, the Israelites, without their knowing it, live in the wilderness by the grace of Jesus Christ. It is he who gives them food and drink (I Cor. 10:3-4; cf. Ex., chs. 16 to 17:7), just as it is he who rescues them from death.

This is why the elect in heaven sing the song of Moses and the song of the Lamb at one and the same time. (Rev. 15:2-4.)

3. THE COVENANT AT SINAI
(Ex., chs. 19; 24; 32 to 34)

Israel as " God's People "

At Mt. Sinai, God renews the covenant he had made with Abraham, but this time he does it with *all* the people. He makes Israel his own people:

> You have seen what I did to the Egyptians, and how I bore you on eagles' wings and brought you to myself. Now therefore, if you will obey my voice and keep my covenant, you shall be my own possession among all peoples; for all the earth is mine, and you shall be to me a kingdom of priests and a holy nation. (Ex. 19:4-6.)

" All the earth is mine. . . ." God is sovereign Lord over all the peoples of the earth, but he fixes his choice on the humblest and least impressive of them all, and decides to make this tribe of slaves " his own possession." Anything is holy that is consecrated to the Lord, and Israel is set apart henceforth for the exclusive service of God. Just as the priest stands before the altar of God on behalf of all the people, so this " nation of priests," this royal priesthood, will stand before him on behalf of all the people of the world. From this time on, Israel is the church of the Old Covenant, and I Peter merely repeats the phrases of Ex., ch. 19, in defining the church of the New Covenant (I Peter 2:9).

The unique thing about Israel consists in the fact that Israel is to be both a *people* and a *church*, set in the very midst of the rough and tumble of the life of nations. In other words, Israel is to be at the same time both a religious and political community, a theocracy.

The Obligations of the Covenant

In his relationship with this people who become his own people, God first of all establishes certain boundaries. No one, on pain of death, is to go near the holy mountain without being summoned there (Ex. 19:12-13, 24). God appears in the midst of a fire and Israel trembles. (Ex. 19:16-18; 24:17.) For no man can see the face of the most holy God and live. Only Moses, who thereby becomes a symbol of the Mediator to come, can live on the mountain of the Lord and receive his commandments (Ex. 19:20; 24:1-2, 12-18).

God ratifies a solemn covenant with the people. The Book of the Covenant is read to the whole assembly and Moses sprinkles them with "the blood of the covenant" (Ex. 24:8). The seventy elders referred to in Ex. 24:9 probably represent the rest of the nations.[14] The priestly people stand before God on behalf of all the earth, and the covenant that this people ratifies contains a promise of salvation for all the nations.

The covenant was not ratified simply with one single generation on Mt. Horeb. On the contrary, it binds every Israelite forever: " Not with our fathers did the Lord make this covenant, but with us, who are all of us here alive this day " (Deut. 5:3).

God is the only God who loves his people with a " jealous " love, a love that has no place for divided loyalties. This is why idolatry, in whatever form it takes, is *always* the basic sin of God's people. Idolatry is treason against the divine love, a treason that the Bible does not hesitate to call " prostitution."

One of the most dramatic pages in the Bible is the one that describes the first breaking of the covenant, the story of the golden calf:

> When the people saw that Moses delayed to come down from the mountain, the people gathered themselves together to Aaron, and said to him, " Up, make us gods, who shall go before us; as for this Moses, the man who brought us up out of the land of Egypt, we do not know what has become of him." (Ex. 32:1.)

In this situation, Moses emerges as the true mediator between God and his people. He reproves and chastizes the people in God's name, but when he is alone before God he does not try to separate himself from the guilty people: "Forgive their sin — and if not, blot me, I pray thee, out of thy book" (Ex. 32:32). His intercession softens God's anger. God agrees to lead his people, but he will not permanently live in their midst (Ex. 33:3, 14-15), for he means to safeguard his sovereign freedom. No one shall ever have control of him. He is the Almighty, who "will be gracious to whom he will be gracious, and will show mercy on whom he will show mercy" (cf. Ex. 33:19).

The Special Role of Moses

Why is it said, within the space of a few verses, that God spoke to Moses face to face as a man speaks to his friend (Ex. 33:11), and yet that no one, not even Moses, can see God's face and live? (Ex. 33:20.) "Natural man," man as sinner, cannot gaze upon the brightness of the divine glory, for the holiness of God is a consuming fire — and Moses is no exception to this. But, by a special privilege, at certain times Moses is admitted into the presence of the Most High. More than that, he enters into the *favor* of God, and is his spokesman and his confidant. Could it not be that at these times he is the forerunner of one greater than himself, namely, the unique Mediator between God and men, in terms of whom Moses' mediation is only a foretaste and a foreshadowing? (Ex. 33:7-11; cf. ch. 34:29-35, also ch. 17:8-13, and, on the other hand, chs. 33:17-23; 40:35; Heb. 3:1-6; II Cor. 3:12-18.)

4. THE PLACE OF THE LAW IN GOD'S UNFOLDING PURPOSE OF SALVATION
(Ex., chs. 20 to 40; Deut., chs. 5 to 10; 28 to 30)

The Law as the Expression of God's Will

God enters into a solemn covenant with his people. His first gracious deed is to reveal his law to them in order that they may *live*. By his law is meant, of course, his *will*. In separating themselves from God, men lost the meaning and understanding of God's will. Since God reveals himself to them by his Word, Israel becomes from this time on the bearer and witness to God's commandments. The law is " the guardian of the freedom we have received " (R. de Pury). It marks the boundaries beyond which the people of God may not trespass without breaking the covenant and falling once again into the darkness of a world without God. The law shows clearly that *all of life* must be placed under God's commands, for it has to do not only with the relationship of man with God and with his neighbor, but with every aspect of religious and civil life. And, again and again comes the refrain, like a signature that makes the decree valid, " I am the Lord . . . I am the Lord . . . I am the Lord " (Lev., ch. 19).

The Ten Commandments

The first four commandments deal with the relationship of man with God; the remaining six deal with the relationship of man with his neighbor.

1. " *I am the Lord your God, who brought you out of the land of Egypt, out of the house of bondage.*" These are the significant words with which the Ten Commandments begin. It is the Savior-God, the Holy, the Almighty, who is speaking, he who rescued Israel from slavery and death. The validity of the law depends totally upon the authority of the one who declares it. Here God declares who he is.

2. " *You shall not make yourself a graven image.*" The Lord and Savior of Israel will not allow his children to have divided loyalties; all resort to other gods or to other powers is an insult to his honor, and is what the prophet Elijah later calls " limping with two different opinions " (I Kings 18:21). However, this is the temptation that always faces Israel. Yahweh is Israel's ostensible God, the one to whom it will turn in time of crisis, but in ordinary situations Israel prays to the local gods, the Canaanite Baals. The first two commandments condemn idolatry. The most prevalent form of idolatry at that time consisted in making idols of the god which were then equated with the god itself, as in the case of the golden calf. It is not without good cause that the throne placed in the center of the Tabernacle is *empty,* for the God of Israel is Spirit and Truth and does not dwell in houses made with human hands. From the very outset this essential point distinguishes the worship of Israel from that of the pagan religions that surround it. But it is important to remember that it is not simply the huge idols made of wood or metal that our text attacks; these idols symbolize more profound realities. An idol is anything that takes first place in the heart of man, a place that belongs to God alone. " You cannot serve God and mammon," Jesus says, " mammon " standing for wealth or riches. Any authority that gives man the final say, whether it be the authority of an individual or a social group or an ideology, sets itself up in place of the legitimate authority of God. One of the most terrible idolatries described in the Bible, for example, is the deified state, considered as an end in itself (cf. the treatment of Babylon in the book of Revelation).

3. " *You shall not take the name of the Lord your God in vain.*" God's name is holy. To take this name in vain must be understood not only as blasphemy but as an attack on God's honor. The people of God are called to be holy as God is holy (Lev. 19:2). Every Christian carries the

name of Christ and must glorify the name that he carries by his obedience and his whole frame of mind.

4. " *Remember the sabbath day, to keep it holy.*" The commandment dealing with the Sabbath is a transition between the first and second portions of the Ten Commandments. It is based on the fact that God rested on the seventh day of creation (Gen. 2:2-3). The Sabbath thus becomes a reminder and a pointer toward the eternal rest into which the elect will enter on the last day. On the Sabbath, God lets men withdraw from the feverish pace of day-to-day life, so that they may concentrate on the unchangeable and eternal. But this commandment also has a human and a social meaning: " You shall rest; that your ox and your ass may have rest " — the Creator wants this even for dumb brutes! — " and the son of your bondmaid, and the alien, may be refreshed " (Ex. 23:12).

The last six commandments deal with the neighbor.

5. " *Honor your father and your mother.*" The authority of the father and mother is vigorously stressed not only here but in a whole series of passages (Ex. 20:12; Deut. 21: 18-21; Prov. 1:8; 23:22; etc.). More is involved here than a simple commandment about human deference. The family is ordained by God. (Gen. 1:27-28; 2:24.) Parents are answerable to God for their children and to this responsibility corresponds a God-given authority. Fatherhood and motherhood are seen as an earthly reflection of the Fatherhood of God: " For this reason I bow my knees before the Father, from whom every family in heaven and on earth is named," wrote Paul (Eph. 3:14-15).

6. " *You shall not kill.*" The prohibition of murder reminds us of the commandment given to Noah and the warning that accompanied it (Gen. 9:5-6): he who kills will be held accountable for his murder before God himself, for God has made man in his image. Therefore God will demand the soul of anyone who strikes another. These are grave words, for there are many ways of killing not

only the body but also the soul. Only God gives life and only God has the right to take it away. (It should be noticed that the Old Testament speaks here of murder, and is not dealing with the question of the legal death penalty.)

7. " *You shall not commit adultery.*" The condemnation of adultery is based upon the order of creation, which proclaims the indissolubility of marriage (Gen. 2:24; cf. Mark 10:1-11). Here again the unity of the human couple must reflect a higher unity. Two beings are to become " one," and it is in Christ alone that we are able to grasp the full extent of the vocation of marriage, understood as a mutual giving where each one no longer belongs to himself or herself but to the other. Husbands are to love their wives " as Christ loved the church " (Eph. 5:25).

8. " *You shall not steal.*" The Biblical concept of property rights is very different from that of Roman or modern law. God is the only absolute proprietor of all earthly goods and we are his tenants, answerable to him for the use we make of our belongings: " The land is mine " (Lev. 25:23); " The silver is mine, and the gold is mine, says the Lord of hosts " (Hag. 2:8). This means that an Israelite should not be dispossessed forever of his heritage (Lev., ch. 25), nor should he expend it ruthlessly (Isa. 5:8), exploit or deceive his brother (Amos 2:6-8), or trample down the poor (Ex. 22:21-27; Lev. 19:35-36; cf. Amos 8:4-6).

9. " *You shall not bear false witness against your neighbor.*" God's law severely punishes false witness. (Ex. 23:1-8; Deut. 19:15-21.) Bearing false witness makes truth and justice impossible in men's relationships with one another. " Let what you say be simply ' Yes ' or ' No,' " Jesus says; " anything more than this comes from evil." (Matt. 5:37.) A world in which false witness becomes the pattern is a world in which law no longer exists, in which demonic powers are in control.

10. " *You shall not covet.*" Covetousness is the hidden

root of murder, theft, and adultery; it destroys not only the relationship of individual to individual but also of group to group and of nation to nation. It is the evil power that enters into the heart and tries to dominate it, the evil power that refuses to recognize the limits set out by God and makes us trespass them in spirit before we do so in actuality (Gen. 4:7; Matt. 5:28-30).

God's Will Relates to All of Life

The Ten Commandments (Ex. 20:2-17) are the basis of all that God decrees. The laws that follow in Ex., chs. 21 to 23 are a concrete application of the Ten Commandments to the particular circumstances of the time. They evolve with the times, as can be seen by comparing the stipulations concerning slaves and property rights in Exodus, Deuteronomy, and Leviticus, each of which represents a different period in Israel's history. As a result, we do not apply these latter laws to our contemporary situation in a literal way. But they do give us real guidance, for they furnish us with certain criteria by means of which we can judge the laws and institutions of our own time. From this point of view it is instructive to reread the laws concerning the protection of the poor, of widows and orphans, and particularly of strangers (Ex. 22:21-24; 23:6-9; Deut. 10:17-19; Lev. 19:33-34) ; the laws concerning work and rest (Ex. 20:8-11; 23:12) ; and the laws dealing with property rights (Lev. 25:23-28, 35-38, 47-55) .

Side by side with the civil laws, we find in Exodus, and even more in Leviticus, whole chapters devoted to ritual laws, to the construction of the Tabernacle, and to the organization of the priesthood. Israel is a priestly people. Its very *raison d'être* is to glorify God and render to him the worship that is his due. But in order to please him, this worship must conform with his will in every particular. Here especially Israel must do nothing that is not dictated to it by the Word of God.

The Tabernacle is the Holy Place where God reveals

himself to his people. God does not stay there all the time. When he enters, he does so in the dazzling splendor of his glory. (Ex. 40:34-38.)

The pagan temples contained statues of the gods whom the pagans worshiped. Israel's Holy of Holies contains only the Ark of the Covenant, within which are the Tables of the Law. The throne above it is empty, for God does not dwell in temples made with human hands. The seraphims set above the throne are a reminder of the majesty of God. The ephod of the high priest has the names of the twelve tribes of Israel inscribed upon it. His vestments are sumptuous, adorned with gold and precious stones, and all these ornaments emphasize the solemnity of his office as the priest of God's covenant.[15]

The modern world tends to separate the " sacred " and the " secular." This does not happen in the Biblical revelation. Civil and religious laws cannot be separated, for they both originate in the will of God and their purpose is to glorify God. It is because the earth is the Lord's that the first fruits of the harvest and the first-born of the flocks are to be offered to him. This is also the reason why each person must treat his neighbor's ox and ass with due respect and be sure that everyone is treated justly. It is because God reveals himself as the Savior-God at a decisive point in its history that Israel must always celebrate the Passover of the Lord. It is because Israel remains a sinful people that it must offer sacrifices of expiation for its sins. From this time on, the law really covers *the whole life* of the people of God. It is Israel's charter, not a " bill of human rights," but a charter of God's claim upon men. For the real guardian of human law and liberty is God. The law represents the commands that men and nations may not ignore without bringing about their own destruction.

In making Israel the guardian of his law, God appoints Israel to a unique place among the nations. Israel somehow understood this and across the centuries, in spite of all its failures, maintained a passionate love for this law which is like God's seal on its election (cf. Ps. 119).

The Law as Condemnation and as a " Schoolmaster "

However, this law, which was originally given to Israel as a gift of grace, is transformed by Israel's transgression into a means of *condemnation*. This is already made clear in the threats attached to breaking the law. (Deut. 28:15-68; 30:15.) And this is what Paul expresses so forcefully in Rom., ch. 7:

> The very commandment which promised life proved to be death to me. . . . We know that the law is spiritual; but I am carnal, sold under sin. I do not understand my own actions. For I do not do what I want, but I do the very thing I hate. . . . For I delight in the law of God, in my inmost self, but I see in my members another law at war with the law of my mind and making me captive to the law of sin which dwells in my members. Wretched man that I am! Who will deliver me from this body of death? (Rom. 7:10, 14-15, 22-24.)

This captivity is more tragic and widespread than the captivity in Egypt, and the cry of the Christian is the same as Paul's: " Thanks be to God through Jesus Christ our Lord! " (Rom. 7:25). For the Christian knows that the condemnation of the law has been overcome by Jesus Christ. Jesus Christ accomplishes what no man could accomplish: he lives a life of perfect obedience to God's commandments, a life of obedience even unto death (Heb. 5:8-10). He does more: he takes upon himself the condemnation which men deserve, and in doing this, he satisfies the law's requirement which demands the death of the sinner. By his obedience and sacrifice, Jesus Christ defeats the powers that have bound us, and opens up to us the possibility of a new life, lived by faith in him. He frees us forever from Jewish legalism, and, by the power of his Spirit, introduces us into the glorious liberty of the children of

God. This is the theme of the great Pauline letters, for nobody has ever understood the weight of the law and the miracle of liberation from it as well as Paul, the former Pharisee. In these comments, we anticipate one of the basic gifts of the New Testament with which we must deal later in this book. (Gal. 2:15 to 3:14; Rom. 3:21 to 5:21.)

What was the function of the law? It was to make us aware of what our situation really is. This is what Paul means when he treats it as the " schoolmaster " that leads us to Christ (Gal. 3:21 to 4:7).

The Relationship of the Gospel to the Law

Does this mean that in God's unfolding purpose of salvation the law has only a temporary significance? Not at all. Consider:

1. It remains at the very heart of the gospel, setting forth the terms under which the forgiven are to live. In this sense it is the charter of the citizens of the Kingdom, a constant reminder of what life is like when it is lived under the sign of Christ's victory, and by the power of the Holy Spirit (cf. Matt., ch. 5; Rom. 8:1-17; ch. 12; Gal. 5:1, 12-25; and see below, Part Three, Chapter X).

2. God's commandments revealed in the Mosaic legislation have a further meaning: they show that law is based on God's will. It is because God's grace is continually at work that human society has a kind of stability and does not founder in total chaos. In what we call " normal times," this stability seems to be self-sufficient and we easily forget its source. But when times of crisis come, we are suddenly aware of how inadequate our ethics and laws turn out to be when they have been severed from the transcendent will that justifies and establishes them. It is soon apparent that there are no longer any reliable standards or trustworthy criteria at work, and everything turns into sheer political and social opportunism. A society that violates the Ten Commandments (such as those dealing with

respect for personality, the family, and the dignity of work)
ends in total collapse. And nothing short of a return to the
source of all law and all truth can save the situation. The
Christian must always remember that above all human
laws, relative and frail, is a divine Righteousness, which
both societies and individuals scorn at their peril.

3. The problem of the ritualistic laws of the Old Covenant is quite another matter. They are abolished because
they were only " the foreshadowing of things to come," and
because in Jesus Christ they found their perfect fulfillment. Wilhelm Vischer has explained this in a helpful
figure of speech: just as paper money has value only in
terms of the gold it represents, similarly the sacrifices of
the Old Covenant have meaning only in the light of the
unique and eternal sacrifice of Jesus Christ.[16] They are
signs of the salvation to come and are no longer necessary
after Christ has appeared (Heb., chs. 8 to 10) .

CHAPTER IV

THE PROMISED LAND

Israel, Church and Nation
The Throne and the Temple
(Joshua, Judges, Samuel, Kings)

SUMMARY

In the Hebrew Bible, the historical books of Joshua, Judges, I and II Samuel, and I and II Kings are included under the heading of the prophetic books.[17] It is not so much the " facts " as the *meaning* of the facts, and their place in God's plan of salvation, which concerns the sacred historian. We witness a succession of fulfillments, judgments, and deliverances. The Promised Land, although conquered once, remains a battlefield on which the power of God and the powers of this world continue to be pitted against one another. The question remains: Who will gain permanent possession, the baals or the Lord?

1. THE ENTRANCE INTO THE PROMISED LAND (Joshua)

Just as it was by the hand of God alone that Israel was delivered from the power of Egypt, so it is by his hand alone that Israel is led across the Jordan into the Promised Land. But the condition that God lays down to his people is that they maintain a radical separation from the nations that surround them. At Shechem the people renew their vow to serve the Lord and to serve only him (Josh., ch. 24).

2. THE RHYTHM OF JUDGMENT AND DELIVERANCE (Judges)

The history of The Book of Judges is a monotonous and almost hopeless rhythm, consisting of a succession of infidelities and revolts followed by momentary repentance. The Israelites are seen as " a stiff-necked people " who try God's patient endurance. Over and over again he has compassion on them and raises up a deliverer for them.

3. THE ESTABLISHMENT OF THE MONARCHY. THE HOUSE OF DAVID (I and II Samuel)

    a. Samuel, the last of the judges, combines the functions of judge, priest, and prophet. He is the one who anoints Israel's first two kings.

    b. Because of his disobedience, Saul fails to find favor in God's sight.

    c. David, in spite of his sins, is a king "after God's own heart," on account of his faith, the reality of his repentance, and his understanding of what he can and cannot do as king. After this, the house of David is the object of God's special concern, for in spite of the unfaithfulness of David's successors, the Savior of the world will be one of his descendants.

4. THE THRONE AND THE TEMPLE (II Sam. 7:1-16; cf. I Kings, chs. 5 to 8)

The task of constructing the Temple at Jerusalem is given to Solomon, the wise and peaceful king. Israel's life as church and nation henceforth has two poles: *the throne of David* and *the Temple,* both visible signs of the sovereignty and presence of God in the midst of his people. Their disappearance will be the great tragedy of the exile. Only the Temple will be restored in the postexilic period, and from that time on it will be the living symbol of the nation's unity.

5. THE EARTHLY AND THE HEAVENLY JERUSALEM

The Promised Land is a kind of prefiguring of the Kingdom of God that will be established in the future. From the time of the reign of David, the faith of the believers is centered on Jerusalem because it is the location both of the Davidic dynasty and of the Temple. The prophets of the Old Covenant see the nations coming to it in great numbers, while those of the New Covenant realize that the earthly Jerusalem is only a symbol of the heavenly Jerusalem, for the latter is God's creation and can only come from on high (II Sam. 5:6-16; Ps. 87; Isa. 2:2-4; ch. 60; 62:1-7; Rev. 21:1-4.)

We now begin an examination of the series of historical books that the Hebrew Bible describes as the " Prophets." This title is more important than we might think, for the history with which these books deal is not just history as such, it is the history of God's people. The thing that interests the sacred writer is the unfolding purpose of salvation that is revealed through this history. God enters into a conversation with his people; he summons them, and they respond — or fail to respond. He summons them particularly through the events of their history. These events, whether victories or defeats, losses or gains, have a *prophetic meaning:* they are judgments or deliverances, by means of which the sovereign God of history reveals who he is, and proceeds with his own unchangeable plan. These are also foreshadowings of the Last Judgment and the deliverance to come.

1. The Entrance Into the Promised Land
(Joshua)

" As I was with Moses, so I will be with you; I will not fail you or forsake you. Be strong and of good courage." (Josh. 1:5-6.)

These are God's first words to Joshua, at the moment when he entrusts Joshua with the difficult task of succeeding Moses and leading his people into the Promised Land. We can observe in this connection that the root of the name " Joshua " is the same as that of the name " Jesus," and means " Savior ": " he who delivers, . . . who brings to pass."

God " exalts " his servant Joshua before all the people (Josh. 3:7), just as he had exalted Moses in order to establish his authority. The crossing of the Jordan dry-shod is a reminder of the crossing of the Red Sea (Josh., chs. 3; 4) ; but this time it is the Ark of the Lord that stops the waters of the river from flowing. Joshua then sets up twelve stones (representing the twelve tribes) as a monument to the

Lord. (Josh. 4:20-24; cf. Ex. 24:4.) After this he celebrates
the Passover of the Lord. (Josh. 5:9-12.) The holiness and
power of the Lord is revealed to him in precisely the same
way that it had been revealed to Moses. (Compare Josh.
5:15 with Ex. 3:5.) The conquest of Canaan is achieved
not by the power of men but by the hand of God. This
is what the capture of Jericho symbolizes. (Josh., ch. 6.)
Joshua, like Moses, stands firmly against the unbelief and
disobedience of the people. A series of stern punishments
demonstrates to the Israelites that they cannot mock God:

> Joshua laid an oath upon them at that time, saying,
> "Cursed before the Lord be the man that rises up and
> rebuilds this city, Jericho.
>
> At the cost of his first-born shall he lay its foundation,
> At the cost of his youngest son shall he set up its gates."
> (Josh. 6:26; cf. also the whole of Josh., ch. 7.)

We have great difficulty understanding this, and particular difficulty understanding the very cruel order that
follows, i.e., placing under an interdict, or destroying
whole towns and populations. What the sacred writer is
trying to emphasize is that no compromise is possible with
the enemies of God and that obedience to God must be
unconditional. Whatever is " offered up by interdict " is
consecrated to the Lord. After that it is wrong to take any
of it for one's self, no matter how little. " Divine politics,"
if such a phrase can be permitted, necessitates a *radical*
separation of God's people from the conquered populations. This is the only way of preserving them from rapid
assimilation, and of maintaining the integrity of their message of salvation. Subsequent events make this quite clear,
for Israel is always slipping into paganism, and the men of
God have to fight a constant battle for the maintenance
of Israel's integrity. Humanly speaking, the consequences
of Israel's special vocation are taxing to the uttermost, for
unless it denies its very being, Israel is dedicated to remain-

ing forever an *unassimilated* and *unassimilable* people. This relationship of Israel to the Canaanite peoples is something like the relationship of the church to the world. For the church also there is a perpetual temptation to transfer allegiance from God to the world. The most destructive instances of this occur precisely when the church is not aware of its own defection. That is why God sometimes makes use of violent means, in order to safeguard the faithful remnant who witness to his salvation.

Certain pages in The Book of Judges, together with the findings of " secular " history, lead historians to think that the settlement of the Israelite tribes in Canaan was accomplished by a process of slow infiltration that took several centuries. The Book of Joshua, of course, gives us a schematic presentation of these events. But this doesn't make much difference, for here, as we also saw to be the case in the exodus, the part stands for the whole.

Israel renews its covenant with the Lord at Shechem, a place reminiscent of the God of the patriarchs whose purposes never fail, and who comes to re-establish Israel in the Promised Land. (Josh., ch. 24.) Joshua warns the Israelites of the gravity of the promise they are making: " You cannot serve the Lord; for he is a holy God; he is a jealous God "; and in the light of the people's affirmative response he cries out, " You are witnesses against yourselves that you have chosen the Lord, to serve him." (Josh. 24:19, 22.)

In this way the people freely reaffirm the decision of the patriarchs. Once for all, they entrust themselves to the gracious yet formidable hands of the Living God.

2. THE RHYTHM OF JUDGMENT AND DELIVERANCE
(Judges)

Unfortunately, faith does not perpetuate itself. Each new generation has to decide for itself whether it will serve the false gods (the baals) or the Living God. The Book of Judges is well aware of this fact: " And all that generation also were gathered to their fathers; and there arose another generation after them, who did not know the Lord or the work which he had done for Israel " (Judg. 2:10). God's work, like ours, is always beginning again!

Consequently, the history of this period follows a monotonous and melancholy rhythm: " And the people of Israel again did what was evil in the sight of the Lord. . . . But when the people of Israel cried to the Lord, the Lord raised up for them a deliverer " (Judg. 3:12, 15; cf. 2:11-22; 4:1; 6:1; etc.). The Israelites sin over and over again; when things are going well they forget all about God, but when things take a turn for the worse, " they cry to the Lord." And the Lord has compassion on them.

Let it be very clear that this is not only Israel's history that is being described, it is also the church's history. It is, in fact, *our* history. We are included from this time on in the great mystery of God's patient endurance.

The time of the Judges is a dismal time of anarchy and warfare. But again and again God raises up witnesses who, in his name and by his power, stand forth and deliver Israel. These are the " judges." Their commission is not hereditary, and each one of them receives a special call from God. It must be confessed that these judges are disconcerting figures, and are often quite bloodthirsty individuals. They are not concerned with the problem of ends and means; they are, in fact, very much men of their own time, and they are not above its particular moral customs and prejudices. Only one thing sets them apart from their contemporaries, and this is their faith in the Living God and their obedience to his commands. As soon as his hand is withdrawn they are nothing, and all their power collapses.

Samson is a good example of this. He is a great hero who boasts that he has killed a thousand men with the jawbone of an ass, but he is unable to keep the secrets of the Lord and is betrayed by his Philistine lover, Delilah, a treacherous " fifth columnist " who is more faithful to the concerns of her own people than Samson is to God. (Judg., chs. 13 to 16.)

The incident that leads to the nearly total destruction of the tribe of Benjamin, and the methods that were used to bring about its disappearance, illustrate the customs of the time.[18] They also show how hard it was for the Israelite tribes to maintain their unity and their freedom in the land that God had given them.

Another judge, Gideon, refused to be king. " I will not rule over you, and my son will not rule over you; the Lord will rule over you." (Judg. 8:23.) Soon public opinion prevails over him and the Israelites demand a king. And The Book of Judges concludes with this laconic comment: " In those days there was no king in Israel; every man did what was right in his own eyes " (Judg. 21:25).

3. THE ESTABLISHMENT OF THE MONARCHY.
THE HOUSE OF DAVID
(I and II Samuel)

Samuel Anoints the First Two Kings

Samuel, the last judge in Israel, plays a very important part in Israel's history. In a unique way, he combines the functions of judge, priest, and prophet. He stands at the threshold of the Davidic era, just as John the Baptist stands at the threshold of the Messianic era. In response to the Lord's command, he anoints the first two kings of Israel. Like John the Baptist, he is set apart at his birth for the service of the Lord. The song that Hannah sings about the downfall of the powerful and the exaltation of the humble is a pure Messianic hymn, which is echoed later on when Mary sings the Magnificat (cf. I Sam. 2:1-10 and Luke 1:46-55).

The Israelites' desire to have a king " like all the nations " (I Sam. 8:20) runs counter to Samuel's deepest con-

victions (I Sam. 8:1-6), but God commands him to give in
to their request: " They have not rejected you, but they
have rejected me from being king over them " (I Sam.
8:7). The establishment of the monarchy is thus presented
to us from the very first as an example of God's *condescen-
sion.* Samuel paints the people a very bleak picture of the
monarchy, but they will not be dissuaded. In vain has the
Lord led them " with a strong hand and an outstretched
arm " across the sea, through the wilderness, and into battle. Now, when Israel goes to war, Israel wants a king, just
like everyone else! In vain has God revealed himself as the
just Judge who reads the secrets of men's hearts and pronounces his judgments with equity; rather than him, Israel
prefers the services of a human master.

God insists that Israel take the consequences of the decision — but he grants it. More than that, even though the
monarchy will be a tremendous burden for Israel to bear,
it will become, in God's hands, *a new means of grace*
(cf. I Sam. 12:18-25). He will give Israel a king " after his
own heart " and from this Davidic dynasty the Savior of
the world will be born.

Saul, the King Who Is Rejected

The Bible now places two contrasting figures before us:
Saul, the tragic figure who is rejected, and David, the man
after God's own heart, on whom all the Messianic promises
rest. The election and rejection of Saul, together with that
of Judas Iscariot, pose one of the most dramatic problems
in the whole Bible. What happens to these men reminds us
that we can turn away from God's presence, even though
we had once experienced it. In Saul's case, the Spirit of
God possesses him after his anointing (I Sam. 10:6-9), and
he is victorious in everything he does. But the folly of pride
also possesses him; he decides that he can bring about Israel's salvation all by himself. Consequently, when Samuel
is late in coming to offer the customary sacrifices, and bat-

tle is about to begin, Saul offers the burnt offering himself.
In doing this he breaks the law of God; he exceeds his
functions as king by usurping those of the priest (I Sam.
13:8-15). Samuel immediately informs him that he will
lose the kingship: " The Lord would have established
·our kingdom over Israel for ever. But now your kingdom
hall not continue " (I Sam. 13:13-14). It is in man's
power to destroy the purposes of God's grace in this way.

Saul's destiny crumbles. Because of a foolish oath, he is
obligated to kill his own son, and the indignant people
have to intercede to save Jonathan's life (I Sam., ch. 14).
He disobeys the Lord by sparing Agag the Amalekite (who
was Israel's " Public Enemy Number One ") and also the
better portion of his flocks, on the pretext that he intends
to offer the latter as sacrifices. Samuel stands up once more
before the guilty king and utters the verdict that condemns
him:

Has the Lord as great delight in burnt offerings and sacrifices,
    as in obeying the voice of the Lord?
Behold, to obey is better than sacrifice,
    and to hearken than the fat of rams. . . .
Because you have rejected the word of the Lord,
    he has also rejected you from being king.

(I Sam. 15:22-23.)

Saul abases himself and entreats. But the prophet with-
draws from the presence of one whom God has already forsaken. At least, however, Samuel does not dishonor him in
front of the people: Saul pleads with Samuel that he may
" worship the Lord *your* God " (I Sam. 15:30), and Samuel agrees. He still honors the royal function that Saul
represents, but he executes Agag " before the Lord." Then
he leaves, " and Samuel did not see Saul again until the
day of his death " (I Sam. 15:35).

From this time on an evil spirit has possession of Saul.
He goes insane and finally commits suicide (I Sam. 31:4-6).

David, the King " After God's Own Heart "

David, the young and handsome shepherd from Bethlehem (cf. I Sam. 16:12), has all the allure of a legendary hero — in his youth he snatches lambs from the jaws of lions, he kills the giant Goliath with a slingshot, he soothes the black moods of King Saul, he is affectionate to friends such as Jonathan, and he is a terror to his enemies. But his true greatness as a king lies elsewhere. It is in *the understanding he has of what is and is not proper to a king who is the servant of the Lord.* It is because Saul is " the Lord's anointed " that, until the very end (and then only because the demented king is pursuing him out of hatred), David refuses to raise his hand against Saul, and has the one killed who dares to boast that he was Saul's murderer (I Sam., chs. 24; 26; II Sam. 1:1-16). David knows that his own authority comes from God, and that he is no more than a *servant* of the Lord: " Who am I, O Lord God, and what is my house, that thou hast brought me thus far? " (II Sam. 7:18).

David is the architect of Israel's unity, and this unity is the result of long conflict. Although acknowledged as king of Judah at Hebron, he is not proclaimed king by all the tribes of Israel until seven years and six months later (II Sam., ch. 5). After this he conquers Jerusalem and makes it the capital of his kingdom, a very astute move that soothes the touchiness of the various tribes: " David took the stronghold of Zion, that is, the city of David " (II Sam. 5:7). Thus, the history of Jerusalem is properly bound to the Davidic dynasty. The promises of God and the hope of Israel rest both on the throne of David and the city of David.

David's first act, after his installation in Jerusalem, is to bring the Ark of the Lord back to Jerusalem. It had previously been stolen by the Philistines (I Sam., chs. 4 to 6), subsequently returned by them, and left in the house of

Abinadab at Kiriath-jearim (I Sam., ch. 7; II Sam. 6:1-5).
The Ark is shown to be dangerous company for God's enemies; no man can touch it without dire results, as Uzzah
discovers when he tries (II Sam. 6:6-11). The entrance of
the Ark into Jerusalem is an occasion of great rejoicing,
for it is the visible sign of the presence of God in the midst
of his own people (II Sam. 6:2, 12-23). David dances
wildly in front of the Ark of God, and is the victim of
scornful taunts from Michal, his wife, who is the daughter
of Saul. Thus, at every turn in David's life we see the hate
of the rejected dynasty standing in his way.

Psalm 24 is almost certainly a recollection of this entry
of the Ark into Jerusalem:

> Lift up your heads, O gates!
> and be lifted up, O ancient doors!
> that the King of glory may come in.
> (Ps. 24:7, 9.)

The Christian tradition has made this the great psalm of
Advent and Ascensiontide, for it has seen in it the announcement of the coming of the Savior.

David's major concern, of course, from this time on, is
to build a house for the Lord that will be worthy of him:
" See now, I dwell in a house of cedar, but the ark of God
dwells in a tent " (II Sam. 7:2). But the Lord replies,
" Would you build me a house to dwell in? " (II Sam. 7:5.)
It is not David who will build a house for the Lord, but the
Lord who will build a house for David, by establishing his
Kingdom forever (II Sam. 7:11). Later on, The First Book
of the Chronicles gives a more surprising interpretation of
the Lord's refusal to let David build him a house, namely,
that a warrior whose hands have shed blood may not build
God's house. This task will be reserved for his son: " He
shall be a man of peace, . . . for his name shall be Solomon [peaceful] " (I Chron. 22:9).

David was a truly great king, but he was nonetheless a

man and a sinner. We may recall, among other possible examples, the story of his adultery, which jeopardized the
whole future of his dynasty. There is scarcely a more magnificent page in the Bible than that which describes how
the prophet Nathan asks for justice from the king, and
tells him the parable of the man who stole a poor man's
sheep. The parable makes David cry out, " The man who
has done this deserves to die "! And then Nathan says
quite simply to him, " You are the man " (II Sam. 12:5, 7) .
David does not try to defend himself, but says, " I have
sinned against the Lord." The straightforward acknowledgment of his guilt wins him the pardon of God. But he
must nevertheless expiate his crime. The child born of the
adulterous relationship will die. His household will be
torn apart by civil war. But God shows his grace and pardon by giving a second son to David and Bathsheba: " And
she bore a son, and he called his name Solomon. And the
Lord loved him, and sent a message by Nathan the prophet;
so he called his name Jedidiah [beloved of the Lord], because of the Lord." (II Sam. 12:24-25.) Among all the sons
of David, *this* child, given to David and Bathsheba as a
sign of God's steadfast love and forgiveness, will be the heir
of his household and the anointed of the Lord.

David's life is beset with adversity again, and this time
it is on account of his own children (II Sam., ch. 13 ff.) .
For a time, David is deposed from his throne by his son
Absalom. But it is in these dark hours, when God apparently abandons him and " leaves him to go down to the
grave," that the king's faith and humility are most apparent. Cursed during his flight by a man from the house of
Saul named Shimei, David restrains the servant, a son of
Zeruiah, who wishes to kill Shimei: " What have I to do
with you, you sons of Zeruiah? If he is cursing because the
Lord has said to him, ' Curse David,' who then shall say,
' Why have you done so? ' " (II Sam. 16:10) . And a little
later when this same servant suggests again to the victori-

ious king that he punish the insulter, David retorts:
"' Shall anyone be put to death in Israel this day? For do
I not know that I am this day king over Israel?' And the
king said to Shimei, 'You shall not die'" (II Sam. 19:22-
23). These are the words of a real king.

Tradition has called David the great poet of Israel, just
as it has called Moses the great lawgiver. According to The
First Book of the Chronicles it is David himself who appoints the singing of psalms as an essential part of worship.
He appoints Asaph and his brothers, " that thanksgiving
be sung to the Lord " (I Chron. 16:7). Most critics today
are agreed that many of the psalms attributed to David
really date from a much later period, but we need to remember in this connection that ancient writers did not
have the same notions that modern writers have about
rights of authorship. They gladly attributed a piece of
writing to some well-known person, and it was natural for
them to attribute to the king himself certain songs that
had been inspired by his exploits. The psalms attributed
to David sing the praises of the Lord, but they also contain
cries of distress and deliverance. It is significant that the
confession of sin of Ps. 51 should have been placed on the
lips of Israel's greatest king. Actually, this king represents
the living incarnation of his people, for the Lord took him
" from the pasture, from following the sheep " (II Sam.
7:8), and chose him by the free choice of his grace. The
Lord was with him in his battles, he punished and humiliated him, he raised him up and comforted him.

Thus the promise made to Abraham begins to be fulfilled in David. It is renewed and clarified. But, as in the
case of Abraham, the promise goes beyond the bounds of a
single life and even beyond the bounds of the history of a
single nation. The words of the psalms attributed to David
evoke and foretell one greater than David — he who will
make expiation for all the people, he whom God will not
permit to know corruption, he who will be the King of

Glory, the Savior to whom the Lord will say, " Sit at my right hand," he who will receive all the nations as an inheritance. The Psalter throughout shows us in David a forerunner of the Messiah to come. (Cf. especially Ps. 2; 16; 18; 22; 24; 69; 110; etc.) The early church did not mistake this connection, and at numerous points it links Jesus and David (see, for example, Luke 24:44; Acts 2:22-36).

4. THE THRONE AND THE TEMPLE
(II Sam. 7:1-16; cf. I Kings, chs. 5 to 8)

In the Hebraic tradition, Solomon, the son of David, the pre-eminently wise king, represents the high point of Israel's glory (I Kings, chs. 3; 4:29-30). He is given the task of building the Temple. (I Kings, chs. 5 to 8.) But the ostentatiousness of Solomon's reign indicates that there has already been pagan infiltration, and it ends in outright idolatry (I Kings, ch. 11). As early as the reign of Solomon's son, Israel's unity is broken by division. The schismatics henceforth have only " evil kings," according to the judgment of the books of Kings and Chronicles. The constant repetition of the same formula, " he did what was evil in the sight of the Lord," shows that the thing that really interests the sacred writer is God's judgment and not human accomplishments. Some of the kings were, humanly speaking, great kings; but in separating themselves from the Davidic throne, the ten tribes cut themselves off from the power and the promises that rest with the house of David. The political schism brings with it a religious schism, and Jeroboam, in order to keep his subjects away from the sanctuary at Jerusalem, erects two golden calves, one at Dan and the other at Bethel (I Kings 12:26-33).

From now on, the Kingdom of Judah represents the true Israel, but Judah's faithfulness is only relative. The comment made about one of its kings, Abijam, is true of most of them:

And he walked in all the sins which his father did before him; and his heart was not wholly true to the Lord
his God, as the heart of David his father. Nevertheless for
David's sake the Lord his God gave him a lamp in Jerusalem, setting up his son after him, and establishing Jerusalem. (I Kings 15:3-4.)

Of only three kings — in three centuries — is it said without reservation that they " did what was right in the eyes
of the Lord " and walked in the way of David their father
(I Kings 15:11; II Kings 18:3; 22:2).

The disappearance of the Kingdom of Israel in 722 B.C.,
and the similar fate of the Kingdom of Judah a century
and a half later, are the chosen people's punishment for
not being faithful to the task that had been entrusted to
them. Only a remnant will be saved. But God remains
faithful to his promises, and the " lamp," referred to in
the quotation above, will be handed on through the hard-
ships of the exile and the humiliations of the restoration
until the true heir is born, the Christ, " descended from
David according to the flesh and designated Son of God in
power according to the Spirit of holiness " (Rom. 1:3-4).

The *throne of David* and the *Temple* are the two sup-
ports on which the existence of Israel, as both a nation and
a church, is based. Just as in the time of wanderings the
Ark of the Covenant had been the visible sign of the presence of the Lord in the midst of his people, the place
where he revealed his glory, so, during the reign and reform of Josiah (621 B.C.), the Temple in Jerusalem becomes the only place where God can be properly worshiped.[19] In fact, burnt offerings made elsewhere are
looked upon as acts of idolatry. Henceforth, the suppres-
sion of the Temple is identical with the supression of true
worship. But God does not bind his revelation to a building; that is what the prophet Jeremiah tries to say to the
people, without any success.

After the hard lesson of the exile, the first thought of

the faithful Israelites is to reconstruct the ruined Temple. It becomes the rallying point for the chosen people, the living symbol of their faith. Destroyed a second time, rebuilt by Herod, it had not been finished during Jesus' lifetime, and it never ought to be. For God does not dwell in temples made with human hands. It is in a temple of flesh, in the person of Jesus Christ, that God fully reveals himself to men, and after this, the other temple becomes useless, just as the sacrifices that were offered there are seen to have been no more than " the shadow of things to come " (Heb. 10:1).

The New Testament gives us an echo of Jesus' words foretelling the destruction of the Temple and relating this fact to his death and resurrection. This, as a matter of fact, becomes one of the principal accusations that the Sanhedrin makes against him. (Matt. 26:61; John 2:13-25; 4:20-24.)

Henceforth, the true sanctuary of God is *the church,* of which Christ is the cornerstone and believers are the "living stones" (I Peter 2:4-6, 9-10).

5. The Earthly and the Heavenly Jerusalem

The Promised Land is like a rough sketch of the Kingdom of God, drawn on the canvas of history. The chosen people enter it and remain in it only by the grace of God. The struggle of faith never ends in it, for this land is only a pointer and a promise of the world to come. Little by little, the hope and the faith of the believers is concentrated on Jerusalem, the city of peace. The Temple is there, the throne of David is there, and finally all peoples will come in great numbers to "the mountain of the Lord" (Isa. 2:2-3; Zech. 8:1-3, 20-23). The Old Testament believes that Israel has a mission to all people, but the movement of conquest does not go from the center to the periphery. It could rather be compared to the powerful attraction of a magnet. The city of David is the lamp that

illumines the nations and draws them into the radiance of
its flame. Love for Jerusalem burns in the heart of the
believing Israelite:

> On the holy mount stands the city he founded:
> the Lord loves the gates of Zion
> more than all the dwelling places of Jacob.
> Glorious things are spoken of you,
> O city of God.
>
> (Ps. 87:1-3.)

The greatest honor that can be given to pagan peoples is
to grant them citizenship in the Holy City:

> The Lord records as he registers the peoples,
> " This one was born there."
>
> (Ps. 87:6.)

We shall feel this passion for the earthly Jerusalem, and
this faith in its destiny, vibrating through the utterances
of the prophets. We shall see it giving life to the believers
when they return from the exile and rebuild its walls. And
even today, two thousand years after the destruction of the
city, Jews weep at the Wailing Wall. What other ruins
have been kissed with such ardor for twenty centuries?

But here again, the earthly city is only the reflection of
another city, which is not made with human hands, a city
that is not here below but is on high:

> Arise, shine; for your light has come,
> and the glory of the Lord has risen upon you.
> For behold, darkness shall cover the earth,
> and thick darkness the peoples;
> but the Lord will arise upon you,
> and his glory will be seen upon you.
> And nations shall come to your light,
> and kings to the brightness of your rising.
>
> (Isa. 60:1-3; cf. chs. 62; 66.)

All the splendors of earth are only poor parables by
which to describe the beauty of the City to come (cf. Rev.,
ch. 21).

CHAPTER V

THE EXILE

Prophetism: The Proclamation of Judgment and the Messianic Age

(Amos, Hosea, Isaiah, Micah, Jeremiah, Ezekiel, cf. II Kings)

SUMMARY

The period that extends from the eighth to the sixth century B.C. is characterized by the appearance of great prophets whose speeches are still available to us. They all proclaim an imminent judgment by God. This judgment takes the form of enemy invasions. It results in deportation and *exile*. By uprooting Israel's elite and tearing Israel away from its secular institutions, the exile becomes a means of testing Israel's faithfulness, and makes it necessary for Israel to place its faith and hope in God alone. Thus, the punishment of the exile is also a *call:* a winnowing process is at work, separating the nominal Israelites from the faithful remnant. The exile, brief as it is, marks a decisive turning point in the history of the chosen people.

The prophets see beyond this time of testing, and they foretell the restoration of the throne of David. Their visions of this restoration, described in what are often very materialistic terms, are too vast to be merely historical in character. They become a proclamation, a sign of the Messianic Age to come, of the great Day of the Lord when his judgment will blaze forth and his Kingdom be established.

The prophet's predictions apply to historical events, but the

end toward which all history is moving is the coming of the
Kingdom of God, the showing forth of his salvation. The direct interventions of God in history, the punishments, and the
deliverances are all signs pointing to this coming.[20]

1. THE PROPHETIC TASK
   a. The prophet is " God's mouthpiece " (cf. Jer. 1:9; 15:16;
   Ezek. 2:8 to 3:3), his " delegate " (cf. Isa. 6:8). He is the
   " watchman " (Ezek., ch. 33) who keeps his eye on Israel
   and stands before the king or the priest or the people to
   remind them of what they owe to God and to declare
   what God tells them to declare:

   > The lion has roared;
   > who will not fear?
   > The Lord God has spoken;
   > who can but prophesy?
   > (Amos 3:8.)

   b. Beside the true prophet stands the false prophet, whose
   lips repeat " pleasing lies " (Jer. 6:14; cf. chs. 23:15-32;
   28; Micah 3:5-8).

2. GOD'S JUDGMENTS — GOD, THE SOVEREIGN LORD OF HISTORY
   a. *God's judgment on Israel*
   Israel's basic sin is that of *ingratitude:* although Israel
   is the object of a unique love, it " prostitutes " itself with
   strange gods (cf. I Kings 16:29 to 18:46; Hos., chs. 1 to
   3; Jer., chs. 2 to 3:5; etc.)
   Israel tramples law and righteousness underfoot and
   abandons them for an easy life (Amos 2:6-8; 5:10-15;
   6:1-7; 8:4-6; Isa. 5:8-24; Micah 2:1-2; etc.).
   Thereafter, Israel's " piety " offends God more than
   honoring him (Amos 5:4-7, 21-27; Micah 6:6-8; Isa. 1:10-
   15; ch. 58; Jer., ch. 7).
   In order for Israel to return to God, every vestige of
   human security must be taken from it. This is *the meaning of the exile* (Hos. 2:13-23; Ezek. 20:33-38).
   b. *God's judgment on the other nations*
   The pagan nations have a place in God's unfolding
   purpose of salvation; they are under his control and subjected to his judgment (Amos, chs. 1; 2; Jer. 25:15-31).

They serve as God's instrument for Israel's punishment and also for its salvation (Isa. 5:26-30; Jer. 25:8-9; Isa. 45:1-6).

Their basic sin is pride, which is why they too are destroyed (Isa. 10:5-19; chs. 13; 14 ff.; Jer., chs. 25; 50 ff.; Ezek., ch. 28; etc.). However, even for these nations there is a possibility of redemption (Isa. 19:18-25; 60:1-5).

3. THE PROCLAMATION OF THE MESSIANIC AGE AND THE MESSIAH HIMSELF

a. The prophetic writings proclaim both the restoration of Israel and the coming of the Kingdom of God; often the two are mixed together (Isa. 2:1-4; 8:22 to 9:6; 11:1-10; Jer. 31:1-14, 23-24; ch. 32; Isa., ch. 40).

b. Israel's deliverance is rightly linked to the coming of a King, the Lord's anointed, the Messiah (Isa. 9:6; 11:2; Micah 5:3; Jer. 23:5-6; Ezek. 34:23-24). This righteous servant will redeem and deliver Israel by his suffering (Isa. 42:1-9; 49:1-13; 50:4-10; 52:13 to 53:12; cf. Ps. 22; 69). His coming will inaugurate a new era of righteousness and peace (Isa., chs. 55; 60; 61; 66).

INTRODUCTION: *Historical Background for the Period*

Prophetism as such is not a special characteristic of Israel's life, any more than the priesthood or the monarchy are unique to it. God makes use of the ordinary institutions of most of the nations of the ancient world, but he gives them a new meaning and uses them as the instruments of his purposes. Thus all ancient religions had their oracles and " seers," who were consulted in critical times (I Sam. 9:9). When Saul goes looking for Samuel for the first time, he is trying to find his lost asses, but he finds himself confronted by a man of God who tells him " all that is on his mind " (cf. I Sam. 9:19). We see the prophets of Baal competing with those of the Lord (I Kings, ch. 18), but Elijah shows the difference between them, for he is Israel's living conscience, the one who speaks to king and people in God's name.

Elijah occupies an important place in the Israelite tradition. As an implacable foe of idolatry, he is a living example of what it means to be faithful to the God of the patriarchs. King Ahab trembles before this formidable prophet, whose words are always followed by results and who has the power to bring drought and ruin, or rain and blessing, upon the country. His victory over the prophets of Baal and their extermination is a pointer to the ultimate victory of God over his enemies. (I Kings, chs. 17 to 21.) But what God, soon after, reveals of himself to the prophet is a reminder that God's last word is not violence but mercy (I Kings 19:1-18). Elijah is one of only two persons in the Old Testament of whom it is said that they were raised into heaven without having known death. (II Kings 2:1-12; cf. Gen. 5:24.) Elijah is regarded as the preacher of repentance par excellence, and his return must precede and foretell the Messianic Age (Mal. 4:5-6). The New Testament interprets John the Baptist as the Elijah who must come (Mark 9:11-13), and on the Mount of Transfiguration, Jesus converses with " Moses and Elijah," who together represent the Old Covenant — Moses as the Law and Elijah as the Spirit of prophecy (Mark 9:4).

From the eighth century on, the prophets occupy an important place both spiritually and politically in Israel's history. The prophet stands before king and priest as the guardian of the law of God. He always speaks first to the responsible leaders, such as the king, the military leaders, the magistrates, or the priests. But if they will not listen, the prophet, scarcely stopping for breath, does not hesitate to carry the debate to the public square and appeal there from the leaders to the people. The predictions thus spoken frequently take the form of rhythmic complaints, either spoken or sung. The impact is so powerful that the leaders will go to almost any lengths to silence " the man of God." But precisely because he is a man of God, most people are afraid to lay hands on him. (Cf. Amos 7:10-17;

Jer. 26:10-19.) Although this provided a certain immunity, there were still a good many prophets who died as martyrs (Jer. 26:20-24; cf. Matt. 23:29-30, 37).

If we really want to understand the prophetic message, we must know something about the historical situation in which each prophet lived and prophesied. For there is something very specific about all of this, and it is only when we understand that God works through concrete historical events that we can see the "suprahistoric" or hidden meaning in them, the ultimate aim of history which is revealed to us through these specific happenings.

We can sketch only briefly the important events of Israel's history during the great prophetic era from the eighth to the sixth century B.C.

Until the middle of the eighth century B.C. the wars in which the Kingdoms of Israel and Judah are involved keep them in constant conflict with the other Semitic tribes that populate Palestine. But toward the end of the eighth century, the political scene changes. Syria and Palestine become the battlefield of the great powers who are struggling for control of the East. During the eighth century, the Assyrian power, which is essentially military, wins its greatest victories. To maintain its superiority, it transplants entire conquered populations. This is the beginning of the period of deportations. Toward the end of the seventh century, Assyria is conquered and replaced by Babylonia, which, in the sixth century, is likewise replaced by the Medes and Persians. Henceforth, Palestine simply passes from the hands of one great power to another.

The prophets see the tornado coming and they foretell its coming with startling accuracy. But in their eyes, the great conquerors of the earth are merely *instruments* of the all-powerful God. They recognize that the root of all Israel's trouble lies in its sins rather than in a fatalistic view of history. Their call to repentance resounds when disaster is still far off: gradually it becomes more and more urgent, more and more menacing, as the disaster comes nearer and as the people still refuse to listen.

Toward the middle of the eighth century B.C., while Amos and Hosea are uttering their warnings, the Northern Kingdom is actually winning battle after battle. It recaptures practically all the territory held during the time of David. It grows rich. It also becomes more and more paganized. And precisely when their contemporaries are taking tremendous pride in such achievements, the prophets discern the seeds of death. And within thirty years, Samaria is destroyed and the kingdom of the ten tribes disappears forever!

The civil war between the kings of Israel and Damascus on the one hand and the king of Judah on the other hand serves as a pretext for the king of Assyria to invade Palestine. The prophet Isaiah pleads in vain with King Ahaz to trust in God alone, rather than to call upon the great foreign power for help against the " two smoldering stumps of firebrands," the kings of Israel and Syria (Isa. 7:4) . The Assyrian conquers the Kingdom of Israel, and soon takes control of the Kingdom of Judah. Then the prophet has to say something different. He urges the kings of Judah to submit, but they plot with their neighbors, looking for help from Egypt and Babylon (Isa. 30:1-5; 31:1-3; cf. chs. 20; 39) . In 701 B.C., the king of Assyria is at the gate of Jerusalem: Isaiah pleads with King Hezekiah to trust God and promises him deliverance — and the armies actually depart (II Kings, chs. 18; 19; cf. Isa., chs. 36; 37) !

The Kingdom of Judah enjoys a reprieve for a whole century. But this deliverance serves only to give it a false sense of security that the prophet Jeremiah (628–586 B.C.) tries in vain to shatter. The reform of King Josiah, who destroys the " high places " and centralizes worship in Jerusalem (621 B.C.) , does not really take hold. The king foolishly becomes involved in the struggle between Egypt and Assyria and perishes in the battle of Megiddo (608 B.C.). Nebuchadnezzar, king of Babylon, captures

Jerusalem for the first time in 598 B.C. and again in 586 B.C. And this is the end of the Kingdom of Judah.

After all is lost, Jeremiah, who had been a prophet of disaster, becomes the prophet of the restoration. He pleads with the exiles to be patient and obedient and promises them that they will be set free. (Jer., chs. 30 to 33.) This message is taken up in another form by Ezekiel, who is among those deported, and also by the great unknown prophet to whom we owe chs. 40 to 55 of Isaiah. And later on (539–538 B.C.), Jerusalem is actually restored by Cyrus' order.

However, as Isaiah had prophesied, only a remnant returns to the Promised Land, and Israel's political glory disappears forever. Henceforth, Israel is nothing but a priestly people, from among whom the Messiah will be born.

1. THE PROPHETIC TASK

Who are these men before whom kings and empires tremble, and what is the secret of their power? The Bible tells us: they are " God's mouthpiece." Their predictions are " words of the Lord," and therefore unfailing in their consequences.

God has " taken " these men (Amos 7:14-15) and thrust them into the thick of the battle (Jer., chs. 1; 15:15-21; 26:12-15). They are prompted by a power they cannot control. For the word of God is " a fire " and " like a hammer which breaks the rock in pieces " (Jer. 23:29). God gives his word to the one who must speak, and imposes silence on the one who must hold his tongue (Ezek. 3:22-27). The prophet must respond to the word he has heard:

> The lion has roared;
> who will not fear?
> The Lord God has spoken;
> who can but prophesy?
> (Amos 3:8.)

His flesh quivers with fright as he hears the message he proclaims (Jer. 4:19-21) ; he feels his very life to be in danger, for he is like "a gentle lamb led to the slaughter" (Jer. 11:19; cf. vs. 18-23). The ways of the Lord upset him and trouble him (Jer. 12:1-4), but he must lead the way under pain of being rejected himself (Jer. 12:5-6). And if he remains silent when he ought to speak, he feels within him "as it were a burning fire" (Jer. 20:9).

The Prophet Speaks of Judgment and Deliverance

The prophet is in part, at least, by definition a "prophet of doom," for he is the one who takes the king and the faithless people to task. His temptation is always to please men rather than God, by disguising the truth that has been entrusted to him, or by trying to make it more palatable. "Behold," the king's messenger says to the prophet Micaiah, "the words of the prophets with one accord are favorable to the king; let your word be like the word of one of them, and speak favorably." But Micaiah answers in the tones of a true prophet, "As the Lord lives, what the Lord says to me, that I will speak" (I Kings 22:14). The false prophet says, "'Peace, peace,' when there is no peace" (Jer. 6:14), or, as it might be put, "'All is well, all is well,' when all is not well." The false prophet has not been present at the heavenly council. He runs without having been sent, he speaks the words of his own heart and not those which the Lord has spoken to him, and he behaves like a liar (cf. Jer. 23:21-32). A prophet who announces peace and prosperity need not be believed until events actually confirm what he says. The prophet of prosperity must be suspect from the very beginning. (Jer. 28: 7-9.)

This rather grim understanding of the prophetic task is characteristic of the whole pre-exilic period. The task of the prophets of the eighth and seventh centuries B.C. is to undermine the false security of the chosen people.

Israel becomes established in the Promised Land, secure in its possessions, its victories, its way of doing things, secure even in its faith. But from the moment that Israel believes that it is " the master of its fate," it begins to lose its own soul. It is subtly corrupted by its Canaanite surroundings. It compromises with the Canaanite gods, the Canaanite customs, and the Canaanite way of doing things. It seeks military security by the number of its chariots, political security by alliances with foreign nations, and spiritual security by sacrifices offered on the one hand to the foreign gods (the baals), and on the other hand to the Lord.

In the midst of all this, a strange conviction gets ahold of the prophets: *in order for Israel to find God again, Israel will have to lose everything else.* Everything. This means all those possessions of which it had been so proud, everything that, without Israel's even being aware of what was happening, had crowded the Living God out of Israel's heart. This means that Israel must lose its riches, its glory as a free and independent people, its land, its king — everything, even up to and including the Holy City, which it believed could not be destroyed, and the Temple, the visible sign of God's presence. Israel must go back " to the wilderness," into a dreadful solitude, where, no longer having anything of its own, it will learn to look to God alone for everything.

The wonderful words of Hosea, " I will . . . bring her into the wilderness, and speak tenderly to her," underlie the whole of prophetic thought. God will lead his people into the valley of death (i.e., " the valley of Achor ") so that he himself may open a " door of hope " (Hos. 2:14-15). In order to be saved, Israel must acknowledge its guilt and go through the fire of judgment. Only then can the message of the resurrection reach Israel, a message that can be heard as a muted yet blessed promise even in the midst of the threats of Hosea, Micah, Isaiah, and Jeremiah.

This is the promise that shines forth afterward like the brightness of dawn during the night of exile.

In the eighth century B.C., Hosea and Amos predict the death of the Northern Kingdom. Thirty years after their preaching, Samaria is destroyed (722 B.C.) and the Kingdom of Israel loses its independence forever. A century later Jeremiah predicts that the same thing will happen to Judah — and the judgment unfolds before his very eyes (598 B.C. and 586 B.C.).

Today, one can travel through the deserted regions where the cities once flourished that are described in the Biblical prophecies. But he cannot do so without feeling a shudder of dread pass over him, for he realizes that God *carries out* his judgments. Here is ample historical confirmation of what God at a certain time foretold " by the mouth of his prophets."

His judgments are certain. His salvation is just as certain. But while his judgment is painfully evident in the ruins of the world, his salvation is evident only to faith. Only the believer can discern the foretastes of salvation and identify the mysterious purpose of salvation at each stage along the way.

The prophet realizes that the sufferings of his people are not God's final word. He realizes that deliverance will follow. He realizes that there will be a final judgment and an ultimate deliverance, even though the time and circumstances of this final coming remain hidden from him. This is why he often shifts without warning from the plane of history to the plane of eternal reality. For example, the restoration of the earthly city makes him think of the eternal City, the New Jerusalem, which he realizes will be " different " from all the cities of the world. The figure of the king becomes that of the Lord and Savior of the universe.

The Prophet Experiences That of Which He Speaks

The prophet does not merely *describe* the judgment and the steadfast love of God. To a certain extent he actually *experiences* them in his own life, and carries their marks in his flesh. Persecution is the normal lot of the messenger of God. " Blessed are you," Jesus later says to his disciples, " when men revile you and persecute you and utter all kinds of evil against you falsely on my account. Rejoice and be glad, for your reward is great in heaven, for so men persecuted the prophets who were before you." (Matt. 5:11-12.)

Jesus Christ, the faithful and true Witness of the Living God, will be a sign of contradiction among men; he will be the Defeated One whom history rejects. The prophet himself is exposed to the same contradiction. He embodies the whole tension of Israel's vocation as the bearer of both the promises and the condemnation of God. He is the faithful witness who in his own body and soul pays the price for the people's wrongdoing. He is wholly involved in the message that he proclaims, and this is why the events of his life and even his very existence become " signs " that speak to Israel's heart more directly than his words alone possibly could. This is particularly true in the case of Hosea, whose marriage portrays the reality of the drama that unfolds between God and his people; Hosea's love for Gomer, the prostitute, is a reflection of Yahweh's love for Israel. Hosea gives his children symbolic names, and thus in his own life he participates in the agony of God and the mystery of his grace.

Jeremiah recognizes that he must be a celibate as a sign of the condemnation that burdens his generation. And the struggles of his vocation foreshadow those of Jesus Christ in such an amazing way that when Jesus asks, " Who do men say that I am? " some people answer, " Jeremiah " (cf. Matt. 16:14).

But the prophet is not bound to the Lord whose coming he awaits only by sharing in suffering. He is bound fully as much by the hope of the glory to come.

God's activity among his chosen ones usually runs counter to the mood of the moment. When everyone is optimistic and the word is " All is well! " the prophet speaks of doom. But when Israel is at the bottom of the pit, when there is nothing but desolation and ruin, the solitary voice of the prophet is lifted up afresh, this time to proclaim the God of all comfort. Jeremiah, a prisoner during the siege of Jerusalem, buys a field because God tells him to: " For thus says the Lord of hosts, the God of Israel: Houses and fields and vineyards shall again be bought in this land " (Jer. 32:15) . Although Ezekiel has been deported, he draws plans for the future Temple in Jerusalem. And the song of Isa., ch. 40, bursts forth in the midst of the exile as a hymn of joy to the praise of the Almighty.

The man of God often speaks out of season. For the Holy Spirit who speaks through him enables him to puncture illusions. The prophet smells death in the air at just the place where others are dazzled by the brilliance of a civilization still at the heights of its glory. And on the other hand, just when life seems buried and condemned, he perceives the secret work of God and receives the promise that resurrection lies ahead.

2. GOD'S JUDGMENTS — GOD, THE SOVEREIGN LORD OF HISTORY

God is the Lord of history. He maintains sovereign control over the history of the world so that he may bring to pass whatever he has ordained. This is the assurance on which the prophets base their understanding of history.

This divine sovereignty, seen from our human perspective, has two aspects — one of wrath, and one of mercy. Only in eternity will we fully understand that these two aspects are actually only one, and that God's justice is simply one aspect of his love.[21] The prophets understand this, and they also understand that judgment always begins with the house of God (cf. I Peter 4:17).

God's Judgment on Israel

Israel has been the object of a unique kind of love. For this reason it will be the object of a unique kind of " wrath ":

> You only have I known
> of all the families of the earth;
> therefore I will punish you
> for all your iniquities.
> (Amos 3:2.)

The deep mystery of election is contained in this jealous and terrible love which will never loosen its hold until the Last Judgment. But throughout all of its history, Israel discovers that the punishments that God inflicts upon it are really signs of his concern, and that his silence in the face of the triumph of sin is the real mark of being abandoned (Heb. 12:4-11; cf. Deut. 8:2-5).

For all the prophets, punishment is before all else a *call*, a plea to repent and return to God. Israel is the perpetual prodigal son who remembers its father only when it finds itself in the exile without food fit even for swine (Luke 15:16).

For the true theme of the drama of Israel is the theme of ingratitude. *Israel has forgotten whom it must love above all.*

> Can a maiden forget her ornaments,
> or a bride her attire?
> Yet my people have forgotten me
> days without number.
> (Jer. 2:32.)

The wrath of God is the wrath of a love that has been deceived and betrayed. And this love is alternately menacing and beseeching:

When Israel was a child, I loved him,
  and out of Egypt I called my son.
The more I called them,
  the more they went from me. . . .
How can I give you up, O Ephraim!
  How can I hand you over, O Israel! . . .
My heart recoils within me,
  my compassion grows warm and tender.
I will not execute my fierce anger,
  I will not again destroy Ephraim;
for I am God and not man,
  the Holy One in your midst,
  and I will not come to destroy.
                              (Hos. 11:1-2, 8-9.)

Having forgotten God, Israel " prostitutes itself " in the
service of idols. It succumbs to all the lusts of the flesh and
all the lusts of pride.

The *social* message of the prophets is powerful indeed.
This fact is often emphasized, and with good reason. But
the real root of the social corruption that the prophets attack is always the same. Their indictment goes like this:
Israel no longer acknowledges God; wherever his sovereignty is disregarded, or his love is mocked, righteousness
and law disappear, for the knowledge of God is the basis
of all life and truth. Consequently it is actually Israel's
atheism that is the cause of its moral chaos.

Indeed, this atheism hides under a religiosity of outward
customs. False religious zeal is no more than a pretense
that horrifies God even more than impiety does:

I hate, I despise your feasts,
  and I take no delight in your solemn assemblies.
Even though you offer me your burnt offerings and your cereal
    offerings,
  I will not accept them,
and the peace offerings of your fatted beasts
  I will not look upon.

Take away from me the noise of your songs;
  to the melody of your harps I will not listen.
But let justice roll down like waters,
  and righteousness like an ever-flowing stream.

(Amos 5:21-24.)

The corruption of the mighty, the readiness of the
judges to accept bribes, the misuse of power by the great
landowners, the disorder of a society that rides roughshod
over the inviolable rights of the poor — these things are
regarded by the prophets as symptoms of a social and moral
disintegration that is a forerunner of disaster, and that
cannot help but bring down failure and war upon any
nation that has become so corrupt.

But if the prophet sees the hand of God in the great
events of history, he is not on that account less aware of
" secondary causes." He sees and takes account of the whole
realm of human responsibility. He knows that those who
sow the wind shall reap the whirlwind. (Hos. 8:7.) With
an astuteness that would do credit to a skillful politician,
he sees the precarious situation of a small nation torn apart
by civil war. For lurking on the horizon are the great
powers of Assyria and Babylonia, waiting for the least sign
of weakness that they can use as a pretext for interfering.

When the call to repentance is not heeded, the prophet
realizes that the eleventh hour has struck, that it is *too late,*
and that judgment must be carried out and undergone,
right to the bitter end. Only by losing its life can Israel
save its soul.

God's Judgment on the Other Nations

Israel involves even the pagan nations in the sphere of
God's redemptive concern. They become the instruments
through whom God carries out his punishments, and thus
they further his cause without realizing it. God uses Assyria
as the rod of his anger against Israel, and Babylonia is
similarly used against Judah. But disaster will overtake

these nations if they believe that they have fulfilled their
commission by their own self-sufficient power. God's flail
will be shattered even more disastrously than those whom
it has struck!

The nation to whom God " whistles," and who comes
" from the ends of the earth " (Isa. 5:26) to fulfill his
orders, soon finds out who is in charge:

> Shall the ax vaunt itself over him who hews with it,
>   or the saw magnify itself against him who wields it?
> As if a rod should wield him who lifts it,
>   or as if a staff should lift him who is not wood!
>
> (Isa. 10:15.)

> Woe to you, destroyer,
>   who yourself have not been destroyed;
> you treacherous one,
>   with whom none has dealt treacherously!
> When you have ceased to destroy,
>   you will be destroyed;
> and when you have made an end of dealing treacherously,
>   you will be dealt with treacherously.
>
> (Isa. 33:1.)

There are few pages in the whole Bible as impressive as
those describing the king of Babylon's downfall into the
kingdom of darkness:

> Sheol beneath is stirred up
>   to meet you when you come,
> it rouses the shades to greet you,
>   all who were leaders of the earth;
> it raises from their thrones
>   all who were kings of the nations.
> All of them will speak
>   and say to you:
> " You too have become as weak as we!
>   You have become like us! "
> Your pomp is brought down to Sheol,
>   the sound of your harps;

maggots are the bed beneath you,
    and worms are your covering. . . .
Those who see you will stare at you,
    and ponder over you:
" Is this the man who made the earth tremble,
    who shook kingdoms,
who made the world like a desert
    and overthrew its cities,
    who did not let his prisoners go home? "
All the kings of the nations lie in glory,
    each in his own tomb;
but you are cast out, away from your sepulchre,
    like a loathed untimely birth,
clothed with the slain, those pierced by the sword,
    who go down to the stones of the Pit,
    like a dead body trodden under foot.
You will not be joined with them in burial,
    because you have destroyed your land,
    you have slain your people.
                                (Isa. 14:9-11, 16-20.)

After having prophesied Judah's punishment, Jeremiah is ordered to make all the nations drink " the cup of the wine of the wrath of God " (cf. Jer. 25:15). Their crime is always the same: overweening pride has led them to claim that they are divine. Ezekiel states the indictment in his prophecy against Tyre:

Your heart is proud,
    and you have said, " I am a god."
                                (Ezek. 28:2.)

And for nations as well as for individuals, the fruit of revolt against God is always *death*.

What happens, however, is that in the hands of the Almighty a pagan king becomes an instrument of salvation — not only negatively, as the " rod of God's anger," but positively, as the vehicle for the deliverance of the chosen people. This is Cyrus, whom the Lord calls "his servant," and even his "anointed" (Isa. 45:1).

> For the sake of my servant Jacob,
>   and Israel my chosen,
> I call you by your name,
> I surname you, though you do not know me.
>   (Isa. 45:4.)

Thus, whether they are aware of it or not, the other nations fulfill the unchangeable purposes of God. They think that they are autonomous, but actually an almighty hand governs them and determines what they shall do. By nature, they are sinners just as much as the rest of humanity. But the covenant of grace that God makes with Israel can include them also. More than that, the real aim of the covenant is *their* salvation:

> And the Lord will smite Egypt, smiting and healing, and they will return to the Lord, and he will heed their supplications and heal them. And the Lord will make himself known to the Egyptians; and the Egyptians will know the Lord . . .
> In that day there will be a highway from Egypt to Assyria, and the Assyrian will come into Egypt, and the Egyptian into Assyria, and the Egyptians will worship with the Assyrians.
> In that day Israel will be the third with Egypt and Assyria, a blessing in the midst of the earth, whom the Lord of hosts has blessed, saying, "Blessed be Egypt my people, and Assyria the work of my hands, and Israel my heritage." (Isa. 19:22, 21, 23-25.)

The prophet Israel sees the nations "flowing" to "the mountain of the house of the Lord" (Isa. 2:2-4; cf. ch. 60: 1-5), and the seer of the book of Revelation can only repeat Isaiah's description of a universal salvation, the shining center of which is a transfigured Jerusalem (cf. Rev., chs. 21; 22).

3. The Proclamation of the Messianic Age and the Messiah Himself

The proclamation of the Kingdom of God is like a great breath of hope in all the prophecies. Judgment, as we have seen, is never God's final word. The times of testing act as a purifying fire. A winnowing process is at work separating Israel according to the flesh from Israel according to the spirit. The latter is reduced to a faithful remnant, and the remnant itself is finally reduced to the lone figure of the Servant of the Lord, who raises up a new people, the church.

The Restoration of Israel and the Coming of the Kingdom

But Israel and the church are only, as it were, anticipations in the midst of a sinful world, of the Kingdom to come, of the glorious age when God will be all in all.

In the prophetic vision, time scarcely exists, and the prophets' understanding of it seems confused to us. The prophets can move without a pause from a description of an earthly kingdom to a state of things that transcends all earthly realities. Or they can interpret Israel's victory over its enemies as a sign of God's final victory over all the powers of evil and death.

The thing that is most characteristic of this coming Kingdom is that it will be an era of *righteousness and peace*. There will be no more war: " They shall beat their swords into plowshares, and their spears into pruning hooks " (Isa. 2:4; cf. ch. 9:4). God's benevolent concern will reach out to include the whole creation. (Isa. 11:6-8.) Men will enjoy the fruits of their labor in peace, and suffering will be no more. (Isa. 65:17-25; cf. Jer., ch. 31.) The knowledge of God will fill their hearts and light up the whole world.

For the earth shall be full of the knowledge of the Lord
    as the waters cover the sea.

                                    (Isa. 11:9; cf. Jer. 31:14.)

The Messianic King as a " Suffering Servant "

From the very first prophets of the eighth century, this
vision of the Kingdom of God is linked with the appearance of a *King*. This King will be a son of David. He will
be adorned with the wisdom and power of God.

For to us a child is born,
    to us a son is given;
and the government will be upon his shoulder,
    and his name will be called
" Wonderful Counselor, Mighty God,
    Everlasting Father, Prince of Peace."

                                    (Isa. 9:6.)

" The Spirit of the Lord shall rest upon him." (Isa. 11:2.)

He shall not judge by what his eyes see,
    or decide by what his ears hear;
but with righteousness he shall judge the poor,
    and decide with equity for the meek of the earth;
and he shall smite the earth with the rod of his mouth,
    and with the breath of his lips he shall slay the wicked.
Righteousness shall be the girdle of his waist,
    and faithfulness the girdle of his loins.

                                    (Isa. 11:3-5.)

This child shall stand " as an ensign to the peoples," and
he will assemble all the outcasts (Isa. 11:10-12) . He will
rule " in the strength of the Lord " and will be glorified
to the ends of the earth (Micah 5:4) .

A century later, when Jerusalem is about to be destroyed, the prophet Jeremiah proclaims to the last kings
of Judah the judgment that awaits them; but God will
raise up from David a " righteous Branch " who will lead
the sheep of Israel back to the sheepfold. He will execute

"justice and righteousness in the land" (cf. Jer. 23:4-5). He will be the instrument of a new covenant written upon the heart. (Jer. 31:31-34.)

The prophet Ezekiel proclaims the judgment of God on the unfaithful shepherds of Israel. God himself will feed the dispersed sheep and gather them together:

> And I will set up over them one shepherd, my servant David, and he shall feed them: he shall feed them and be their shepherd. And I, the Lord, will be their God, and my servant David shall be prince among them; I, the Lord, have spoken. (Ezek. 34:23-24.)

But it is the unknown prophet of the exile, to whom we owe Isa., chs. 40 to 55, who must be given credit for describing the figure of the *Servant of the Lord* in all of its wonder and mystery. The poem in Isa., chs. 40 to 55 (to which perhaps we must add Isa., chs. 60 to 62 as representing the same point of view), has often been called the "gospel" of the Old Testament. In it we penetrate to the very heart of the meaning of redemption.

In the midst of the Babylonian exile a voice breaks forth and begins to sing "a new song" (Isa. 42:10). "Comfort, comfort my people." (Isa. 40:1.) And the subject of this comfort is none other than *God himself*, coming to deliver his people from the yoke of the oppressor. As was the case in the Egyptian captivity, this involves more than simply a liberation from actual physical bondage. It also involves a resurrection from the dead. The condemnation is removed. The people who are "blind and deaf" (cf. Isa. 43:8) can understand the word of their Lord in a new way, and can walk in the light of their God as they never did before.

The "Servant" in these chapters is first of all Cyrus, the means of Israel's actual deliverance (Isa. 41:2-3; ch. 45). Secondly, the servant is Israel, "the offspring of Abraham, my friend" (Isa. 41:8).

> You are my servant,
> I have chosen you and not cast you off.
> (Isa. 41:9.)

And finally this corporate figure is reduced to a single figure. He is no longer Cyrus; he is no longer Israel. His characteristics are steadfast love and righteousness:

> A bruised reed he will not break,
> and a dimly burning wick he will not quench.
> (Isa. 42:3.)

He is given

> as a covenant to the people,
> a light to the nations,
> to open the eyes that are blind,
> to bring out the prisoners from the dungeon,
> from the prison those who sit in darkness.
> (Isa. 42:6-7; cf. ch. 49:6.)

This servant, before whom kings will " prostrate themselves," is " abhorred by the nations " (Isa. 49:7) . His appearance combines both humiliation and glory. He is exposed to blows, to spitting and to shame (Isa. 50:6) . He is the one who drinks to the dregs the cup of wrath that Israel itself should really drink (Isa. 51:17, 22) . Nobody understands the atoning character of his suffering until God exalts him and lifts him up. And then all those who had looked upon him with revulsion are filled with joy at the sight of him (Isa. 52:13-15) . Israel, God's cherished plantation, his vineyard, which for so long had produced nothing, now produces a little plant, which may be scorned but which will be its salvation:

> Who has believed what we have heard?
> And to whom has the arm of the Lord been revealed?
> For he grew up before him like a young plant,
> and like a root out of dry ground;
> he had no form or comeliness that we should look at him,
> and no beauty that we should desire him.

He was despised and rejected by men;
  a man of sorrows, and acquainted with grief;
and as one from whom men hide their faces
  he was despised, and we esteemed him not.

Surely he has borne our griefs
  and carried our sorrows;
yet we esteemed him stricken,
  smitten by God, and afflicted.
But he was wounded for our transgressions,
  he was bruised for our iniquities;
upon him was the chastisement that made us whole,
  and with his stripes we are healed.
All we like sheep have gone astray;
  we have turned every one to his own way;
and the Lord has laid on him
  the iniquity of us all.

                                              (Isa. 53:1-6.)

Who *is* this executed criminal? Some people have answered that he is one of the prophets who, like Jeremiah, carries the whole weight of the sins of his people and suffers persecution. Others have seen in this servant the chosen people themselves, punished, humiliated, suffering for the salvation of the nations. (This is the usual interpretation of the rabbinic schools, which refuse to see a Messianic prophecy in Isa., ch. 53.) Neither of these answers is wrong, but neither one is sufficient. For there is only one servant who has really borne the sins of his people, only one who, being righteous, has suffered for the unrighteous, and thereby justified all men (Isa. 53:8-12). This one servant is Jesus Christ, the Son of God.

And the faithful people — Israel and the church — participate in his shame and in his glory.

The prophets were able to grasp the meaning of his suffering in advance, and they were able to live victoriously because they were, by faith, already living under the sign of the resurrection. For as the apostle Peter says:

The prophets who prophesied of the grace that was to be yours searched and inquired about this salvation; they inquired what person or time was indicated by the Spirit of Christ within them when predicting the sufferings of Christ and the subsequent glory. (I Peter 1:10-11.)

Five centuries before the coming of Jesus Christ, this mystery of our redemption, " into which angels long to look " (I Peter 1:12), was disclosed to a prophet in the bleakest moment of the exile. He is not concerned about times and seasons, for chronology does not matter here. He does not distinguish the coming of the Spirit of God in the humiliation of the incarnation from the coming of that same Spirit in glory. For him these are simply two aspects of the same reality. The Lamb who is slain is the King of Glory before whom the nations will prostrate themselves forever. The desert will blossom as the rose. Jerusalem, the desolate city, will be the mother of many children. (Cf. Isa. 54:1-8.) The nations will run to her. (Isa. 55:5.) The glory of the Lord will rise upon her. (Isa. 60:1.)

> Violence shall no more be heard in your land,
> devastation or destruction within your borders;
> you shall call your walls Salvation,
> and your gates Praise.
> The sun shall be no more
> your light by day,
> nor for brightness shall the moon
> give light to you by night;
> but the Lord will be your everlasting light,
> and your God will be your glory.
>   (Isa. 60:18-19.)

In these passages, Jerusalem is the church, the bride who will rejoice at the coming of the Bridegroom:

> I will greatly rejoice in the Lord,
> my soul shall exult in my God;
> for he has clothed me with the garments of salvation,
> he has covered me with the robe of righteousness,

as a bridegroom decks himself with a garland,
and as a bride adorns herself with her jewels.

(Isa. 61:10.)

We are already in the presence of God's new creation:
" For behold, I create new heavens and a new earth " (Isa.
65:17; cf. II Peter 3:13; Rev. 21:1).

The characteristic of the new heavens and the new earth
is that *righteousness* dwells within them. The entire Old
Testament yearns for this righteousness and awaits it, realizing that it can come only from God. It realizes that
man's heart is unable either to produce it or to satisfy its
demands. It realizes that God prefers " a broken and con-
trite heart " to burnt offerings and sacrifices (Ps. 51:16-
17). And it awaits the Righteous One who will suffer for
the unrighteous. (Cf. Zech. 9:9-10; 12:10.) Not until Jerusalem is adorned with the mantle of *his* righteousness
will it be able to enter into the gaiety and joy of its Lord
(cf. Mal. 4:2).

CHAPTER VI

THE REMNANT OF ISRAEL

Judaism
After the Exile

SUMMARY

The main characteristic of this final period of Israel's history is that it changes from a nation into a religious community. Its life is centered on the Temple and on worship. The persecution suffered under Antiochus Epiphanes is a further sorting out, and the faith of the Israelites who remain loyal is centered on the coming of the Messiah.

1. THE RESTORATION (Ezra, Nehemiah, Haggai, Zechariah)
   a. The great deprivation of the exile is that Israel is no longer able to worship God as he should be worshiped. This leads to a basic concern with the reconstruction of the Temple (Ezra, chs. 1 to 6; Haggai; Zech., chs. 1 to 8).
   b. After Israel has endured a hundred miserable years, Nehemiah undertakes the reconstruction of the walls of Jerusalem. Ezra publishes the law, reorganizes the priesthood and the worship. The reconstituted community is solemnly dedicated to the Lord.

2. PERSECUTION UNDER ANTIOCHUS EPIPHANES, AND THE MACCABEAN PERIOD
   The Maccabean period marks a turning point in the life of postexilic Judaism. For a brief time, Israel experiences political independence, and its characteristics as a religious community crystallize.

3. THE PIETY OF THE JUDAIC COMMUNITY (Job, The Psalms)
   a. Alongside the tide of ritualism and legalism, mention

must be made of a new growth of individual piety. This
is expressed in The Book of Job.

b. The depth of the Israelite community's life in the days
following the exile is particularly portrayed in The
Psalms; these songs express the prayers, the faith, and
the hope of Israel.

4. THE END OF TIME AND THE COMING OF THE KINGDOM
(Daniel)

The apocalyptic visions of The Book of Daniel show us
the final epoch-making struggles in which God reveals himself as the Sovereign Master of the earth and makes an end
to the kingdoms of this world. The Messiah comes on the
clouds of heaven and manifests himself as King and Judge.
The Book of Daniel is a message of comfort addressed to
the persecuted remnant of Israel, for it proclaims the ultimate victory of God.

INTRODUCTION: *Historical Background for the Period*

Before the exile, the prophets had proclaimed that only
a remnant of Israel would be saved. And if at times the
promised restoration is described in poetic and rather
grandiose terms, we must remember that this vision of the
re-establishment of the kingdom of David in all its former
glory is actually more eschatological than historical. (Isa.
6:13; 9:5-6; 11:10-16.)

The "worm Jacob," to use the language of the great
prophet of the exile (Isa. 41:14), goes through a painful
return from exile, and a laborious reconstruction of the
ruins of its homeland. Once more, Israel must learn to
walk by faith.

In 538 B.C., Cyrus allowed the deportees to return to Jerusalem and rebuild the Temple. But not all of them immediately returned to their native land. " Yet did many of
them," as Josephus wrote much later," stay at Babylon, as
not willing to leave their possessions." [22] Those who did
return found the city in ruins and their lands occupied by
those who had remained there.

The Persian domination was relatively peaceful. Respect was shown for the traditions and customs of the conquered populations, and Cyrus even consented to have the Temple rebuilt at his own expense, although he probably arranged this by a previous deduction from the royal taxes. But internal coups and insurrections followed one another in the Persian Empire until it was conquered by Alexander the Great in 336 B.C. When Alexander's empire was divided among his generals, Palestine and Syria became a bone of contention between the Ptolemys, rulers of Egypt, and the Seleucids, inheritors of the ancient empires established on the borders of the Tigris and Euphrates rivers (320-168 B.C.). Throughout all of this, the Jews managed to retain a good deal of freedom, and adapted themselves to the Greek world where their military aptitude, among other things, was appreciated.

But things changed quickly under the reign of Antiochus Epiphanes, King of Syria. He took possession of Jerusalem, desecrated the Temple by building a pagan altar in it, and massacred the people. This led to the Maccabean revolt, which resulted in the independence of Judea (142 B.C.). This independence lasted until 63 B.C., when, following a number of internal feuds, Jerusalem was conquered by Pompey. This marked the beginning of the Roman occupation. Herod, an Idumean prince, succeeded in gaining the favor of the Roman authorities, and the last of the Maccabean princes was beheaded in 37 B.C. Next came the bloody reign of Herod the Great, to whom the Romans had given the title " King of Judea."

Consequently, except for the reign of the Maccabees, Israel did not experience political liberty in the postexilic period. The great dream of the restoration of the Davidic dynasty was not realized in historical terms. Rather, Israel became a *religious community,* and henceforth the Temple and the law were the primary concerns. From now on, Judaism develops in the direction that we see fulfilled in Jesus' own lifetime.[23]

1. THE RESTORATION
(Ezra, Nehemiah, Haggai, Zechariah)

Israel Cut Off from the Temple

We have already seen that the exile is a time of suffering for faithful Jews, particularly because of its effect upon their spiritual life. They are cut off from the Temple — and it was in the Temple and in the Temple alone that proper sacrifices could be offered; it was in the Temple that the first fruits of the harvest were to be offered, as well as the first-born of the cattle, and it was in the Temple that the rites of purification were to take place. Consequently, the exiled Israelites feel that they are unclean people living in the midst of unclean people. Their pain is not only the pain of being exiled but also the pain of the believer who has abandoned God and whom God seemed to have abandoned. Certain psalms help us to understand how poignant this homesickess was. Psalm 137 is the classic example:

> By the waters of Babylon,
>> there we sat down and wept,
>> When we remembered Zion.
> On the willows there
>> we hung up our lyres. . . .
> How shall we sing the Lord's song
>> in a foreign land?
> If I forget you, O Jerusalem,
>> let my right hand wither!
> Let my tongue cleave to the roof of my mouth,
>> if I do not remember you,
>> if I do not set Jerusalem
>> above my highest joy!
>> (Ps. 137:1-2, 4-6.)

Psalm 42 also comes from this period:

> My tears have been my food
>> day and night,
> while men say to me continually,

" Where is your God? "
These things I remember,
    as I pour out my soul:
how I went with the throng,
    and led them in procession to the house of God,
with glad shouts and songs of thanksgiving,
    a multitude keeping festival.

(Ps. 42:3-4.)

The book of Lamentations reflects these days of fasting and mourning. The believing remnant, in the loneliness of the exile, sings its song of unutterable sadness:

How the Lord in his anger
    has set the daughter of Zion under a cloud!
He has cast down from heaven to earth
    the splendor of Israel;
he has not remembered his footstool
    in the day of his anger. . . .
He has broken down his booth like that of a garden,
    laid in ruins the place of his appointed feasts;
the Lord has brought to an end in Zion
    appointed feast and sabbath,
and in his fierce indignation has spurned
    king and priest.

The Lord has scorned his altar,
    disowned his sanctuary.

(Lam. 2:1, 6-7.)

Plans for the Restoration of the Temple

If the destruction of the Temple was a sign of God's anger, its restoration will be the mark of the faithful remnant's re-entry into his grace. That is why, in the midst of the exile, we see Ezekiel, who is both a prophet and a priest, drawing extraordinarily detailed plans for the future Temple, and devising the regulations for worship in it (Ezek., chs. 40 to 46). But the prophet knows that there are spiritual conditions attached to this restoration. What is involved is nothing less than a *resurrection:* the breath

THE REMNANT OF ISRAEL

of the Spirit must pass over the dried bones of Israel and
give them life (Ezek. 37:1-14). The river of life that nour-
ishes the earth must flow forth from the Temple. (Ezek.,
ch. 47.)

According to The Book of Ezra, it is due to the command of the Lord himself that Cyrus decides to rebuild
the Temple in Jerusalem (Ezra 1:1-4). The civil admin-
istration of the country is entrusted to a prince of Judah,
who is a descendant of the king who had been deported.

When worship is re-established in Jerusalem, Jeshua (or
Joshua) becomes the first high priest (Ezra 2:2; Hag.
1:12). The derivation of his name is identical with that of
Jesus, and it means " he who delivers," or " he who brings
to pass."

Although the Temple has been destroyed, the ancient
stones on which the sacrifices had been offered are still
there. Some burnt offerings are made, although the foundation of the Temple has not yet been laid. (Ezra 3:6.)
The first task is to rebuild the Temple. But a conflict
breaks out between the repatriated Israelites, who were
Jews believing in strict cultic observance, and the people
who had remained in the country, particularly the Samari-
tans. The repatriates want to restore worship in all of its
purity; therefore, no outsider can be allowed to participate
in the work of reconstruction. Those who feel that this rul-
ing excludes them from the new community try to sabo-
tage the whole enterprise by writing to Darius, who has
succeeded Cyrus as king of Persia, but their plot is foiled.
(Ezra, chs. 5; 6.)

Actually, the considerable delay in the rebuilding of the
Temple seems much harder to justify. This becomes clear
in the prophecies of Haggai. It is true that the exiles had
lamented the loss of Jerusalem, and that the best of them
had been forced by the exile to develop a new depth of religious sensitivity. But when they get back to their homes,
they become caught up in the concerns of daily living. Certainly one must serve the Lord, but first of all one must

live! The fields must be sown, the houses must be rebuilt.
But the first harvests are inadequate, the cost of living is
high, and wages are low. As a result it is all too easy for the
people to say, " The time has not yet come to rebuild the
house of the Lord " (Hag. 1:2).

This is a very human way to think. But when the people
of God think this way, they are actually denying God. We
must not forget that the issue is not simply the building
of a building. For the Temple is more than just a place
of worship, it is the place where God himself dwells, the
sign of his presence in the midst of his people. This issue is nothing less than the issue of knowing *whether
Israel is going to rebuild its national life with or without
God.*

This is the way things stand in the year 520 B.C., about
eighteen years after the edict of Cyrus, in the second year
of the reign of Darius. The prophet Haggai can keep silent
no longer:

> Is it a time for you yourselves to dwell in your paneled
> houses, while this house lies in ruins? Now therefore says
> the Lord of hosts: Consider how you have fared. You
> have sown much, and harvested little; you eat, but you
> never have enough; you clothe yourselves, but no one is
> warm; and he who earns wages earns wages to put them
> into a bag with holes. (Hag. 1:4-6.)

Why has Israel " sown much, and harvested little," and
accumulated things without really thriving? Because *it has
built without being the least bit concerned about God.*
(Hag. 1:7-11.) Then, as The Book of Haggai reports:

> Zerubbabel the son of Shealtiel, and Joshua the son of
> Jehozadak, the high priest, with all the remnant of the
> people, obeyed the voice of the Lord their God, and the
> words of Haggai the prophet, as the Lord their God had
> sent him; and the people feared before the Lord. (Hag.
> 1:12; cf. Ezra 5:1-2.)

As a result, " all the remnant of the people " (Hag. 1:14) give themselves wholeheartedly to the building of the Temple of the Lord on which the solemn promises from on high are based.

Two months after Haggai's prophecies, Zechariah re-echoes a solemn warning: " Return to me, says the Lord of hosts, and I will return to you " (Zech. 1:3). The cause of disaster had been the faithlessness of Israel; henceforth, the only important thing is to discover whether the present generation will be more attentive to the Word of the Lord than its fathers were.

Zechariah's message takes the form of visions whose language is very clear. We see horsemen patrolling the earth (Zech., ch. 1). Everything is peaceful. The powerful nations reign securely. The question is, When will God avenge his people and deliver them from their enemies? An angel consoles the prophet: deliverance is at hand! The second vision foretells the reconstruction of Jerusalem. The Day of the Lord is at hand, for he has " roused himself from his holy dwelling " (Zech. 2:13). Then Zechariah sees the high priest, Joshua, clothed in filthy garments: in his own person he is bearing Israel's defilement. But an angel removes his garments, clothes him in rich apparel, and puts a clean turban on his head. Thus, God himself removes the guilt of his people.

Joshua and his associates are foreshadowings of the Messiah who is to come, the *Branch* whom God is going to raise up from the midst of Israel: " I will remove the guilt of this land in a single day " (cf. Zech., ch. 3). A perceptive prophecy! Joshua is a figure pointing toward the Messiah to come, who " in a single day " — namely, Good Friday — will remove the guilt of his people forever.

Joshua is the high priest of God. Zerubbabel, the king, stands in the Davidic succession. (Cf. Matt. 1:12-13.) His job is to complete the work of restoration. To reassure him in the face of the unpromising beginning that has been

made, the Lord of hosts tells him that he will fulfill his task
" not by might, nor by power, but by my Spirit " (Zech.
4:6). Joshua and Zerubbabel " are the two anointed who
stand by the Lord of the whole earth " (Zech. 4:14). What
they do has as much prophetic meaning as who they are.
For in this same place a " Branch " will rise who will assume both their functions:

> It is he who shall build the temple of the Lord, and
> shall bear royal honor, and shall sit and rule upon his
> throne. And there shall be a priest by his throne, and
> peaceful understanding shall be between them both.
> (Zech. 6:13.)

Jesus Christ will actually unite the functions of king and
priest in his own person, but the temple which he builds
will not be made by human hands, and it will certainly not
be a temple of stone: " *We* are his house," says the letter to
the Hebrews (ch. 3:6). The community that God intends
to establish is a community of " living stones," a " spiritual
house " (I Peter 2:4-6). The cornerstone of the new temple will be Jesus Christ himself. (I Peter 2:4-6; cf. Isa.
28:16-18a; Mark 12:10-11.) It is through him that God
will reveal his glory, and he will be the living tabernacle
where God will make himself known to men (Ex. 40:36;
John 2:18-22; Heb. 8:1-2; Rev. 21:3, 22).

Nehemiah and Ezra

The edict of Cyrus and the first return of the deportees
took place in 538 B.C.; the prophecies of Haggai and Zechariah, in 520 B.C. In spite of the momentary enthusiasm
engendered by their message, and in spite of the reconstruction of the Temple, the life of the repatriates continued to be miserable. About a century later, two men of
note return to their native land. They go in response to
God's command, and with the approval of Artaxerxes,

King of Persia. One, Ezra, is a priest, and the other, Nehemiah, is a layman. Ezra goes to reinstate the " Law " of the
Lord in full force, Nehemiah to rebuild the walls of Jerusalem.

The story of Nehemiah is a great story of indomitable
faith. The news of the misery in which the returned Israelites are living in their homes had reached Susa, the capital:
" The survivors there in the province who escaped exile
are in great trouble and shame; the wall of Jerusalem is
broken down, and its gates are destroyed by fire " (Neh.
1:3). The news comes to Nehemiah as a shock. He fasts
and prays. Then God helps him to find favor in the sight
of the king, and he sets out in possession of the necessary
authority to rebuild Jerusalem.

He kindles the courage of both the leaders and the people and they rebuild the walls. (Neh., chs. 2; 3.) Judah's
ancient enemies try to thwart the whole undertaking
(Neh., ch. 4), but Nehemiah's faith conquers every obsta-
cle: " Those who carried burdens were laden in such a
way that each with one hand labored on the work and
with the other held his weapon " (Neh. 4:17). God fights
with his people and watches over them. There is a magnificent symbol here — the people carrying a weapon in one
hand and a trowel in the other, in order to rebuild the
City of God, and keeping watch night and day so that they
will not be surprised by the enemy!

In addition to all these external difficulties, there are internal difficulties as well. The people, overburdened by
taxes, experience famine and desolation. People of means
take advantage of the situation and lend money at exces-
sive interest rates, with the result that their insolvent debt-
ors are reduced to selling their own sons as slaves. In this
situation the builder becomes the judge, and Nehemiah
re-establishes order by his impartiality and his justice. He
even arranges things so that the creditors repay their debts
to those whom they have exploited. (Neh., ch. 5.) The

Lord protects Nehemiah by defeating the plots of all his enemies. (Neh., ch. 6.)

Why is so much importance attached to the matter of rebuilding a few stone walls? The reason is that these are the walls of Zion, the walls of the City of God. God is its protector and defender, its " shield and buckler." The integrity of Jerusalem must be upheld because its role is to act as a witness among the nations; it foretells the City to come, which will not be the work of men's hands. And although Jerusalem is built by human hands, it is God who, by the power of his Word, is really its architect and builder (cf. Ps. 87) .

> Unless the Lord builds the house,
>   those who build it labor in vain.
> Unless the Lord watches over the city,
>   the watchman stays awake in vain.
>   (Ps. 127:1.)

When Jerusalem rejects its Lord, it seals its own fate. Its own house will be forsaken and desolate. (Matt. 23:37-39; Luke 19:41-44.)

So Nehemiah is the city's builder. Its priest is Ezra. He gives all his attention to the re-establishment of *worship*. He reads the law in public to all the assembled multitude (Neh., ch. 8) . The law of God is explained to the people " so that the people understood the reading " (Neh. 8:8) . And the Day of the Lord is to be a day of joy. (Neh. 8:9-12.) The covenant is solemnly renewed. (Neh., ch. 10.)

Strong measures are taken against those who marry foreign women, for a religious community that is trying to reform itself must remain free from pagan contamination. (Ezra, chs. 9; 10; Neh. 13:1-3, 23-30.) These measures may seem rigid to us. Actually they represent the beginnings of " Judaism," a rigid exclusivism and emphasis on the letter of the law which will later issue in a Jewish sect, the Pharisees. But this rigor, which, in its spirit if not its form, recalls the rigor of the first entry into the Promised Land, is a necessary reaction against the syncretistic spirit that threatens the faith on all sides. Pure Jewish monotheism must pay this price if it is to survive.

For this tiny remnant of Israel, the only ones who had survived disaster, faithfulness means specific obedience to God's commandments. This involves an attachment to ceremonies and institutions that to us today may seem outdated, but that then were the only means of safeguarding religious integrity. The role of the priests becomes predominant: the Israel of the restoration is correctly defined as a hierocracy — a government by priests.

During the grim days of the exile, the Israelites had made the most of those aspects of their religion which they could still observe, namely, fasting and the Sabbath. After the exile these are of basic importance. But once again there are prophetic voices to remind the Jews that real fasting consists in the practice of righteousness and steadfast love, and that this is the only kind of worship that is pleasing to God. (Zech., ch. 7; cf. Isa., ch. 58.)

Even in this time of religious exclusivism, there are prophetic reminders of the universal character of Israel's calling. This is the real meaning of the books of Ruth and Jonah, both of which come from this period. The story of Jonah is a magnificent parable of God's love for his creation. Jonah is not at all concerned about the fate of Nineveh, but he becomes very cross because God allows the plant that gave him shade to die! And God answers:

> You pity the plant for which you did not labor. . . .
> And should not I pity Nineveh, that great city, in which there are more than a hundred and twenty thousand persons who do not know their right hand from their left, and also much cattle? (Jonah 4: 10-11.)

The Living God raises up the walls of Jerusalem, but his love and concern continue to embrace the world.

2. PERSECUTION UNDER ANTIOCHUS EPIPHANES, AND THE MACCABEAN PERIOD

The Temple and the walls are rebuilt. But the hope of the restoration of the monarchy, which had kept Israel going during its darkest hours, was not fulfilled.

Four centuries after the return from the exile, however, Israel had a brief period of eighty years of political liberty. This period is an important one in the history of post-exilic Judaism. The Maccabees take up arms in order to defend Israel's existence as a *religious community*. Once again the question is whether Israel will preserve the faith of its fathers without compromise, or whether it will sell out to the surrounding culture.

The Persians had given full religious liberty to the Jews in Jerusalem, but things change under the domination of the Seleucids, who attempt to *assimilate* the Jews. According to I Maccabees,[24] a good many Israelites succumb to the influence of Greek culture; they are tired of being *a nation set apart* and assert that " since we separated from them many evils have come upon us " (I Macc. 1:11). They set up a gymnasium in Jerusalem (it is a curious thing that assimilation begins with athletics!) and conceal their circumcision — which had without doubt been the cause of much humiliation and scorn. King Antiochus Epiphanes, then the ruler of all Judea, gives real encouragement to the movement. And then, quite abruptly, he attacks Jerusalem, and ransacks the treasury of the Temple (143 B.C.). He builds a stronghold in the heart of the Holy City.

Antiochus Epiphanes has a totalitarian understanding of the state. Throughout his kingdom, he tries to suppress all the laws and customs of particular cultures. He makes a frontal attack on Jewish practices, particularly the burnt offerings made in the Temple, and the laws relating to Sabbath observance, circumcision, and unclean animals. (I

Macc. 1:43-54; cf. II Macc., ch. 6.) It is said that "Many even from Israel gladly adopted his religion." (I Macc. 1:43.) The faithful minority is driven into hiding under pain of being put to death. "The abomination of desolation," probably a pagan altar or an idol, is set up in the heart of the Temple at Jerusalem (cf. I Macc. 1:54).

Notice here that for the first time in its history, Israel is persecuted on account of its faith; an attempt at forced assimilation is made. Most of the people succumb, but a faithful remnant remains, which courageously endures the most frightful martyrdoms (I Macc. 1:25-28; cf. II Macc., ch. 7). This faithful remnant is embodied in the strong personality of Mattathias, his son Judas surnamed Maccabaeus, and his brothers. We need not linger over the denouement of their struggle. The thing that is really important is the spirit in which it is undertaken. It is really faithfulness to the law of God which is involved, faith doing battle with the enemies of the Living God. And the author of the books of the Maccabees particularly stresses that the sufferings that are undergone *have a single meaning:*

> Now I urge those who read this book not to be depressed by such calamities, but to recognize that these punishments were designed not to destroy but to discipline our people. In fact, not to let the impious alone for long, but to punish them immediately, is a sign of great kindness. For in the case of the other nations the Lord waits patiently to punish them until they have reached the full measure of their sins; but he does not deal in this way with us, in order that he may not take vengeance on us afterward when our sins have reached their height. Therefore he never withdraws his mercy from us. Though he disciplines us with calamities, he does not forsake his own people. (II Macc. 6:12-16.)

There is a mighty certainty that sustains Israel throughout the many trials of its history, and that the church appropriates later on for its own use (cf. Heb. 12:4-13). The certainty is that discipline is a call to order that God directs *toward those whom he loves*. His silence is much more to be feared, for this simply means that the crime is remaining unpunished until " they have reached the full measure of their sins."

The trials of the Maccabean period help to sort out those in Israel who are really faithful, and those for whom " Israel " is only a name. What emerges from all this is an even greater rigor in the observance of the law. The faithful make renewed efforts to *separate themselves* from everything that might soil them, and out of this movement comes the caste of Pharisees ("Pharisee" means "separated"). The stern judgments leveled against the hypocrisy of the Pharisees by Jesus ought not to blind us to the fact that in a time of crisis the Pharisees were the defenders of the orthodox faith, and that they stood for unyielding faithfulness to the law of God. But not content to defend the law, they begin to write commentaries on it, and under the pretext of explaining it, they become victims of a subtle casuistry, adding precept upon precept. This is what Jesus calls " the tradition of men " (Mark 7:8).

Alongside the Pharisees we find the Sadducees, who try to hold strictly to the written law, to a purely legal idea of righteousness (the word " Sadducee " means " righteous "). Their notion of God is so transcendent that before long their beliefs become totally unrelated to life itself. Very quickly they become materialists and opportunists who are always ready to go along with the tendencies of the moment and the politics of the party in power. This group gets its members particularly from the priests.

It is also in the third century B.C. that a new aspect of Jewish religion comes into being, the *synagogue*. The centralization of worship in Jerusalem made it impossible for Israelites living in other parts of the world to make their ritual sacrifices. Many of them were able to go up to the Temple only once a year, during the great Passover festival. This made it necessary to institute another form of worship without sacrifices if the community of the faithful was to be maintained. The first synagogues mentioned in documents known to us are those of Egypt, in the third century B.C. By the time of Jesus, we find them everywhere, even in Palestine. Synagogue worship consists of prayers and a reading of the Law and the Prophets, together with exposition. Thus, little by little a religion of the Book develops, centered on the Word of God, alongside the sacrificial religion that had prevailed until then. It is this important transformation which will make the continuation of Judaism possible throughout the world, even after the Temple is finally destroyed in A.D. 70.

3. THE PIETY OF THE JUDAIC COMMUNITY
(Job, The Psalms)

The prophets of the exile had concentrated their attention on the omnipotence and the holiness of God. This sense of the greatness of God and his terrible holiness is recovered in postexilic Judaism to the point that circumlocutions are necessary to avoid pronouncing his name.

We have examined the ritualistic and legalistic character of postexilic Judaism. But it also manages to affirm the personal character of salvation in a brand-new way. Until this time, it was the spiritual destiny of the *nation* that had been the concern of the narratives of the chroniclers and the sermons of the prophets. For them, the individual existed only in relation to this collective destiny. After the exile, the notion of salvation becomes individualized, and each human being is personally responsible before God for what he does (Jer. 31:29-30; Ezek. 33:12-16).

The Book of Job

The danger in such a notion is that it can easily lead to moralism. Virtue and good fortune, sin and bad fortune, tend to be related to each other in terms of cause and ef-

fect. Later on, of course, this whole idea of retributive justice is condemned by Jesus. Even at this time it is attacked in one of the strongest books of the Old Testament,
The Book of Job. The sufferings that Job endures are not
the direct consequence of some shortcoming of his, as the
belief of his friends would suggest. Rather, they are a test
of his faith, with the purpose, when all is said and done,
of glorifying God.

The prologue to the book clearly poses the problem: Satan raises a question about the purity and the unselfish
character of Job's faith. After all, he says, it is to Job's own
best interest to have faith, but if God should take away
his gifts, then Job's faith would collapse! God consents to
test his servant. Job loses his possessions, his family, and
his health. He has nothing left. He goes through a terrible
spiritual struggle. He complains to God in his doubt and
pain; but his complaints clearly remain the complaints of
a believer. He scornfully rejects his friends' efforts to help
him, for he can receive help from God alone. And God reveals himself to Job, who then replies:

> I had heard of thee by the hearing of the ear,
>   but now my eye sees thee;
> therefore I despise myself,
>   and repent in dust and ashes.
>
> (Job 42:5-6.)

The Book of Job reveals the true nature of faith. The
assault to which this " righteous man " is subjected at the
hand of Satan foreshadows in an amazing way the assault
to which the soul of Jesus is subjected on the cross.

The Psalms

The most vital expression of Jewish piety following the
exile is not found in its official documents, its legal texts,
or its histories, but in its prayers and songs. The clearest
example that has been left to us is that most powerful of

witnesses, the book of The Psalms. Certain psalms, it goes without saying, come from an earlier time, but most of them do not go back farther than the exile. Some of them are specially written for use in worship, or on the annual pilgrimages. Many of them express the joys and the sorrows, the conflicts and the victories, that take place in the personal life of the believer. But these joys and sorrows, these conflicts and victories, are expressed in such a way that they have a universal meaning. When the Christian community sings the psalms today, it has no trouble recognizing that it is singing about its own temptations and deliverances. It transposes them without any difficulty into a Christian key. Nothing on earth will ever surpass the power of these songs of praise and thanksgiving, the deep self-knowledge revealed in the penitential psalms and their cries for deliverance. Even today, anyone who wants to learn to pray must nourish his spiritual life with the psalms. The Christian church has understood this so well that it has given the psalms an unrivaled place in its liturgy.

We have already discussed the Messianic character of certain psalms attributed to David, and we shall have occasion to return to them when we come to study the witness of the New Testament. But it is not enough just to say this, for the over-all impact of these songs, which express the faith and hope of the faithful remnant, is *prophetic* in character. Only in the light of Jesus Christ can they be fully understood. When, for example, the psalmist extols the virtue and the victorious power of " the righteous man," he means one who is in a right relationship of trust and obedience with God; but human righteousness is always relative, and the only righteous man to whom these words can strictly be applied is Jesus himself. We know that it is in him, and in him alone, that the faith and hope of the psalmist can find their fulfillment. Just as in the case of the prophets, it must be remembered that the psalmist is a man who is involved in the specific struggles of exist-

ence. When he speaks of his temptations, his doubts, the
enemies who assail him, the deliverances that God grants
him, it is all existentially real for him. But these hopes,
these struggles, these victories, only have meaning because
One who is greater than he will confront all God's enemies
and vanquish them. The psalmist's sins are, so to speak,
pardoned beforehand, because they will be atoned for on
the cross, because there is One yet to come who alone is
able to " create in him a clean heart " (cf. Ps. 51:10) . The
psalmist, like the prophet, understood ahead of time " the
sufferings of Christ and the subsequent glory " (cf. I Peter
1:10-11; Luke 24:44) . He experienced these sufferings himself and discerned this glory with eyes of faith (cf. particularly Ps. 2; 22; 59; 110) . Thus, in anticipation his piety
was enlightened, strengthened and sealed with the seal of
the Spirit. Anyone who has understood this mystery will
see that the psalms are striking evidence of the victorious
Christ.

4. THE END OF TIME
AND THE COMING OF THE KINGDOM
(Daniel)

The restoration did not bring the promised deliverance.
The hope of a restored monarchy, although it was aroused
for a moment, did not materialize. Consequently, the believing Israelites see more and more clearly that the reign
of the Messiah can be established only by God's act. It will
come at the end of time, on that glorious day when God
places all his enemies under his feet and all the nations
turn toward Mt. Zion.

We have seen many indications of this eschatological
faith in the prophets, and it is particularly emphasized in
the later ones, Zechariah and Malachi. But in postexilic
Judaism it leads to the creation of a new literary style,
called " apocalypse." An apocalypse describes the last times
and the Kingdom to come by means of visions that are usu-

ally presented in symbolic language. The language is purposely cast in a form that will hide its meaning from the uninitiated. The Biblical canon has preserved only one Old Testament apocalypse, The Book of Daniel.

The Book of Daniel was written during the Maccabean era. It has two distinct parts. The first part (Dan., chs. 1 to 6) recalls the story of Daniel at the court of the kings of Babylon. By their faithfulness to the God of Israel, and by their refusal to compromise in any way, Daniel and his two friends embody the faithful remnant that will suffer martyrdom rather than kneel before strange gods (cf. Dan., chs. 1; 3; 6). This is almost certainly a veiled way of talking about the current persecutions of Antiochus Epiphanes. God gives Daniel a prophetic ability that enables him to interpret the king's dreams. And these dreams correspond to world-wide history and to the end of the times. (Dan., chs. 2; 4; 5.) For example, Nebuchadnezzar sees a marvelous statue made in the image of four empires. But a stone " cut out by no human hand " falls off the mountain, hits the feet of the statue, and destroys it. Thus the hand of God will destroy the empires of men. The stone itself becomes a great mountain that fills all the earth; this symbolizes the reign of God. (Dan. 2:31-45.)

The second part of The Book of Daniel presents the same themes again in the form of visions. Four great beasts come out of the sea (and we need to remember that to the Israelite the sea is the great abyss, the place where the evil powers reside). The beasts devour all those whom they can find on earth. The last beast has ten horns; and suddenly one very small horn takes the place of three of the others. This horn has " eyes like the eyes of a man, and a mouth speaking great things " (Dan. 7:8). Suddenly the scene changes: the Ancient of Days (the Lord) takes his place on a throne of fire; myriads of angels stand before him: " the court sat in judgment and the books were opened." The Last Judgment has begun. The beast is killed, the others have their lives spared for a while, but " their dominion was taken away." Then Daniel sees someone coming on the clouds of heaven, " like a son of man." He comes to the Ancient of Days, " dominion and glory and kingdom " are given to him and " all peoples, nations, and languages " serve him (cf. Dan. 7:10-14).

Daniel, anxious and alarmed, asks for the truth concerning all this. He is told that the four beasts are four kings who shall arise out of the earth. " But the saints of the Most High shall receive the kingdom, and possess the kingdom for ever, for ever and ever." (Dan. 7:18.)

It is once more made explicit that the last king can be recognized by the violence of his attacks on the Most High, and by the extent of his persecution of the saints.

The historical allusion is clear. The four animals represent the four empires that waged war among themselves for the control of the East from the fifth to the second century. These were the Chaldeans, the Medes and Persians, the Greeks under Alexander the Great, and last of all and most arrogant of all, Antiochus Epiphanes himself, the man who profaned the Temple and ordered bloody persecutions against the " remnant of Israel." He is the crowning example of the iniquity of men, and his coming is the sign of the end. God, in a mighty theophany, reveals himself as the Lord and Judge of heaven and earth.

And the kingdom and the dominion
and the greatness of the kingdoms under the whole heaven
shall be given to the people of the saints of the Most High.
(Dan. 7:27.)

We have given this extensive attention to Dan., ch. 7, because it is of central importance in the New Testament. In all likelihood, the expression " Son of man," which Jesus uses all through the gospels, is taken from this chapter. Furthermore, Jesus himself proclaims the coming of the Son of Man " on the clouds of heaven " (Matt. 26:64).

The figure of Antiochus Epiphanes becomes the symbol of the antichrist. Later on the apostolic church applies the prophecy to a Roman emperor, probably Caligula or Nero (cf. II Thess. 2:3-4; Rev., ch. 13), and then to an apostate who has come out of the bosom of the church (I John 2:18-19). Several of the visions in the book of Revelation are directly inspired by The Book of Daniel, both in terms of the form they take and the images they employ. The notion of a battle in which the angel Michael is involved (Dan. 12:1) is repeated in Rev. 12:7, and the image of the Book of Life in which the names of the elect are written (Dan. 7:10; 12:1) is repeated in Rev. 5:1-5.

The message of these two books came out of similar situations, i.e., periods of bitter persecution. It is a message of *comfort,* designed to strengthen the faith of the elect by the vision of God's final victory.

Chronologically, The Book of Daniel is one of the last books in the Old Testament. It fastens the attention of believers on the Kingdom yet to come.

Israel's faithful completely give up an expectation that the kingdom of David will be established in the future by men's efforts. They expect it to come by a mighty act of God who will break into the course of history and thus bring it to an end. From this time on David is no more than a figure pointing toward this Kingdom to come, a Kingdom that will be the Messianic Kingdom.

PART TWO

THE FULLNESS OF TIME
OR
THE INCARNATION

JESUS CHRIST *lived in such obscurity (in terms of the usual definition of obscurity) that the historians, writing only about the
"important" things that happen,
have scarcely noticed him at all.* —
Pascal, *Pensées,* No. 785.

INTRODUCTION

God devotes twenty centuries to molding the people from whom his Son shall be born. It takes the same people only three years to turn upon the Son and put him to death.

Several centuries have gone by since the preaching of the prophets has been heard in Israel. The little Palestinian principalities have passed one by one under the yoke of Persian, Greek, and Roman oppression. And all of a sudden a new prophet appears on the scene. His name is John. He proclaims the imminent coming of the Kingdom, and calls the people to repentance. His preaching has all the harshness of an Amos: the Day of the Lord, for which everyone is waiting, will be not a day of grace but a day of wrath. Indeed, the ax has already been laid at the root of the tree of Israel.

A man comes to be baptized by John, a man who is clearly not like other men, even though he looks just like them. John is not deceived by outward appearances, nor are the multitudes. For this newcomer speaks with an unparalleled authority that is corroborated by what he does. He does not merely proclaim deliverance, he actually delivers. He does not merely call men to serve him, he actually shares his own authority with those whom he calls. He moves among men and events with the sovereign freedom of a son who comes to set his father's house in order or, to put it another way, he comes with the loving concern of a doctor who ministers to a sick world, knowing full well that he can heal it. This freedom disturbs and scandalizes "the scribes and Pharisees," who are the acknowledged leaders of Israel; they are bound by custom and tradition,

151

and Jesus stands above and interprets custom and tradition with the liberty of a son. In comparison to him, they are no better than mercenaries. They realize, perhaps obscurely at first, but more and more clearly as time goes on, that there is a total incompatibility between their aims and his. In bluntest terms, it is his neck or theirs. This being so, he must be eliminated as quickly as possible. The hidden conflict very soon becomes an open one. Jesus leaves Galilee and goes apart with his disciples to prepare them for the prospect of his death. Then, his hour having come, he goes to Jerusalem.

The trial takes place. The hatred of the Jewish authorities and the cowardice of the Roman authority are enough to condemn an innocent man. Jesus makes no effort to defend himself. When confronted by his accusers he retains his total freedom. He makes no effort to " save himself." He dies. The matter is closed.

Until the very end the disciples refused to believe that it would end in tragedy. They kept waiting for a miracle, and this was precisely the possibility that Jesus had rejected as a temptation. Consequently, the ignominious death of their Master leaves them defeated and alone.

But to their astonishment, the defeat is transformed into victory. The dawn of Easter breaks through the darkness of Good Friday. The risen Lord appears to the incredulous disciples. He gives them his peace, and he commands them to evangelize the world.

The assurance of the resurrection is the foundation of the church. And the church proclaims to all the world that by Jesus and in Jesus " It is finished " (John 19:30) . Everything that needed to be done has now been done. Everything — that means everything for which Abraham and Moses were guided to the Promised Land; everything for which God had created a people for himself and entered into covenant relationship with them; everything for which the throne and the Temple had been built on Mt. Zion; everything that the prophets had believed and proclaimed; everything that the psalmists had believed and sung about; everything that God had prepared from the beginning of the world so that he might bring it to pass at the appointed time.

This assurance of fulfillment is the message of every page of the New Testament. All is fulfilled. The tomb is empty. Hell has been conquered. Jesus has begun his reign. He will come again to establish this reign throughout the entire world. In him, " the old has passed away, behold, the new has come." (II Cor. 5:17.)

All this is the *good news* that the New Testament proclaims. The whole concern of the apostolic preaching is to make this known far and wide. The whole thrust of the message can be summarized in Peter's affirmation on the Day of Pentecost, " God has made him both Lord and Christ, this Jesus whom you crucified " (Acts 2:36) , and in what follows, " There is salvation in no one else, for there is no other name under heaven given among men by which we must be saved " (Acts 4:12) .

The Gospels were compiled to bear witness to these facts: " These are written that you may believe that Jesus is the Christ, the Son of God, and that believing you may have life in his name " (John 20:31) .[25]

CHAPTER VII

THE INCARNATION
(Matthew, Mark, Luke, John)

SUMMARY

The " good news " that the Gospels proclaim is that Jesus of Nazareth, crucified under Pontius Pilate, is the hoped-for Messiah, the Christ of God, the Son of the Living God.

1. A KING COMES INTO HIS KINGDOM
   a. The genealogy of Jesus Christ, son of David according to the flesh, and Son of God according to the Spirit. The " signs " of his reign and the incognito of his reign (Matt., chs. 1; 2; Luke, chs. 1; 2; 3:23-38; John 1:1-18) .
   b. John the Baptist, the herald who paves the way for the King — the greatest and the last of the prophets (Mark 1:1-8; Matt., ch. 3; Luke, ch. 3; John 1:18-34) .
   c. A king, but of what kingdom? The baptism and temptation (Matt. 3:13 to 4:11; Luke 3:21-22; 4:1-13) .

2. THE " PRESENT REALITY " OF HIS REIGN
   a. " The time is fulfilled ": Jesus consciously inaugurates his reign (Mark 1:15; Luke 4:21; Matt. 4:13-17) . He is the legitimate heir who has come to take possession of what belongs to him (Luke 2:49; John 1:11; cf. Mark 12:6; Matt. 17:26) .
   b. Jesus does not openly declare himself to be the Messiah, but his Messianic consciousness manifests itself in his words and deeds. He speaks " with authority " (Mark 1:22, 27; Matt. 7:28-29) . He commands men to follow

him (Mark 1:16-20; 2:14; cf. Luke 9:57-62). To suffer on his account is to be blessed and to save one's soul (Matt. 5:11; Mark 8:35). To acknowledge or deny him is to acknowledge or deny God himself (Matt. 10:32-39).

c. The Sermon on the Mount is a kind of charter of the Kingdom that Jesus came to establish (Matt., ch. 5). He acts with utter freedom as far as men and institutions are concerned (cf. his " but *I* say unto you," Matt. 5:22 ff.), not out of contempt for the law, but because the hour of its fulfillment has struck and a new era has dawned (Mark 2:18-28; cf. Matt. 5:17-20). Entrance into the Kingdom is by grace (Mark 2:5, 15-17; Luke, ch. 15).

d. Jesus' acts of deliverance — healing, casting out demons, raising from the dead — are " signs " or foretastes of the coming Kingdom and of God's victory over the power of sin and death (Mark 1:24; 2:3-12; 3:11-12, 27; Matt. 8:29; 12:27-28; Luke 10:8-11, 18; John, ch. 9). Wherever Jesus goes, the " present reality " of God's reign and salvation is apparent (Luke 4:21; 19:9; 23:43).

3. THE SECRET OF THE KINGDOM

Why does Jesus prohibit those closest to him from revealing the Kingdom? Why does he insist upon the " Messianic secret "? (Mark 1:25, 43-44; 3:12; 4:11; 7:36; 8:26, 29-30; cf. Matt. 16:20).

a. This is done partly for prudential considerations (John 7:2-9).

b. The " secret of the kingdom " (Mark 4:10-12) applies particularly to the nature of this Kingdom (John 6:14-15; 18:36), for it is the secret of the humiliation of the Son and of his rejection by the very ones he came to save.

c. This secret is revealed only to faith. The decisive question is " But who do *you* say that I am? " Peter's confession, the first profession of the faith of the church. Peter's doubt (Mark 8:27-33; Matt. 16:13-28).

4. THE CRUCIFIED KING

a. The scandal of his suffering: " The Son of Man must suffer " (Mark 8:31-38 and parallels; cf. I Cor. 1:17-25; Mark 3:6; Luke 4:28-30; 19:47-48; Mark 12:1-12).

b. The journey to the cross. Jesus henceforth sets his face toward Jerusalem and his approaching death (Mark, chs. 9:2 to 12:44; cf. Luke 9:51-62; 12:49-56; 13:1-9, 31-35; 19:41-44). He prepares his disciples to be ready both for his being taken from their midst and for his return (Mark, ch. 13; Matt., chs. 24; 25; John, chs. 12; 17).

c. The hour of darkness (Mark, chs. 14; 15 and parallels; cf. Luke 22:53; Matt. 27:45; John 13:30). Jesus states rather than explains the substitutionary meaning of his death (Mark 10:45; Luke 22:14-20). He gives his life freely (John 10:17-18).

5. THE RISEN LORD

a. The assurance of the resurrection as the foundation of the faith and life of the church (Mark 16:1-8; Matt., ch. 28; Luke, chs. 23:50 to 24:42; John, chs. 20; 21; I Cor. 15:1-8).

b. The forty days: Jesus opens the eyes of his disciples so that they may understand the Scriptures (Luke 24:25-27, 44-45). His ascension " to the right hand of God " (Luke 24:51; Acts 1:11).

1. A KING COMES INTO HIS KINGDOM

The Meaning of the Genealogies

The New Testament opens with a genealogy: " The book of the genealogy of Jesus Christ, the son of David, the son of Abraham " (Matt. 1:1). Thus from the very first page, there is an emphasis on the *continuity* of revelation. We are on the threshold of a new dispensation, but this does not involve a break with the past. On the contrary, it is the fulfillment of the past.

Even the name " Jesus Christ " is a profession of faith, for the Evangelist confesses that this Jesus, whose story he is going to tell, is the Christ of God, the foretold and expected Messiah, the true heir of the throne of David, and the heir of all the promises made to Abraham.

The Gospel of Luke thrusts the ancestral line even farther back: Jesus is "the son of Adam, the son of God" (Luke 3:38). Jesus is not only the heir of the chosen people; he is the New Man, the Second Adam who will restore men to their status as children of God, and give them another chance to achieve their original purpose. (Luke 3:23-38.)

Both of these genealogies make the ancestry depend not on Mary, as one would expect, but on Joseph. This is possible because the Jewish understanding of adoption makes the adopting father the legitimate father. A greater difficulty is posed by the fact that the two genealogies are not identical. None of the attempts to explain this fact really gets to the heart of the problem. These discrepancies are disturbing only to those who cling to Biblical literalism. The real significance of these genealogies for us is not found in their historical accuracy or inaccuracy, but in their theological significance. The sacred writers wish to stress two things: the continuity of revelation and the physical reality of the incarnation; and the genealogical tables are included only to illustrate these two essential facts.

With regard to the first of these, Matthew, writing for Christians of Jewish background, insists on the fact that Jesus is the son of David, the son of Abraham, which means that he is the heir both of the throne of David and of the promise made in Abraham to the people of God. Luke, writing especially for Christians coming from a non-Jewish background, goes back to the first Man; with Jesus the new humanity begins, born from on high, born of the Holy Spirit (cf. I Cor. 15:45-49; Rom. 5:12-15).

Why can't the Evangelists say this in general terms? Why do they have to get involved with so many details? We have already seen, in dealing with similar material in Genesis, that the genealogies are a way of emphasizing God's faithfulness and the continuity of his plan of salvation. Civilizations are born and die, but the thread of the redemptive will of God unfolds across the centuries, and no human chance or accident can snap the thread in two. The birth of Jesus happens at the appointed time and marks the climax of the whole history of the people of God; even more than that, of the whole history of mankind. Everything was conceived and created with this single day in mind (cf. Eph. 1:3-10).

But the genealogies in the Gospels clearly have a second purpose as well: they call attention to the physical reality of the incarnation. Jesus' flesh is the flesh of an " adulterous and rebellious " people. Matthew has a very clear purpose in mind when, in his genealogy he lists the names of four women — one of whom was guilty of incest (Tamar, Gen., ch. 38), one a prostitute (Rahab, Josh., ch. 2), one a foreigner (Ruth), and one an adulteress (Bathsheba, II Sam., chs. 11; 12). Could it be more clearly stated that what is involved here is a covenant of grace, in which personal merit simply doesn't count, and where the only thing that counts is faith in God's promises and the fulfillment of his plan of salvation? Thus we see this plan follow its course unalterably through the ups and downs of history, creating, right in the midst of the world of the flesh, a relationship between God and man based solely on grace.

The Birth and the Early Years

The Annunciation is the result of all this. (Luke 1:26-38; cf. Matt. 1:18-25.) The Apostles' Creed has retained the fact of the supernatural birth of Jesus, " conceived by the Holy Ghost, born of the Virgin Mary," because this fact expresses the mystery of the incarnation. The coming of Jesus is God's world invading man's world. It is because Jesus is " true God and true Man," that he is able to take the whole burden of man's sin upon himself and remove it. By her obedience to grace, Mary becomes the tabernacle of the Holy Spirit, the mother of the Savior. The humility of Mary, the Lord's servant, is just the opposite of the pride of Eve, and in God's Son, the promise made by him to the Mother of the Living will be fulfilled (Gen. 3:15).

"She will bear a son, and you shall call his name Jesus," the angel says to Joseph, "for he will save his people from their sins." (Matt. 1:21.) The name of "Jesus" is used twice in the Old Testament. It was the name given to Joshua, the servant of God who led Israel into the Promised Land, and to Joshua, the high priest who had charge of the work of the restoration after the exiles returned to the same Promised Land (Zech., ch. 3). We have seen in our discussion of both of these men that the name means "he who saves," who "brings to pass."

This time, however, we are no longer on the threshold of the Promised Land, and the era that now gets under way is the reign of God. The King himself comes to his own people to bring about their liberation. The foreign Prince from whom Jesus comes to free his people is no longer a Pharaoh or a Nebuchadnezzar, but the real "Prince of this world" himself, of whom the Pharaohs and the Nebuchadnezzars were only fleeting expressions on the scene of history. The yoke from which Jesus comes to deliver men is the yoke of sin, and the exile from which he will bring them back is the continual flight away from the presence of God (Gen. 3:8). For he is "Immanuel," which means "God with us" (Matt. 1:23).

The accounts of Jesus' birth demonstrate both the hope that his coming fulfills, and the resistance that it arouses. For God's invasion of the world can have only the double effect of inciting some men to faith and hardening others to resist. The Prince of this world musters all his forces to defend his empire against the true heir who comes to overthrow him.

The faithful *remnant* that looks for "the consolation of Israel" is embodied in Zechariah and Elizabeth, Simeon and Anna, the shepherds of Bethlehem, and in a special way in Mary and Joseph. The songs of Mary, Zechariah, and Simeon in Luke, chs. 1; 2 (the Magnificat, the Benedictus, and the Nunc Dimittis), express all the hopes of the " poor " in Israel, whose invincible trust spanned the centuries and now sings to the glory of God. Jesus echoes this hope in the Beatitudes: the living piety of the prophets wholly directed toward the reign to come is sustained among the insignificant and the humble.

Alongside this particular hope for Israel is another hope, more hidden and more obscure, but real nevertheless; this is the hope for the pagan world. The prophets had foretold the day when the nations would come to bring their tribute to the King of Kings on the holy mountain. (Isa. 2:2-4; 49:6; 61:6.) The gifts of the Wise Men are symbolic of the beginning of this approach of the pagan world to the throne of grace. (Matt. 2:1-12; cf. Rev. 21:24.)

Herod embodies the whole gamut of the resistance of the powers of this world to the hidden ways of God. The episode of the massacre of the innocents recalls that other massacre described at the beginning of the exodus (Matt., ch. 2; cf. Ex., ch. 1). In both cases, the divine power is more than a match for the enemy's display of force. The Pharaohs and the Herods can find no way to prevent God's purposes from coming to fulfillment. Even though they make the whole world bloody, this does not hold up the coming of God's reign for an hour. And against the soldiers of the kings of this world God sets nothing more than the frailty of a tiny child " with whom he is well pleased " (cf. Matt. 3:17).

The Bible makes a great deal of the humble circumstances surrounding the beginning of Jesus' life. There is no place whatsoever for the Son of God in the inn or even in the world (Luke 2:7; cf. ch. 9:58). He is poor at birth and he will be poor all his life, forever an " outcast," stranger, and pilgrim on the earth. He came to take possession of what is rightfully his, " and his own people received him not " (John 1:11). His is thus from the very first moment, and always will be, a " sign that is spoken against " by men (Luke 2:34). Even over his manger hovers the shadow of the cross. It will loom larger in every critical situation until the day that Jerusalem rejects the One who came to save it and thrusts him outside its wall like a petty malefactor. And even in doing that, without knowing what it is doing or desiring to do it, Jerusalem will be helping to bring about the fulfillment of his purposes.

John the Baptist

" In the fifteenth year of the reign of Tiberius Caesar . . . the word of God came to John the son of Zechariah in the wilderness." (Luke 3:1-2.) In this manner, on the very threshold of the New Dispensation, the last and greatest of the prophets appears on the scene.

For God does not visit his people without proclaiming his coming. At each crisis in its history, Israel witnessed the appearance of someone describing the divine visitation. The " day of the Lord," a great and terrible day, never came unexpectedly. Eight centuries before, another man had been uprooted from the same Judean wilderness to proclaim the end of the kingdom of Samaria — his name was Amos. Seven centuries before, another man had come into the court of the Temple to proclaim its destruction — his name was Jeremiah.

And now, once again, Israel is on the threshold of a decision that could make nonsense of the whole destiny of the chosen people: " Repent," says the voice, " for the kingdom of heaven is at hand " (Matt. 3:2).

John is more than an ordinary prophet; he is the messenger who prepares the way for the coming of the king (Mark 1:3; Matt. 3:3; Luke 3:4-5; cf. Isa. 40:3-5). He is the long-awaited Elijah whose coming must precede the coming of the Messiah (Matt. 3:3; cf. II Kings 1:8; Mal. 4:5-6; Matt. 11:14; 17:10-13). He preaches the baptism of repentance and the remission of sins. He shatters the false security of

the " sons of Abraham." Already the ax is laid at the root
of the tree of Israel. Already the harvest is ripe and the
Lord is coming, his winnowing fan in his hand, poised to
clear the threshing floor. The baptism of John is of water,
but this one's baptism will be of fire, the purifying and
consuming fire of the Spirit.

Does this message of judgment seem too severe? Then
simply remember that within three years Israel will crucify
its king, and that within forty years Jerusalem will be sur-
rounded and the Temple destroyed forever.

John, like Amos and Jeremiah, describes events that have
inner meanings that are greater than they appear to be on
the surface. The cup of wrath is entrusted to him; the cup
of grace is reserved for Another. John's greatness consists
in the fact that he knows this and that he wishes to be nothing more than the precursor of one " greater than he," the
thong of whose sandals he is not worthy to untie (Mark
1:7; cf. John 1:27). He lives on the threshold of the coming reign. He can only proclaim its coming, and his joy is
solely one of hope and expectation. Yet Jesus later says that
among all the men born of woman there was no greater one
than this man. (Matt. 11:7-11; cf. John 3:25-30.)

King of What Kingdom? — Baptism and Temptation

And now the predestined Son comes to John to be baptized in the waters of the Jordan. (Mark 1:9-11; Matt. 3:13-
17; Luke 3:21-22.) What does this baptism of repentance
mean when it is administered to a sinless person? By it,
Jesus identifies himself with his people, and although the
true meaning of his act will not be understood until much
later, he has come " to fulfill all righteousness " (Matt.
3:15). But from the highest heavens, God seals and blesses
this voluntary humility: " Thou art my beloved Son; with
thee I am well pleased " (Mark 1:11). By taking upon himself the whole burden of men, Jesus reveals himself as the
true Son of the Father who is in heaven. To John's bap-

tism of water corresponds the baptism of the Spirit, which
is the Father's gift.

The first act of the Spirit is to " drive Jesus *into the wilderness.*" In the Biblical tradition, the wilderness is the
place where God encounters his people, and tests their
faith. Israel had spent forty years in the wilderness (Deut.
8:2-5), and Jesus, reliving the destiny of his people in his
own experience, symbolically spends forty days there being
" tempted by Satan " (cf. Mark 1:12-13).

There is a tendency today to look upon the New Testament belief in Satan and in demonic possession as " a manner of speech," or as a naïve concept particular to ancient
times. We believe, on the contrary, that this belief has
much deeper theological implications than is commonly
thought. Jesus certainly believes in a power of evil at work
in this world and the purpose of his coming is to break the
dominion of the " ruler of this world " (John 12:31; 14:30;
I John 3:8). It is because he has overcome Satan in a deep
personal encounter (cf. Matt. 4:1-11) that he is able to destroy his works (Matt. 12:24-29).

It is this victory over Satan which gives to the cross its
cosmic significance. " The principalities and powers " that
hold mankind in captivity (Col. 1:13; 2:15) have been
conquered there.

Later on Jesus teaches his disciples to pray, " Lead us
not into temptation." This is surely reminiscent of Jesus'
own hand-to-hand combat with Satan. Only one who has
done battle with the enemy knows the terrible strength of
the tempter. Here is a place where fear is indeed the beginning of wisdom. Jesus must first of all " bind the strong
man " in a decisive battle, before he can " plunder his
house " (Mark 3:27). The only reason he can undo Satan's
work here below, and free men from his yoke, is because
he confronted and conquered him in this initial encounter
in the wilderness, which is a kind of foretaste of the final
encounter with him in the fullness of his power on the

cross. The battle of the forty days in the wilderness depicts in one vivid episode a struggle that actually continues throughout Jesus' entire ministry. The battle that he here endures in spirit is one he will have to endure in the give-and-take of every succeeding day. But because he has unmasked the adversary in this initial battle, Jesus will recognize him at a glance when he reappears at critical moments later on (cf. Matt. 16:23; John 6:15). This constant vigilance is the basis for all the subsequent temptations and victories.

Contrary to his reputation, Satan is not very original. His attack on Jesus is just like the attack that the serpent unleashed against Adam and Eve, except that it has greater variety and subtlety. " If you are the Son of God, command . . ." This is the poison of doubt trying to undermine the love of the Son for the Father, by suggesting that the Son is quite able to take charge of his own destiny. After all, is he not the Son of God? Is he not the Master and Heir of the Kingdom? Must he be expected to live in his own Kingdom as an outcast? Is it really necessary that he experience hunger, thirst, and nakedness? Must he be at the mercy of his subjects? Isn't the maintenance of the required incognito really cruelty to the very multitudes he has come to save, when a real demonstration of his power would convince them of his identity beyond a shadow of a doubt?

At this point, we must remember the nature of the Messianic hope that had existed through the centuries. Scripture itself had led Israel to expect a restoration of the Davidic dynasty, and it appeared that this would be a temporal restoration. The hope also includes a vision of glory which runs through the prophetic writings and the psalms, in which all the pagan nations give their allegiance to the God of Israel.

But Scripture contains another picture — that of the Suffering Servant of Isaiah who takes upon himself the

shame of his people (Isa., ch. 53). This picture is less frequently associated with the Messianic hope than the other,
and it is certainly a less popular picture than that either of
the restoration of the monarchy or the Son of Man coming
on the clouds of heaven (Dan. 7:13-14).

How will Jesus, whose whole life has been nourished by
Scripture, choose between these three conceptions? He deliberately discards the notion of a temporal kingdom,
which to him is only a figure of speech to describe the
world to come — and this is probably the meaning of the
third temptation (Matt. 4:8-9; cf. John 18:36). He does
not, however, discard the notion of the Son of Man's coming on the clouds in power and glory. He is sure that this
will come to pass, but he leaves its fulfillment to the Father, who alone determines and knows the hour. To anticipate this hour would be to " tempt God " (Matt. 4:5-7;
cf. chs. 24:27, 36; 26:53, 64).

Therefore, his immediate vocation will be that of the
Suffering Servant (Mark 10:42-45; Phil. 2:8). By submitting to baptism, he had previously confessed as his own the
sins of his people. He who has come to feed, deliver, and
save men, will not be able to save himself either from
thirst or scorn or death, and his enemies will mock him
with this ironic fact (Matt. 27:39-44).

Was Jesus aware of all the consequences of his choice
when he was undergoing these temptations? We simply do
not know. Scripture tells us very little about his own inner
struggles. But the careful way in which Jesus answers the
tempter shows us something important: to argue with Satan on his own terms is in itself to give him control of the
situation. And this is just what Jesus refuses to do. When
Satan suggests, " If you are the Son of God . . . ," Jesus
refuses to reply on Satan's terms; he counters simply with
" God. . . ." He will have no other nourishment than the
words that proceed from the mouth of God (Matt. 4:4; cf.
John 4:34). He will not tempt the Lord his God, nor will

he try to anticipate the appointed time by his own initiative. (Matt. 4:7; cf. John 2:4; 7:6; 12:27; 17:1.) He will
worship God alone, and will have nothing to do with the
Prince of this world. (Matt. 4:10; 6:24; cf. John 14:30.)

From this moment on there is open warfare between the
one who has the empires of this world in his power and
the One who comes in God's name to denounce and destroy this power. This bloody battle will come to clearest
focus in the cross. But it must be understood as a never-
ending battle, in which all the forces of evil hurl themselves
into the assault, and in which everything in man that does
not desire God sets itself against the coming of his Kingdom.

Scripture tells us that Jesus " in every respect has been
tempted as we are " (Heb. 4:15). He " learned obedience
through what he suffered " (Heb. 5:8). The fact that these
temptations are real makes him truly our brother. It is
because he overcame them that he has power to deliver us
from them.

The whole mystery of the Word made flesh is bound up
with the fact that he is really human, and that his struggles are real struggles.

2. THE " PRESENT REALITY " OF HIS REIGN

The beginning of Jesus' active ministry is related to the
fact of John's imprisonment (Mark 1:14). The career of
the forerunner is now finished. That of the Lord now begins.

What is the difference between the preaching of Jesus
and John the Baptist? On the surface there appears to be
almost none (cf. Matt. 3:2 and 4:17), but actually there is
all the difference between a future hope and a present reality, between expectation and fulfillment. For John the
Baptist had proclaimed that the Kingdom was about to
come — Jesus tells us that it has begun.

The Inauguration of the Kingdom

"*The time is fulfilled.*" (Mark 1:15.) Every Israelite knows that this statement signifies the breaking in of God's reign, the coming of the Messiah. Matthew's Gospel says the same thing when it declares that the prophecy of Isa. 9:1-2 has been fulfilled. (Cf. Matt. 4:12-16.) And Luke's Gospel, describing Jesus' first sermon in Nazareth, reports that after he read Isa., ch. 61, Jesus made a statement of incalculable importance: "*Today* this scripture has been fulfilled in your hearing" (Luke 4:21).

What does Jesus mean by this? The Messianic significance is unmistakable:

The Spirit of the Lord God is upon me,
  because the Lord has anointed me
to bring good tidings to the afflicted;
  he has sent me to bind up the brokenhearted,
to proclaim liberty to the captives,
  and the opening of the prison to those who are bound.
                                                          (Isa. 61:1.)

It is the *present reality*, the " today " of the Kingdom (cf. Heb. 3:7), manifesting itself in grace and judgment, which is proclaimed to the unbelieving people of Nazareth. They are indeed unbelieving — admiration is a far cry from faith. And Jesus quickly exposes the deep skepticism that is hidden under the initial astonishment of these men. Although their hearts are eager enough for miracles of the Kingdom, they are really looking not for the Kingdom itself, but only for its outward signs. And how, they must have thought, can this Jesus, this son of a carpenter whose family is known throughout the village, how can *he* be the King of Israel? It does not take them long to move from disappointed hope to charges of deception, to move from anger to hatred, and from hatred to murder.

" But passing through the midst of them, he went away."

(Luke 4:30.) The message that God's Kingdom is a present reality is proclaimed without effect in Nazareth (cf. the Marcan account of this story, Mark 6:1-6).

It is this *present reality* of God's Kingdom which underlies everything Jesus says and does, which gives unique authority to his words and unique significance to his actions. His whole approach is that of the true heir who has come into the world to be about his Father's business (Luke 2:49) and put his estate in order (Mark 12:6; cf. Matt. 17:26; John 1:11; 2:16; etc.).

Jesus' Authority

According to the Synoptic Gospels, Jesus claimed to be the Messiah only at the conclusion of his ministry; he even imposed silence on those who thus described him. Later on we will examine the reasons for this " Messianic secret." However, his words, his deeds, and his whole attitude toward the religious leaders of his time, indicate an unparalleled authority. The immediate reaction of the crowd to the hearing of his preaching is significant: Jesus speaks " as one who had authority, and not as the scribes " (Mark 1:22; Matt. 7:28-29). Even more important, *his words and his deeds are identical.* Jesus does not merely proclaim that deliverance is available, he actually delivers. The response is one of astonishment: " What is this? A new teaching! With authority he commands even the unclean spirits, and they obey him " (Mark 1:27). " Never was anything like this seen in Israel." (Matt. 9:33.)

Jesus behaves with all the freedom of a son in his father's house, with the sovereign authority of a king who has come to take possession of his kingdom. He orders men to follow him and they leave all to follow him. (Mark 1:15-20.) When he calls, no hesitation is permitted. (Luke 9:57-62.) To suffer for him is to be blessed. (Matt. 5:11 and parallels.) To reject him is to reject God himself. (Matt. 10:32-39.) This claim to share authority with God himself inevitably puts Jesus in conflict with all those who are threatened by his coming. These include the demonic powers who know that the Day of the Lord marks the end of their own kingdom, the powers of this world who have divided up the world as though it belonged to them, and the religious powers who had presumptuously claimed to have exclusive control over man's salvation and who were crushing men's souls under the oppressive burden of a religion of works. All these powers instinctively combine against the reign that has now begun.

The Sermon on the Mount

The Sermon on the Mount (Matt., chs. 5 to 7) is the charter of the Kingdom that Jesus came to establish. To all those who feel satisfied and secure, the materially satisfied who put their trust in their riches, the spiritually satisfied who think themselves justified by their own righteousness (Matt. 5:20; Luke 18:9-14), or by their barns of wheat (Luke 12:16-21), Jesus contrasts the " poor " — those who are poor in worldly goods and poor in spirit, but not poor in heart — all the humble folk of Israel who wait for the Day of the grace of the Lord (cf. Luke 2:25, 38; Matt. 11:25). The Beatitudes are an echo of the Magnificat: God puts down the mighty and exalts those of low degree (Luke 1:50-52). Blessed are those who wait for the coming of the Lord! Blessed are the poor! Blessed are those who mourn! Blessed are the merciful! Blessed are those who hunger and thirst after God's righteousness! It is to such as these that the Kingdom belongs. The coming dawn will be their comfort. Woe to those, on the other hand, who have tried to find their security and comfort here below, for when the Day of the Lord comes, all their possessions will be found worthless. (Matt. 5:1-12; cf. Luke 6:20-26; 16:19-31.)

The righteousness of the Kingdom exceeds that of the scribes and Pharisees. It requires purity of heart (Matt.

5:21-48; cf. ch. 5:8; Mark 7:14-23), and means that the life of the Father must be the pattern for the life of men (Matt. 5:44-45, 48; cf. Luke 6:35-36).

Jesus deliberately elevates his revelation above that of the past. " You have heard that it was said . . . but *I* say to you." (Matt. 5:21, 27, 38, 43.) Who, without blaspheming, could dare to put his own authority above that of Moses, unless he were the Messiah himself? Does this mean that Jesus arbitrarily throws out the ancient law without any concern for the consequences of doing so? Not at all. He acknowledges it to be the " word of God ": he is nourished by this word (Matt. 4:4) during his whole lifetime, and he charges others to submit to it (Matt. 23:3). He did not come to abolish the Law or the Prophets, but to fulfill them. (Matt. 5:17.) He goes so far as to say that not a single iota, not a dot, " will pass from the law until all is accomplished " (Matt. 5:18).

How can these apparent contradictions be reconciled? If Jesus issues a new law, it is precisely because *the hour of fulfillment has sounded.* In his own person the new order has begun. He has come " to fulfill all righteousness " (Matt. 3:15), to take upon himself the weight of the law, and to nail it to the wood of the cross. Even now, without their knowing it, the grace that flows from the cross illumines those disciples whom he introduces into the joy of the Kingdom. And because the hour of liberation has sounded, certain institutions crumble away.

The Son of God has a freedom that makes the reign of God a joyful thing, and this scandalizes the Pharisees more than anything else. For Jesus violates the Sabbath. He allows his disciples to break their fast. He eats with publicans and sinners. He is a " glutton and a drunkard " (Mark, chs. 2:13 to 3:6; cf. Matt. 11:19). In contrast to John the Baptist his approach to life is neither ascetic nor austere. Jesus explains all this in a few words: his coming is like a wedding day, the prelude to an eternal wedding day. The

hour of separation will come soon enough. The true meaning of the occasion demands that one enter into it with
joy rather than in mourning:

> Can the wedding guests fast while the bridegroom is
> with them? As long as they have the bridegroom with
> them, they cannot fast. The days will come, when the
> bridegroom is taken away from them, and then they will
> fast in that day. (Mark 2:19-20.)

To repair the old clothing of Pharisaic righteousness by
adding various patches to it would only make the tear
worse. (Mark 2:21.) In order to enter the wedding cham-
ber one must have brand-new clothing, which the master of
the house, according to Oriental custom, provides for his
guests. (Matt. 22:11-12.) To wish to pour the new wine of
the Kingdom into the old wineskins of Jewish legalism
would result in the loss of both the wine and the wineskins. (Mark 2:22.) Jesus knows that the new wine of the
Spirit will sooner or later burst the bounds of Jewish institutions.

The old distinctions between " pure " and " impure " do
not exist for him any longer, for it is man's *heart* that is
corrupt, and Pharisaic legalism can only construct " whitewashed tombs " (Mark, ch. 7; Matt. 23:25-28) . Jesus did
not come for the " well " but for the sick — for those who
know that they are lost and wait for salvation at his hand.
(Mark 2:15-17.) This is why the pagans, the publicans, and
the prostitutes may rank higher at the heavenly banquet
than the " churchgoers." (Luke 7:36-50; 13:22-30; 14:15-
24; 16:14-15; 18:9-14.) There is more joy in heaven over
one sinner who repents than over ninety-nine righteous
persons who need no repentance. Jesus shares his Father's
joy over each lost sheep who returns to the sheepfold.
(Luke 15:1-7; cf. Ezek., ch. 34; John 10:1-19.) He has come
into the world to lead a prodigal humanity back to the Father's house. He kills the fatted calf and rejoices with sin-

ners. (Luke 15:11-32.) But the shadow of the Pharisee hovers over the feast like that of the older brother in the parable — angry, vindictive, and harsh. He is already living in his father's house, but he does not really understand what the father is like, the father who eagerly watches the horizon, with a daily hope that will be satisfied only by the return to life of the departed child who was lost and dead.

The Pharisee constructs his own scale of sins and good works which must be kept in balance. He does not know that the fruit of sin is death, and that the only way out of this is by a new birth. (John 3:1-8.) The narrow gate to the Kingdom is death and resurrection. Only one person can open the gate and that is the well-beloved Son who is willing to die in order that he might give us life.

The Miracles as Messianic Acts

Jesus' acts of deliverance are like foretastes of the life to come. They are indeed acts of compassion, concrete expressions of God's steadfast love, but more significantly they are Messianic acts, and only as such can they be understood.

In this connection, the casting out of demons has a very special place in the Gospels, for the beginning of God's reign means the end of the demonic reign. The demons know this, and they are greatly disturbed by the mere presence of Jesus. In fact, those who are victims of demon possession are the first to confess Jesus' Messiahship: " What have you to do with us, Jesus of Nazareth? Have you come to destroy us? I know who you are, the Holy One of God " (Mark 1:24; cf. ch. 3:11) . And Matthew's Gospel attributes these significant words to the demoniacs of Gadarene: " What have you to do with us, O Son of God? Have you come here to torment us *before the time?* " (Matt. 8:29) . " The time " referred to here is the hour of Judgment and God's Reign, which will make an end to the power of Satan and his rivals. Has this hour struck? Jesus believes that it has. When the Pharisees accuse him of " casting out demons by the prince of demons," he replies:

> If I cast out demons by Beelzebul, by whom do your sons cast them out? Therefore they shall be your judges. But if it is by the Spirit of God that I cast out demons, then *the kingdom of God has come upon you*. (Matt. 12:27-28, italics added.)

Similarly, when Jesus sends his disciples on their mission, he gives them power to cast out demons (Mark 6:7), to cure illness and to say to those whom they have cured, " The kingdom of God has come near to you " (Luke 10:9).

We no longer believe that illness is always an immediate result of sin or the mark of demonic powers, but illness does demonstrate that humanity is subject to the powers of sin and death. And it is just these powers that Jesus comes to destroy. The healings and the raisings from the dead described in the Gospels have no other meaning. They are so many signs announcing the reign of God. The Gospels make a great deal of the fact that Jesus cures on the Sabbath. Does he do this simply to shock the scribes and Pharisees? Certainly not. But in the process of doing so, he gives the Sabbath its real meaning. The Sabbath reminds us that God rested on the seventh day of creation; it is thus a prefiguring in the present of the eternal rest that is to come, of God's world where there will be neither illness, nor mourning, and where death will be no more. The life of Jesus on earth inaugurates this reign, and gives us a foretaste of it. Every healing is a foreshadowing of his reign, a foreshadowing of the eternal Sabbath, and marks God's victory over sin and death. " The sabbath was made for man, not man for the sabbath; so the Son of man is lord even of the sabbath." (Mark 2:27-28.) To restore bodies and to save souls is to glorify God and affirm his reign — and what work could be more fitting for the Sabbath than

that? (Cf. John 9:1-5, 13-17, 35-41.) The guilt of the Pharisees in this matter is not their zeal for the letter of the law,
but their hardness of heart (Mark 3:5) and their *willful*
blindness, for the most obvious signs of God's reign clash
with their obstinate refusal to believe (John 9:39-41).

The wonderful prophecies of Isaiah describing God's
reign proclaim that the deliverance that is to come will set
men free from illness and death:

> Then the eyes of the blind shall be opened,
>   and the ears of the deaf unstopped;
> then shall the lame man leap like a hart,
>   and the tongue of the dumb sing for joy.
>   (Isa. 35:5-6.)

Jesus' response to John's messengers, who inquire whether
he is the one " who is to come," almost certainly contains
a direct allusion to these prophecies of Isaiah:

> Go and tell John what you hear and see: the blind re-
> ceive their sight and the lame walk, lepers are cleansed
> and the deaf hear, and the dead are raised up, and the
> poor have good news preached to them. And blessed is
> he who takes no offense at me. (Matt. 11:4-6.)

The prophets are realists. Therefore they understand these
signs of the Kingdom in a physical and material way. But
physical deliverance can be a parable of spiritual deliverance:

> In that day the deaf shall hear
>   the words of a book,
> and out of their gloom and darkness
>   the eyes of the blind shall see.
>   (Isa. 29:18.)
> Then the eyes of those who see will not be closed,
>   and the ears of those who hear will hearken.
>   (Isa. 32:3.)
> I am the Lord, I have called you in righteousness,
>   I have taken you by the hand and kept you;

I have given you as a covenant to the people,
  a light to the nations,
  to open the eyes that are blind,
  to bring the prisoners from the dungeon,
  from the prison those who sit in darkness.
                                              (Isa. 42:6-7.)

It is impossible to mistake the double meaning of these predictions. Jesus' words also have this kind of double meaning. The healing of bodies and souls is one and the same thing to him, for it is the *whole* man, body, soul, and spirit, whom he came to save and restore to full integrity. (Mark 2:1-12; 5:25-34.) Physical blindness and deafness are symbols of a much more terrible kind of blindness and deafness, the blindness of those who do not see God and the deafness of those who do not hear his word. This parabolic meaning of the healings is particularly stressed in the Gospel of John (chs. 5 and 9), but it is implicit in the other Gospels as well (Mark 7:31-37; 8:22-26; cf. ch. 8:17-18).[26]

The actual miracles of healing are of secondary importance and consequence in comparison with the preaching of the gospel which is the good news of salvation. For Jesus came to preach this *good news.* (Mark 1:35-39.) It is because he has power to forgive sins that he is able to lift the curse of the illness that is sin's consequence, rather than the other way around. (Mark 2:3-12.) And it is because he has conquered Satan, the prince of demons, that he is able to destroy his work: " No one can enter a strong man's house and plunder his goods, unless he first binds the strong man; then indeed he may plunder his house " (Mark 3:27).

Jesus' coming is the dawn of God's reign. To his disciples who return joyfully from their missionary journey, Jesus declares, " I saw Satan fall like lightning from heaven " (Luke 10:18).

The secret of Jesus' authority lies in the complete identity between his will and that of his Father. Here on earth he is only the instrument, albeit the perfect instrument, of the will of God. (Matt. 11:27-30; Luke 10:22; cf. John 5:17-30.) If the faith of the centurion amazes Jesus, it is because a Roman officer clearly understood that an authority like his could only have come from above, and that henceforth, whatever he might command, that authority was absolute. (Matt. 8:5-13.) The *present reality* of God's reign resounds, sovereign and victorious, wherever he is believed in, acknowledged, and accepted. (Luke 19:9; 23:43.)

3. THE SECRET OF THE KINGDOM

If Jesus has a clear understanding of his Messianic vocation, and if his deeds are so many signs of the Kingdom that is being ushered in, why does he impose silence on the demoniacs whom he delivers, on the ill whom he cures, and even on his own disciples, when they recognize and acknowledge his Messiahship? (Mark 1:25, 43-44; 3:12; 7:36; 8:26, 29-30; cf. Matt. 16:20.)

Here we are confronted by what is usually called the "Messianic secret." When we read the Gospels carefully, we see that from the beginning of his ministry, Jesus is the object of a kind of popularity that he neither seeks nor desires. It is, however, the inevitable consequence of the authority that flows from his person and from his words and deeds. The Gospels, and particularly the Gospel of Mark, emphasize not only that Jesus did not want this kind of popularity, but that on a number of occasions he tried to escape from it (Mark 1:32-39; 6:30-33; 7:24; 8:27; cf. John 6:14-15, 26-29). This easy success interferes with his real work of preaching and teaching. Jesus has no desire to pose as a wonder-worker, but the crowd always pays more attention to his miracles than to his message (John 6:26-29). He constantly has to defend himself against the wrong kind of reputation.

It is interesting to notice that only once does Jesus encourage a man to tell other people that he has been healed.

This takes place in a pagan country. To the Gadarene demoniac who wished to follow him, Jesus replies, " Go home to your friends, and tell them how much the Lord has done for you, and how he has had mercy on you " (Mark 5:19). He makes this man his missionary in the country of Gadara.

It seems clear that Jesus' request for silence with regard to his Messianic titles is dictated on the one hand by prudential considerations and on the other hand by the very nature of the Kingdom he has come to establish. Let us look briefly at these two reasons in turn.

1. *Prudential considerations:* Jesus knows that his days are numbered, for the imprisonment and beheading of John make quite clear what is in store for prophets. The day will come when Jesus will go to his death openly and willingly, but so long as " his hour has not yet come " (John 7:2-9), he avoids open conflict with the Jewish and Roman authorities. To assert that he was Messiah would be to lay himself open immediately to the opposition of the Pharisees and Sadducees who had been looking for ways to get rid of him ever since he first appeared on the scene (Mark 3:6). Such an assertion would also awaken the fears of the Roman authority, which was always on guard against attempts at insurrection, and which would interpret Jesus' proclamation solely in terms of political Messianism. When Jesus confesses before the Sanhedrin that he is indeed the Messiah, the reaction is swift and condemnation is inevitable (Mark 14:61-64; cf. John 19:12-16). And it is as " King of the Jews " that he is crucified (cf. Mark 15:26; John 19:19-22). There is an episode that only the Fourth Gospel recounts, that describes Jesus withdrawing from the crowd that had come to make him king. (John 6:15). The episode demonstrates the misunderstanding that leads the crowd to make a political leader out of Jesus. And this is precisely the misunderstanding that Jesus wishes to avoid at all costs. But these prudential considerations are not the most important reason for Jesus' secrecy.

2. Far more weighty is *the nature of the Kingdom* Jesus

has come to establish. As early as the temptation in the wilderness we saw Jesus reject the idea of a political Messiahship (Matt. 4:8-10). The incident with which we have just dealt is a concrete illustration of this decision. Jesus' Kingdom is not of this world (John 18:36-37). He is indeed the true heir of the throne of David, but in a sense that the Roman authorities cannot understand. This seems to stand out clearly in certain words of Jesus with which he condemns the Zealots' attempts at insurrection. (Matt. 5:38-45; 26:52.) Like the ancient prophets, he sees Israel's trials as a judgment of God (Luke 13:5), and those who are responsible for them as instruments of the Most High (John 19:9-11).

(It is interesting to note that although Jesus recognizes Pilate's authority as legitimate, he has nothing but scorn for Herod, a usurper and renegade, who owes his worldly fortune to his collaboration with Rome. Jesus describes him as a " jackal," [27] the most vile of all animals, who trails huge meat-eating animals and lives off the dead bodies they leave behind [Luke 13:32]. When Herod questions him, Jesus does not answer a single word [Luke 23:9], and this silence is probably the greatest condemnation Jesus ever voiced.)

If Jesus accepts the actual situation of the Roman occupation (Matt. 22:15-22), this does not mean that he has no concern for his peoples' political troubles. But the captivity from which Jesus comes to deliver them, and the freedom that he brings them, are of a different sort. God's reign transcends the realities of this world. This world is actually a " *dead* " world. Its " freedom " is a false freedom, passing itself off as the real thing, and its temporal power is likewise only a pretense. Jesus comes *to raise this dead world to life*. Apart from such a resurrection, all that can be done is to rearrange the corpses, whether the corpses are social or political.

Israel's problem therefore is not to recover a freedom it

never had, but to seek the Kingdom of God and his righteousness, and thus to be raised from the dead to its true
vocation as witness. The poignant way in which Jesus ad-
dresses his people makes clear that his coming confronts Israel with a final decision. It is not a decision for or against
Rome, but for or against the Living God of the patriarchs.
For Jesus as for the prophets, Israel's temporal destiny is
inextricably related to its spiritual destiny, and this is its
specific vocation as a priestly people. Israel's real problem
is not the presence of occupation forces (whether Roman
or any other), but the fact that it does not recognize the
signs of the times, which mean the hour of visitation and
judgment (Luke 12:54-57; 13:1-9). The prophets came
and they were persecuted. The heir of the Kingdom arrives
and Jerusalem refuses to recognize him. In so doing, it signs
its own death warrant:

> For the days shall come upon you, when your enemies
> will cast up a bank about you and surround you, and
> hem you in on every side, and dash you to the ground,
> you and your children within you, and they will not leave
> one stone upon another in you; *because you did not
> know the time of your visitation.* (Luke 19:43-44; cf. ch.
> 13:34-35; Mark 12:1-12; 13:1-2.)

The cities of Israel that refuse to listen to Jesus' call will
suffer a more terrible fate than that of the most pagan cities of antiquity (Matt. 11:20-24; cf. Luke 10:13-15), for
they experienced the first fruits of the reign of God and
were not converted.

The " secret of the Kingdom " is that it must be received
by faith and not by sight. God came among his own and
his own received him not. The Word has been spoken, but
the number of those who have heard it is minimal. (John
1:5, 10-13.) This is the real meaning of the parable of the
sower. (Mark, ch. 4; Matt., ch. 13.) The proportion of seed
that is lost is very high. (Mark 4:3-7.) But those seeds

which fall on good ground bring forth grain, thirty-, sixty-
and one hundredfold. The beginnings of the Kingdom are
hidden and almost infinitesimal, and out of all proportion
to the results. (Mark 4:26-32.) Its fruits will not be visible
until the hour of the harvest, which is the Last Judgment.
(Matt. 13:24-52.) " The kingdom of God is not coming
with signs to be observed; nor will they say, ' Lo, here it
is! ' or ' There! ' for behold, the kingdom of God is in the
midst of you." (Luke 17:20-21.)

The Kingdom has come because Jesus has come. And the
incognito of this coming is another aspect of its " secret."
The kingdoms of this world are established by their splendor. But the splendor of Jesus' Kingdom is of another sort;
it is established only for those who have " eyes to see " and
" ears to hear." It can be recognized by faith alone. The
kings of this world rule their subjects with an iron hand
and take whatever they please. (I Sam. 8:10-20; Mark
10:42.) The King of heaven and the Lord of the earth
comes to his own in the form of a servant (Mark 10:42-
45; Luke 22:25-27; cf. Phil. 2:5-7) and has nowhere to lay
his head (Luke 9:58) . His yoke is easy and his burden is
light, but he takes upon himself all the burdens of the
weary and heavy-laden. (Matt. 11:28-30.) He takes upon
himself all the evils and sins of humanity. (Isa. 53:4-5; cf.
Matt. 8:17.) He comes, as Pascal said, " in the glory of his
own order," which is the order of charity.[28] But humanity
is so constituted that this secret of his humiliation is a
source of doubt and scandal. And the fullest measure of
this scandal will be the sacrifice of the cross.

The Secret of the Kingdom Revealed Only to Faith

" But who do you say that I am? " This question, which
Jesus asks his disciples at Caesarea Philippi, marks a decisive turning point in his ministry. (Mark 8:27-30 and
parallels.) Until this time he had proclaimed the good
news of the Kingdom. The crowds rushed to hear him,

but the opposition gained force, an underhanded and spiteful opposition borne of jealousy and fear, and unwilling to let things proceed any farther. Herod is terribly alarmed by this new prophet, and Jesus is soon forced to flee from Galilee. (Luke 9:7-9; 13:31.) And from this time on, he devotes himself more and more to his little band of disciples, to the intimate circle of the Twelve. He shares his preaching and healing with them. He sends them out to preach and to cast out demons in his name. (Mark 3:13-19; 6:7-13, 30-33; cf. Matt., ch. 10; Luke 9:1-6; 10:1-20.) And now he asks them the decisive, direct, and personal question that every man must finally answer: " But who do *you* say that I am? "

Each member of the tiny band of disciples is faced with an ultimate choice: shall he follow his master to the end or shall he, like the crowd, leave Jesus when he makes plain that the way that must be followed is the narrow way of the cross? The Gospel of John reminds us of the reality of this dilemma: after the miracle of the loaves, it reports that "many of his disciples drew back and no longer went about with him. Jesus said to the twelve, ' Will you also go away? ' " (John 6:66-67.)

Simon Peter is the first to confess his Lord. (Mark 8:29; Matt. 16:16; Luke 9:20; John 6:68-69.) His eyes are opened: Jesus is the long-awaited Messiah, the Holy One of God! The Gospel of Matthew emphasizes the fact that a confession such as this cannot proceed from the natural heart of man. Only the Spirit of God knows who is from God, only the Father knows the Son, only the Son knows the Father: " Blessed are you, Simon Bar-Jona! For flesh and blood has not revealed this to you, but my Father who is in heaven." (Matt. 16:17; cf. Matt. 11:27; I Cor. 2:11; 12:3.)

This is a crucial decision, for between human admiration for the person of Jesus, and faith in Jesus as the Son of God and Savior of the world, there is all the difference between heaven and earth, between a divine revelation and a human sentiment. Only the grace of God enables us to recognize this difference, by revealing the Son of God to us. (Gal. 1:15-16; I Cor. 12:3.) This is why Peter's confession is the foundation and cornerstone of the church, for apart from this revelation, apart from this faith in Christ as the Son of God, there is no such thing as the Christian church. Only a church that is supplied with the full authority of its Lord, and is illumined by his Spirit, has authority to bind and to loosen souls and to withhold the keys of the Kingdom (Matt. 16:18-19; cf. John 20:22-23). The apostles do not fully understand the meaning of Jesus' words until after the resurrection, when, endowed with his Spirit on the Day of Pentecost, they receive full authority to proclaim his salvation to the world, and to pardon and judge in his name. For the present, however, they are again uncertain and perplexed, as we soon discover.

No sooner has Simon Peter confessed his master, than he immediately stumbles over the scandal of Jesus' suffering. When Jesus tells him that he must suffer many things, Peter responds: " God forbid, Lord! This shall never happen to you! " (Matt. 16:22.)

Jesus' reply is one of frightful severity. This time it is not the voice of God that he hears in Peter's words, but the voice of Satan: " Get behind me, Satan! You are a hindrance to me; for you are not on the side of God, but of men " (Matt. 16:23).

The word " hindrance," or " stumbling block " as it is in Greek, refers to something that makes one stumble, or is the reason for a fall (cf. Matt. 11:6). Jesus' reaction to Peter indicates the intensity of the struggle in which he is engaged. What the crowds are waiting for, what even the disciples are waiting for, is a brilliant manifestation of his Messianic glory, and this hope will continue right up to the very end of Jesus' life (cf. Mark 11:7-10). This expectation had even crossed Jesus' mind early in his ministry.

Jesus could have escaped from death. But he rejected the temptation to ask for divine intervention on his behalf (Matt. 4:5-7; cf. Matt. 26:53), and accepted the mysterious destiny of the Suffering Servant of Isaiah as being God's will for him (cf. Isa., ch. 53).

4. THE CRUCIFIED KING

The Scandal of a Suffering Messiah

" And he began to teach them that the Son of man must suffer many things." (Mark 8:31.) " The Son of man *must* suffer. . . ." It is not only Peter who stumbles when confronted with this terrible *necessity*. Everyone does. And woe to him for whom the crucifixion is merely something mentioned in the creed and the liturgy, and who no longer recognizes how scandalous and horrible it is!

" The Son of man *must* suffer. . . ." This has nothing to do with the " fatalism " of ancient philosophy. This kind of necessity is something very different. It is based on who God is and who man is, on how intolerable God's holiness is to man, and how intolerable man's sin is to God. Thus human freedom indulges in a very grim sport: " Away with him, away with him, crucify him! " (John 19:15.) Take away the Holy One from our midst! We can't stand his words, his deeds, his way of looking at us! As long as he is around, we can't do as we please! Away with him, away with him, crucify him! He shows up what's really going on in our inmost hearts! (Luke 2:35.) He exposes the hollowness of our " religion " and the shallowness of our contrition! When he's around we know that we are " whitewashed tombs "! (Matt. 23:27.) Away with him, away with him, crucify him!

But God has a " game " to play too. His game is the terrible game of salvation. If this folly of men is to put the best of his children to death, he will turn the tables by using this same folly to fulfill his own purposes. Let it be

granted that Satan gathers all the powers of this world together against the Lord's Anointed. (Acts 4:26-27.) Let it
be granted that when these hostile forces are mobilized the
leaders of Israel, the inheritors of all God's promises, will
be in the front ranks. Let it be granted, once again, that
Roman law and order will become the cowardly and oblig-
ing accomplices of Jewish intrigue. And let it be granted,
finally, that Satan will persuade the frightened disciples to
renounce their Master, or else will reduce them to silence,
and that one of the Twelve will turn traitor.

Let all that be granted. Nevertheless, in the midst of all
these apparent victories, won by the prince of this world,
his ultimate defeat is hidden. He is merely the instrument
of a higher purpose. For in this single Son whom he
crushes with his might, Israel in all of its faithfulness is incarnate. Satan has all men in his power save this one. He
will subject him to the torture of suffering on a cross — in
vain. He will inflict all the rages of hatred on him — in
vain. He will make mankind forsake him — in vain. The
darkness will be so thick that God himself will seem to
have forsaken him — but all in vain. For Jesus will remain
obedient unto death, even death on a cross. (Phil. 2:8.)
The only prize that the prince of demons really wants will
escape him, for he will be unable to capture God's well-
beloved Son: " The ruler of this world," as Jesus points
out, " has no power over me " (John 14:30). And the victory of this single person will become victory for every
person.

Jesus knows all this; his acknowledgment that he must
suffer is balanced by his assurance of his resurrection " on
the third day " and his return in glory (cf. Mark 8:31, 38).
But only those who have followed him and believed in him
in his disgrace, and have been willing to lose their lives
for him, will know the glory of his reign. (Mark 8:34 to
9:1 and parallels.) And in order that the testing may be
to the full, the master and his disciples must enter into the
darkness of abandonment, separated from one another.

The Journey to the Cross

The vision of the transfiguration is given to the disciples as a foreshadowing of the resurrection. For a moment the veil is set aside, and then immediately it is shut again. (Mark 9:2-13.) They see Moses and Elijah conversing with Jesus, and this serves to emphasize once again the unity of the two covenants. Once more God affirms his good will toward the One who comes to take up his cross, by enfolding him in his glory, and by acknowledging in the humble Servant his beloved Son (Mark 9:7; cf. Mark 1:11). Following this, Jesus and the disciples go back down into the daily struggles of earth and the disciples' incredulity draws a sad comment from the Lord: " O faithless and perverse generation, how long am I to be with you and bear with you? " (Luke 9:41; cf. Mark 9:14-29.)

From this time on there is an invisible barrier set up between Jesus and his followers. Jesus " set his face to go to Jerusalem " (Luke 9:51). Mark's Gospel describes him as walking alone in front, while the disciples follow far behind him, " full of fear," and continue their discussion about what it all means. While Jesus thinks of death, they think of glory. They ask him who among them is greatest, and argue with one another about the places they will occupy in the coming Kingdom. At the time when their Lord is approaching total humiliation, they are dreaming only of their own exaltation. (Mark 9:30-37; 10:32-45.) The sober character of the accounts only underlines the tragic gulf that exists between the master and the disciples. It involves not only a difference of opinion concerning when the Kingdom will come, it also hinges on the very nature of this Kingdom. For Jesus, it is by losing one's life that he finds it: " Greater love has no man than this, that a man lay down his life for his friends " (John 15:13). The new birth is found when the self is denied and life is centered on God and the neighbor. By contrast, all that the disciples have succeeded in doing is to transfer their egocentricity into the spiritual realm. They are less concerned about the reign of God than they are about how much status they will have in it.

Jesus' final conversations with his disciples show how clearly he understood the two great temptations that will always assail his church: the real meaning of spiritual authority (Mark 10:42-45; Luke 22:24-30; John 13:1-17), and the problem of internal division (John 13:34-35; 15:1-17; 17:20-26). It is as the sons of the Kingdom are united that the world knows whose disciples they are. This unity, which he is to ratify with his blood, is the subject of the Lord's final prayer for his church.

The entry into Jerusalem is a display of Messianic faith, which Jesus makes no effort to stop. To those who urge him to silence his disciples, he replies, " If these were silent, the very stones would cry out " (Luke 19:40). But the very character that he gives to this entry shows how he conceives of his Kingship:

> Lo, your king comes to you;
> triumphant and victorious is he,
> *humble and riding on an ass,*
> on a colt the foal of an ass.
> (Zech. 9:9, italics added.)

Jerusalem must be given a final opportunity to hear the summons of her King, for her destiny cannot be separated from his, and by condemning him she will be signing her own death warrant. (Luke 19:41-44.) The parables of the vineyard and of the wedding feast emphasize the seriousness of this final decision, for they show that God's vineyard can be taken away from the leaders of Israel and entrusted to others. (Cf. Matt. 21:33-43; 22:1-10.) Jesus knows that his hour has come: the Messianic secret is now out in the open, and rather than trying to escape from his accusers, he seems to be deliberately provoking their anger, as chapters 21 to 23 of Matthew make very clear. The Pharisees are guilty not only because they have closed the gates of the Kingdom to themselves, but even more because they have prevented others from entering that Kingdom (Matt. 23:13).

We need to remember that in his strictures against the "Pharisees," Jesus is not condemning a particular sect, but rather the attitude of all those who assume that faith is their permanent possession, and who consequently slip almost imperceptibly into spiritual pride and hypocrisy. The Pharisees were the inner circle of Jews who were held to be "pure." Little by little they had made a "merit" of this virtue. They had stopped living by the grace of God, and their religion had become a religion of works. Jesus struggles until the end of his life to tear their mask away from them so that they can see what they truly are. His severity is a last effort to break through the awful shell of self-righteousness in which they live, and which makes them "whitewashed tombs" and walking corpses. The whole church is constantly threatened by this hardening of the spiritual arteries which we call "pharisaism," and the church must always read these particular chapters of Matthew with fear and trembling. The whole church lives under the threat that God may desert his dwelling place. (Matt. 23:38; Rom. 11:19-21; Rev. 2:3-5.)

Jesus' disciples are frankly impressed by the Temple that Herod the Great had undertaken to build, and that was still unfinished. But Jesus prophesies that not one stone of it will be left upon another. (Matt. 24:1-2; cf. Mark 13:1-2.) Matthew, ch. 24, and Mark, ch. 13, describe a historic event, the destruction of Jerusalem (which actually took place in A.D. 70), and an eschatological event (the return of the Lord at the end of time and the Last Judgment). The first generation of Christians may have believed that these two events would occur simultaneously. We have already seen, in our study of the ancient prophets, that historical events were like signs foretelling "the last things."

Jesus makes clear that no one knows the day or the hour of these last things, not even the Son, but only the Father. (Matt. 24:36 and parallels.) Nevertheless, the assurance of God's final victory shines through all these last discourses of Jesus: blessed will be those who endure during the time of testing (Matt. 24:12-13), blessed will be the servants whom the Master finds awake and watchful (Matt. 24:43-51; 25:14-30; cf. Luke 19:11-27), blessed will be the church that is waiting, with lamps lighted, for the coming of the Bridegroom (Matt. 25:1-13).

The Hour of Darkness

Jesus simply asserts the meaning of his sacrificial death, rather than explaining it in so many words. He emphasizes that it is done freely, and that it fulfills a substitutionary function: " The Son of man also came not to be served but to serve, and to give his life as a ransom for many " (Mark 10:45). The anointing at Bethany is like the royal anointing of the Crucified One, and the woman's action will be remembered throughout the whole world. (Mark 14:3-9; John 12:1-8.) The words spoken by Jesus at the Last Supper indicate more clearly than any others the double assurance that sustains him during these last hours: the assurance of the atoning worth of his death, and the assurance of the coming of the Kingdom. " This is my body which is given *for you*. Do this in remembrance of me." (Luke 22:19, margin; cf. I Cor. 11:24.) While distributing the cup Jesus declares, " Take this, and divide it among yourselves; for I tell you that from now on I shall not drink of the fruit of the vine until the kingdom of God comes " (Luke 22:17-18; or, according to other versions, " until that day when I drink it new in the kingdom of God," Mark 14:25).

The Lord's Supper, according to the Gospels and the Pauline tradition, has a double meaning: it is both commemorative (" in remembrance of . . .") and eschatologi-

cal (". . . until he come "). It is the communion of the
body broken for us, of the blood shed for us, and it is
also the foreshadowing of the great banquet of the Kingdom.

Jesus stresses the free and voluntary character of the gift
that he makes of himself. (John 10:18.) When the hour
has come, he goes consciously and deliberately to Jerusalem, for that is where a prophet is supposed to die. (Luke
13:31-33.) According to the Synoptic Gospels, it is his discourses in the Temple and concerning the Temple that
lead to the death sentence. (Mark 12:12; cf. Matt. 21:15,
45-46; 26:3-5, 60-61.) According to the Fourth Gospel, the
decision of the Sanhedrin seems to be connected with the
resurrection of Lazarus and the effect that this had on the
people. (John 11:47-57.) Jesus asserts the terrible responsibility of those who betray him (Matt. 21:38; 23:29-39;
26:20-25), but he is sure, to the very end, that God could
deliver him from their hands if he so wished (Matt. 26:39,
53). Consequently, Jesus sees his betrayers as instruments
in God's hands, for through them is fulfilled the purpose of
salvation for which God had sent him to earth (John
11:51; 12:27-33; 13:27; 14:29-31; 18:1-5; 19:9-11; cf. Mark
8:31, " the Son of man must suffer "; ch. 14:26-31, 43-52).
During his trial Jesus plays into his accusers' hands by uttering the " blasphemy " that leads to his condemnation.
To the question, " Are you the Christ, the Son of the
Blessed? " he replies, " I am; and you will see the Son of
man sitting at the right hand of Power, and coming with
the clouds of heaven " (Mark 14:62; cf. Matt. 26:63-64).
Throughout his whole trial, Jesus is so completely free in
his attitude toward his judges that they, with their uncon-
trolled rage and their secret fear, are the ones who really
seem to be on trial. His words and even his silences are
marked by such kingly dignity that Pilate himself is said
to have been troubled. (Luke 23:1-25; cf. Matt. 27:19-36;
John 18:28-40.) But the people, excited by their leaders

demand the death of their king, even (according to the Gospel of Matthew) to the extent of saying the terrible words, " His blood be on us and on our children! " (Matt. 27:25.)

Jesus gives his life freely. But the freedom of this gift does not diminish either the horror or the fear connected with it, and the Gospels make no attempt to conceal this from us. John's Gospel has preserved an account of the inner struggle through which Jesus must have gone: " Now is my soul troubled. And what shall I say, ' Father, save me from this hour '? No, for this purpose I have come to this hour. Father, glorify thy name " (John 12:27-28). And to his disciples he can say, " The hour is coming, indeed it has come, when you will be scattered, every man to his home, and will leave me alone " (John 16:32).

Nevertheless, it is in the first three Gospels that Jesus' inner struggles are reported to us in all their bloody realism. The Synoptics are not afraid to let us see the Son of God engaged in mortal combat within his soul, and sweating drops of blood at the very moment when he is consenting to the supreme sacrifice: " Father, if thou art willing, remove this cup from me: nevertheless not my will, but thine, be done " (Luke 22:39-46).

Why should Jesus have been afraid of death?

Greek paganism understood the Stoic notion of " dying serenely." Modern paganism likewise understands the notion of a " noble death." But the Bible does not understand anything of the sort — in the Bible death remains " the king of terrors " (Job 18:14). It is the wages of sin, the direct result of condemnation. (Gen. 3:19, 22; 6:3.) It is the gateway to Sheol, the place of darkness to which God never goes, because in his very being he is Light and Life. And it is truly the darkness of his absence that surrounds the cross on which Jesus dies. It is from the very midst of the darkness of hell into which Jesus has voluntarily descended that his cry rises up, " My God, my God, why hast

thou forsaken me? " (Matt. 27:46) . But he who utters this
cry is the only one who is innocent, the only one who is
pure — he is the Son of God. The darkness into which he
descends is the darkness of the world he has come to save.
Describing the moment when Judas went out to betray his
master, the Gospel of John says, " It was night " (John
13:30) . It is also " night " at the time when Jesus struggles
and dies: " Now from the sixth hour there was darkness
over all the land until the ninth hour " (Matt. 27:45;
cf. Mark 15:33) . It is in the night of the world, in the
night of sin, in the night of death, in the inexorable night
of the tomb, that Jesus goes down into the utter darkness:
" And Jesus cried again with a loud voice and yielded up
his spirit " (Matt. 27:50) .

In Matthew's Gospel, we see the earth itself staggering
under the weight of this death, trembling on its very foundations. For is not this death indeed the condemnation of
the present world and the definitive sign of its destruction?
(Matt. 27:51-54.)

A new world will emerge from the tomb where Jesus is
buried on the evening of Good Friday. But it will be able
to emerge only through the miracle of the resurrection.

5. THE RISEN LORD

The Gospels make clear that the disciples were hope-
lessly confused on the day after the crucifixion. All their
hopes had collapsed. Jesus was dead and buried. He could
be spoken of only in the past tense: " He *was* a prophet
mighty in deed and word before God and all the people.
. . . We *had hoped* that he was the one to redeem Israel "
(Luke 24:19, 21).

Why didn't the disciples take Jesus' repeated predictions
about his suffering, resurrection, and return more seriously? The Gospels simply report their blindness without
trying to explain it. Until the very end, the disciples had
expected God to perform a miracle; now they no longer

expect anything. They return to their ordinary occupations. The incident is closed.

The Assurance of the Resurrection as the Foundation of the Church

If anything stands out clearly in the final chapters of the four Gospels, it is that without the fact of the resurrection there would never have been any Christian church. In their inmost hearts, a few men would have cherished the memory of this extraordinary master in whom, for a moment, they had placed all their hope. Then, one by one, these men would have died, and Jesus of Nazareth would have been buried in oblivion.

Apart from the victory of the resurrection, the cross is no more than a terrible verdict of condemnation. What is in store for a humanity that does such a thing to the best of its children: " If Christ has not been raised," cries Paul, ". . . we are of all men most to be pitied " (I Cor. 15: 14, 19).

That is why the disciples are in the deepest darkness, weighed down by their denials, their cowardice, their deluded hopes, and the dark and forbidding silence of God.

A church that did not live by the fact of the resurrection, and that did not preach the resurrection, would also be in the deepest darkness, and Paul's word would have to be applied to it: " Your faith is futile and you are still in your sins " (I Cor. 5:17).

But away with all this talk, for the Lord is risen! He appears to the women who have gone to the sepulcher to embalm his body on Easter morning. He appears to Peter, then to the Eleven in the upper room. He appears to the disciples at Emmaus and to the fishermen on the Sea of Tiberias. He appears afterward, according to the witness of Paul, to more than five hundred brethren at one time (I Cor. 15:6), and finally to Paul himself.

These appearances are enveloped by a mystery that the

accounts make no effort to hide. It is he, and yet even those closest to him do not recognize him. (Luke 24:16; John 20:15; 21:4.) It is clearly a bodily resurrection, for all four Gospels emphasize the fact of the empty tomb. Jesus invites his disciples to touch his wounds. He even eats before them. But his body is no longer subject to the ordinary laws of nature, for Jesus can enter and leave a room whose doors are locked (John 20:19, 26).

The way in which Jesus lets himself be recognized is very significant. Mary's eyes are opened when he says her name. (John 20:16.) The eyes of the disciples at Emmaus are opened when he breaks bread with them. (Luke 24:30-31.) The eyes of the Eleven are opened when he says, " Peace be with you " (John 20:19). To the more incredulous, he shows his pierced hands and side. (Luke 24:39; John 20:20-27.) Simon recognizes him because of the miraculous catch of fishes. (John 21:6-7.) And later on Jesus says to his persecutor, Saul of Tarsus, " I am Jesus, whom you are persecuting " (Acts 9:5).

Notice that in each case the Lord's identity is revealed not in general terms, which are equally available to everyone, but by some intimate and special trait that each time is related to the memory of an earlier encounter. The manner in which these men and women are borne into faith remains God's secret, as befits all new birth. Their companion of former times, whom they had loved and respected, but who was one of them, whom they had even rebuked on occasion (Mark 8:32), has become the LORD, he before whom men bow down and adore (John 20:28; cf. Matt. 28:17; Luke 24:52). From now on, the difference between Jesus and his disciples is the difference that separates man from God.

The resurrection is the *disclosure* of the victory that Christ won on the cross: by his resurrection, it is clear that sin and death have been conquered. This is the meaning of the amazing victory of Easter. Not only does God roll

away the stone from the tomb of Jesus, he also rolls away
the stone from the tomb of mankind. For the earth on
which we live is nothing more than a huge sepulcher in
which generation after generation returns to the dust
from which it came (Gen. 3:19). We must accept in its
rugged realism the Biblical affirmation that reminds us
that the fruit of sin is *death* (Rom. 5:12). For it is only if
we understand the universality of death's reign that we can
understand the extraordinary quality of the divine act in
which Jesus descends into the abode of the dead, so that
afterward he may be raised up from it, and raise us up with
him (cf. Eph. 4:8-10). Jesus, " the Prince of Life," broke
the bonds of death, for he could not possibly be held in
death's power (Acts 2:24; 3:15). Henceforth he bequeaths
life eternal to all those who belong to him: " Death is
swallowed up in victory. O death, where is thy victory? O
death, where is thy sting? " (I Cor. 15:54-55). This is a
rescued humanity's cry of thanksgiving.

In Jesus Christ we are *dead persons who have been raised
to life*. He has vanquished the powers that held us in bondage. He has removed the condemnation that weighed on
mankind. The peace that the risen Lord gives to his disciples is a peace that the world cannot give (Luke 24:36;
John 20:19; cf. ch. 14:27). It is the peace that comes from
the cross, the peace of the remission of sins, and the peace
of pardon. It is that peace for which the believers in Israel
yearned down through the centuries, the peace of reconciliation with God (Isa. 1:18; Jer. 31:34; Ps. 51:9-14;
Rom. 5:8-10). " He is our peace," Paul writes (Eph. 2:14).
The greeting of peace becomes the apostolic greeting par
excellence: " Grace to you and peace from God our Father
and the Lord Jesus Christ " (Eph. 1:2).

The resurrection of Jesus Christ is the blessed sign of
our own resurrection and of the resurrection of the world.
He " is the first fruits of those who have fallen asleep."
(I Cor. 15:20.) Through him this dead world is promised

a new life that will be life with God.

We shall deal later with the cosmic import of this victory. For the moment we must emphasize that ever since the first Easter Sunday morning, the defeat of the " Prince of this world " has been an accomplished fact: " It is finished." To be sure, the struggle continues to be waged, but the decisive battle has already taken place. The resurrection is God's seal upon the redemptive work of his Son.

The apostles' task, henceforth, will be to be *the witnesses of the resurrection*. Their task will be to proclaim, in the name of the risen Lord, the forgiveness of sins (John 20:21-23; cf. Luke 24:44-49; Matt. 28:18-20; Acts 2:32, 37-38; I Cor. 15:1-11) .

The cross, the rock of offense, has become the power of salvation.

The Forty Days

Jesus promised his disciples that the Spirit of truth would guide them into all truth. (John 16:12-15; 20:22-23.) During the mysterious period of the forty days, during which Jesus has not yet gone up to heaven and yet during which he is no longer an earthly creature, he opens the minds of his disciples so that they can understand the meaning of his coming. For this he refers them to *Scripture*. Henceforth, it is Scripture that will teach them about him as they read it illumined by the Holy Spirit.

The instruction begins on the road to Emmaus as Jesus walks at the side of the disciples without their having recognized him as yet:

> And he said to them, " O foolish men, and slow of heart to believe that all the prophets have spoken! Was it not necessary that the Christ should suffer these things and enter into his glory? " And beginning with Moses and all the prophets, he interpreted to them in all the scriptures the things concerning himself. (Luke 24:25-27.)

Jesus pursues the same subject in his conversations with the Eleven:

> Then he said to them, " These are my words which I spoke to you, while I was still with you, that everything written about me in the law of Moses and the prophets and psalms must be fulfilled." Then he opened their minds to understand the scriptures, and said to them, " Thus it is written, that the Christ should suffer and on the third day rise from the dead, and that repentance and forgiveness of sins should be preached in his name to all nations, beginning from Jerusalem. You are witnesses of these things. And behold, I send the promise of my Father upon you; but stay in the city, until you are clothed with power from on high." (Luke 24:44-49.)

These two passages are tremendously important. They emphasize the indissoluble unity of the Biblical revelation, for the witness of the church will depend upon the double foundation of the apostles and the prophets (Eph. 2:20). These passages lay the foundation for a Christological interpretation of the Old Testament. They enable us to assert that Moses and the prophets and the psalms, and indeed all the Scriptures, *speak of Jesus* and proclaim his coming. Scripture has a hidden meaning that is accessible only to faith, which can only be revealed by the Holy Spirit. Indeed, apart from this revelation, the Old Testament remains a closed book (cf. also John 5:45-47; 8:56-58; II Cor. 3:12-16).

From this time on, the apostles' commission is clearly defined; it will be to proclaim that Jesus of Nazareth, crucified under Pontius Pilate, raised on the third day, is indeed the Christ proclaimed throughout Scripture, the King of Israel. But this commission already goes beyond Israel; it reaches out to " the nations " (Matt. 24:14; 28:19; cf. Acts 1:8). Jesus' Lordship is universal.

Lastly, the apostles realize that they cannot fulfill this commission simply by their own human resources. There

must be the outpouring of the Holy Spirit, the baptism of
fire at Pentecost. And so they wait for this in the peaceful
contemplation and silence of the upper room. (Acts 1:12-
14.)

The event of the ascension occupies only a few lines at
the end of the Gospel of Luke and in the first chapter of
The Acts. But this double mention is significant. For this
is the final act in the earthly life of Jesus of Nazareth, and
it is also the act that inaugurates his reign. With the Lord's
exaltation, *the time of the church* begins.

Jesus blesses his followers, and, in so doing, blesses the
whole church that will be born. Then he leaves them. He
is " lifted up into heaven." It would seem as though the
separation ought to fill the disciples with sorrow (John 16:
5-6), but it is said on the contrary that they return to Jerusalem " with great joy," and that they remain in the
Temple praying and blessing God (Luke 24:52-53). What
has happened is that their eyes have been opened. They
know that their Lord lives, that he reigns, and that he is
" at the right hand of God." And this joyful certainty is
stronger than separation and waiting.

The apostles have learned to look at Christ rather than
at themselves.

The book of The Acts gives us a picture of the disciples
looking into heaven just after the ascension. But " two men
in white robes " send them back to their work in the world
of men, for earth rather than heaven is the place where
they are to witness and live in obedience. The Lord himself
will come to them and will be with them through his Holy
Spirit. He will be with them invisibly but truly, all the
days of their life. (Matt. 28:20.) And he will come again
in power and glory, at the end of time. (Acts 1:11.)

PART
THREE

THE LAST TIMES
OR
THE TIME OF THE CHURCH

Just as Jesus Christ dwelt unknown in the midst of men, so his truth dwells in the midst of ordinary points of view, without seeming the least bit different. So also the body of Christ dwells in the midst of ordinary bread. — Pascal, Pensées, No. 788.

Introduction

The Reign of Christ and the
Time of the Church

(Acts, the Letters, Revelation)

The Reign of Christ

We have just seen that the ascension marks the entrance of Christ into his reign. His exaltation opens up a new and *final* period in the history of the world. The apostle Paul puts a definite limit on the duration of this reign when he declares that Christ will rule " until he has put all his enemies under his feet. . . . Then comes the end, when he delivers the kingdom to God the Father after destroying every rule and every authority and power " (I Cor. 15:25, 24) . In reality, Christ performs the function of a mediator. When the work of reconciliation has been completed, his role of mediator will be finished and " God will be all in all."

This mediatorial work of Christ can be described in terms of two essential moments — the incarnation and the return of Christ.

1. By his *incarnation* and his sacrifice on the cross, Jesus took upon himself the condemnation of the world. He vanquished " the principalities and powers," all the hostile forces that are in revolt against God's sovereignty. In Paul's

201

vigorous language, "he disarmed the principalities and powers and made a public example of them, triumphing over them in it" (i.e., the cross, Col. 2:15, margin).

This victory is decisive in the sense that the condemnation passed upon Satan and his satellites is definitive. It is also decisive in the sense that by his resurrection from the dead, Jesus has already conquered death in his own person; he is "the first fruits of those who have fallen asleep" (cf. I Cor. 15:20-21), the assurance of the resurrection at the last day of those who belong to him (v. 23). In exalting him to his right hand, God is already restoring to him *at the present time* all authority in heaven and on earth (Matt. 28:18). This restoration of authority is the specific meaning of the expression "exalted at the right hand of God," which occurs so frequently in the apostolic writings.

Jesus is the true king of heaven and earth, although, in fact, a certain latitude is still left to the hostile powers. His reign is a period of transition, between the old world as it was before his coming and the final establishment of the Kingdom of God. This is why it belongs to "the last times."

2. The ultimate establishment of the reign of God will be preceded by *a second direct intervention of Christ* in the struggles of earth. This second moment is that of his coming again. Christ will return to judge the world. There will be a great final battle. The book of Revelation describes a reign of a thousand years, after which Satan is given one last chance to deceive the nations (Rev., ch. 20). After that comes his final destruction, followed by the establishment of the new heaven and the new earth (Rev., ch. 21).

From that time on, Christ's mediatorial work is completed. The authority that God had conferred on him so that he might lead the world to obedience is no longer necessary. This does not mean that the person of the mediator disappears. Rather, the glory of God illumines the

New Jerusalem, and *its lamp is the Lamb* (Rev. 21:23; cf. ch. 11:15).

We must notice again that in the thought of the apostles, the Son's mediatorial action is not limited to the redemptive action that he exercises upon the fallen world. It is also " in him " and " by him " that the world was created (Col. 1:12-16; Heb. 1:2-4; John 1:1-3). And he performs the same role as the agent of the second creation. (Rev. 1: 12-18; ch. 5; 19:6-16; 21:22; 22:17.)

This role of Christ in relation to his Father has been defined with admirable clarity by Paul:

> For us there is one God, the Father, *from* whom are all things and *for* whom we exist, and one Lord, Jesus Christ, *through* whom are all things and *through* whom we exist. (I Cor. 8:6, italics added.)

And again:

> [God] chose us in him before the foundation of the world, that we should be holy and blameless before him. He destined us in love to be his sons through Jesus Christ, according to the purpose of his will, to the praise of his glorious grace which he freely bestowed on us in the Beloved. (Eph. 1:4-6.)

Jesus Christ is the predestined Son of God, the one in whom we see our own true destiny as sons created in God's image. It is because God sees us *in him,* not as we are but as he will fashion us, that God has created us, sustained us, and pardons us. Through him we shall finally be included " in the kingdom of his love." It is in him that we are able to say to God, " Abba, Father! " (Gal. 4:4-6; cf. Rom. 8: 11-17).

The Time of the Church

We have said that from the time of his ascension Jesus Christ is the Sovereign Ruler of the world. But this sovereignty remains hidden from the eyes of the world. It re-

mains *an object of faith,* as it did during his earthly ministry. The church is the place where this sovereignty is
recognized and confessed. The specific task of the church is
to proclaim the Lord until he comes (I Cor. 11:26). The
aim of the church's preaching is to prepare men for this
coming (II Peter 3:8-12). For the Lordship of Jesus Christ
and the redemptive power of his cross must be proclaimed
to the farthest reaches of the whole earth. Only then will
the end come. (Matt. 24:14; Acts 1:4-8.)

The church lives under the sign of the reign that is
coming. It exists by faith in the risen Lord and by the hope
of his coming. It is already participating in the new creation, through the baptism of the Holy Spirit. It is the
body of Christ, whose head is in heaven, the living organ-
ism that guides and gives life through his Spirit. The
church has a twofold nature: through the Spirit it shares
in God's life; but since it is also made up of the stuff of
human existence, it remains a gathering of sinful men and
it shares fully in the present world.

We can therefore say that in a certain sense the mystery
of the incarnation continues in the church, for it is the
visible body, on earth, of the invisible Lord who reigns in
the heavens.

We have seen God humble himself by making his divine
Word ring out even through the weakness of human words.
We have also seen God humble himself by taking the form
of a human being and concealing his divinity under the
figure of the suffering and crucified Servant. And now we
see him humbling himself for a third time, in allowing this
body of believers, this weak and sinful body which is the
church, to represent him on earth, to speak, to judge, and
to prophesy in his name. And of these three kinds of humiliation to which God submits, the last is perhaps the
most difficult to understand from our point of view. Didn't
the group of the twelve apostles include a traitor and a
renegade? It is Peter's confession and his denial that give

the clearest example of both the grandeur and misery of the church. The church is a body composed of sinners, but even so it is empowered by the Holy Spirit. It is a body that, because it is of the earth, is involved in condemnation, and yet because it is the body of the glorified Lord, it has within it the promise of eternal life.

Thus Jesus will continue to be crucified in the life of the church. This will happen not only or even especially because Christians will be involved in his shame and will suffer at the hands of the world. It will happen even more because, since they are still sinners, they will continually drive new nails into his flesh by their denials and their indifference.

The Lord of glory chose once again to make his glory known through the weakness of human flesh. Why did he do it? Why has he made faith so difficult to a world that looks to us, the believers, for life? He has his own reasons, which we do not know. It is enough for us to know that he consented to this last and ultimate humiliation, and as a result we feel ourselves bound to this church of his, no matter how wretched or disappointing it may be. (And who of us has not been disappointed or led astray by the deficiencies, the narrowness, and the divisions of the visible church?) But how dare we disavow that which Jesus chose and loved? (Eph. 5:25.) He made its distress his own, and in its turn it makes our personal distress its own. With it and in it we are under both the judgment and the grace of God. In it and by it our sins will be forgiven. (Acts 2:38; cf. Matt. 16:19; 18:18-20; John 20:23.) It has been granted, incomprehensibly, mysteriously, and in spite of its unworthiness, the full authority of God. (Luke 10:16.) He has given it the keys of the Kingdom, and the glorious ministry of reconciliation (II Cor. 5:11-21). It is his ambassador in the world of men. But the greatness of its message is communicated through the weakness of the messenger, in order that no one " might boast in the presence of God "

(I Cor. 1:26-31; II Cor. 4:7-18; 6:4-10; 12:1-10).

Since it is the visible body of the Lord, the church will necessarily be the object of the attacks of the world just as Jesus Christ himself was (John 15:18-20). Satan has claimed the right to sift it like wheat. (Luke 22:31.) The church in its turn must resist to the point of shedding its blood. (Cf. Heb. 12:4.) But it will enter this battle in the strength of the risen Lord, in the assurance that the victory is already won (Rom. 8:31-39; Phil. 3:7-11), and in the assurance of the final victory which is the object of its waiting and of its hope (II Tim. 2:11-12).

Faith looks upon disgrace that is suffered for Jesus' sake as a sign and condition of close union with him. The body must continue to engage in battle against the powerful enemies of God just as the head of the body has done (Col. 1:24). Neither Jesus nor his apostles make any attempt to conceal the fact that the battles will become more and more intense until the final battle itself. It is enough for them to be sure that God will have the last word. This is the real meaning of the majestic visions of the book of Revelation.

The first and last books of the New Testament are particularly dedicated to Christ the King, with this difference, that the first bears witness to his *hidden* glory, while the second bears witness to his *self-evident* glory.

The time that separates these two comings is the time of the church, the time of its mission, the time of God's patience (II Peter 3:8-9), a final reprieve offered to a condemned world, so that it may accept the message of the resurrection.

CHAPTER VIII

THE BEGINNING OF THE REIGN OF CHRIST AND THE BIRTH OF THE CHURCH

(The Acts of the Apostles)

SUMMARY

1. THE ASCENSION: JESUS "EXALTED AT THE RIGHT HAND OF GOD"

The meaning of the ascension: Jesus Christ begins his reign (Luke 24:50-53; Acts 1:9-11). The promise that his exaltation includes the church (I Cor. 15:20; Eph. 4:8-10).

a. The change that occurs in the relationship of Jesus with his disciples: they adore him as their Lord and God (Luke 24:52; cf. John 20:28).

b. The meaning of the phrase " exalted at the right hand of God " (Ps. 110; Acts 2:22-36; cf. Mark 14:62; Rom. 8:34; Eph. 1:20; Heb. 1:3; Matt. 28:18).

c. The cosmic meaning of the victory of Jesus Christ: he has conquered "the principalities and powers" (Col. 2:15; I Peter 3:22; Eph. 1:20-23; I Cor. 15:20-28). His glory is in direct relation to his humiliation and his sacrifice (Phil. 2:5-11; John 3:13-16; 12:27-33; 17:1-5).

d. Jesus is exalted above the angels as Priest and King of the New Covenant (Heb., chs. 1; 2); Jesus as intercessor is the one who stands for us before God (Heb. 4:14-16; cf. Rom. 8:33-34).

e. The promise of the ascension: the church is a partner in the glory, the judgment, and the reign of Christ (Luke

22:28-30; I Cor. 6:2; I Thess. 2:11-12; II Tim. 2:11-12;
Rev. 1:6).

2. PENTECOST: THE CHURCH AS THE CREATION OF THE HOLY
SPIRIT
   a. The community of the disciples on the day after the
   ascension waits for the baptism of the Spirit (Acts 1:4-8,
   12-14).
   b. The Holy Spirit confers on the church a foretaste of
   Christ's reign: the church belongs to "the last times"
   (Acts, ch. 2; Joel 2:28-32; cf. II Peter 3:8-13; Matt. 24:14).
   Pentecost marks the beginning of the great gathering together of God's children (John 11:49-52; cf. Isa. 2:2-3;
   11:10-12; etc.). The church is built on the double witness of the Word and the Spirit.
   c. The apostolic church receives the "signs" of the reign,
   and sees instances of the power of Jesus' name (Acts,
   chs. 3 to 5).

3. THE FIRST STRUGGLES
   a. Whenever God "attacks," there is a counterattack by the
   adversary. The struggles of the church begin from the
   Day of Pentecost (Acts 2:13). Israel's guilt is denounced
   in Peter's sermons. (Acts 2:36; 3:13-14; 4:10). An account
   of the first conflicts (Acts, chs. 4; 5).
   b. Stephen, the first martyr of the church (Acts, ch. 7).

4. THE MISSION TO THE PAGAN WORLD
   The persecution and the scattering of the church becomes
   the beginning of the mission to the pagan world (Acts, ch.
   8). This raises the problem of the relationship between the
   two covenants, and the problem of fidelity to the law (Acts,
   chs. 10; 11). The story of Paul, the apostle to the Gentiles
   (Acts, 9:13 to 28:31; cf. Gal., chs. 1; 2; I Cor. 15:8-11; Rom.
   1:3-6, 14; 15:17-29).

1. THE ASCENSION: JESUS "EXALTED
AT THE RIGHT HAND OF GOD"

Ascension Day ought to be the greatest day of the whole
Christian year, and yet few people are aware of what it

means. We must therefore make a special effort to understand the real meaning of the ascension in the unfolding of
God's purpose. To do this we not only must refer to the
two brief accounts of the ascension (Luke 24:50-53 and
Acts 1:9-11) but also must try to understand the implications of this belief which can be discovered in the entire
apostolic witness.

When Christendom commemorates the ascension, it
celebrates the beginning of the reign of Christ — his coro-
nation as King. The exaltation of Jesus in glory is, so to
speak, God's seal of approval upon all of Christ's redemptive work. It is the Father's response to the voluntary humiliation of his only Son, the proclamation of his victory
over all the enemy powers, the enthronement of Christ as
Victor and Ruler.

But it means even more than this. For the Son who returns to " the bosom of the Father," as the Johannine expression has it (cf. John 1:18; 17:1-5), does not return by
himself. He returns as God made man. All men redeemed
by Jesus of Nazareth are promised the divine glory, are
brought in by him to the very heart of the Trinity, are reconstituted in their original calling (Gen. 1:27) as children of God (Eph. 4:8-10; Rom. 8:15-17; Gal. 4:6-7;
Heb. 2:10-13; John 17:22-23). This means that the ascension includes the most glorious of promises, that the exaltation of Jesus is the first fruits (I Cor. 15:20) of the exaltation to glory and dominion of the church of Jesus Christ
itself. The church is already aware that it shares in this
reign by faith, even though it must still keep on fighting
the battles of this world. (Rev. 1:6.)

The Change in the Disciples' Relationship to Jesus

The account of the ascension (Luke 24:50-53) clearly
shows the change in the relationship between the Master
and his disciples that takes place after the resurrection.
After Jesus leaves his disciples and is exalted in the heav-

ens, it is said that they *adore* him. After this he is no longer simply a beloved Master, whom on occasion they were even permitted to rebuke (Mark 8:32). Now he is the LORD, the One to whom they must give obedience and faith as to God himself. After the resurrection, Thomas makes a profession of faith, " My Lord and my God! " (John 20:28), which becomes the profession of faith of the whole church.

We must be very clear about this: the foundation of the church is faith in the divinity of Jesus Christ. Without this faith, the Christian church simply does not exist. The decisive moment for our faith is the moment when we recognize that the sovereign authority of Jesus Christ over our lives is identical with the sovereign authority of God himself, when we know that our salvation is in him and that the source of our life is in him.

" Exalted at the Right Hand of God "

The exaltation of Jesus Christ " at the right hand of God " is the concrete expression of this sovereignty. The basic importance of this term is pointed up by the fact that it occurs seventeen times in the New Testament (Ps. 110:1; Matt. 22:44; 26:64; Mark 12:36; 14:62; 16:19; Luke 20:42; 22:69; Acts 2:34; Rom. 8:34; Eph. 1:20; Col. 3:1; Heb. 1:3; 8:1; 10:12; 12:2; I Peter 3:22). We must therefore take time to understand its meaning as clearly as possible.

To say that God " acts by his right hand " is to say that he acts by his power, by the strength of his arm. To be exalted " at his right hand " is thus to be invested with his power, to receive authority like his, to share the throne with him. This is certainly the meaning that the New Testament puts on the exaltation of Christ, and the spatial imagery is only a way of expressing the fact that Jesus is invested with a royal function, endowed with all the prerogatives of God.

The expression itself comes from Ps. 110:

> The Lord says to my lord:
> "Sit at my right hand,
> till I make your enemies
> your footstool."
>   (Ps. 110:1.)

Jesus quotes this psalm and puts a Messianic meaning upon it. (Mark 12:35-36 and parallels.) On the Day of Pentecost, Peter likewise quotes it and applies it to Jesus, along with Ps. 16. David, he says, knew that God had promised to seat one of his descendants upon his throne, and in these psalms he is really predicting and proclaiming the resurrection of Christ. The apostle adds that Jesus, exalted at the right hand of God, has received the Holy Spirit from the Father and has shed it abroad. Thus there is the double witness of *Scripture* and the *Spirit*. And so Peter concludes, "Let all the house of Israel therefore know assuredly that God has made him both Lord and Christ, this Jesus whom you crucified." (Acts 2:22-36.)

The title of "Lord" (*Kurios*) was reserved for divine beings. In ancient times it was used to flatter political leaders. But Israel could not use the term in this way. To confess that "Jesus is Lord," *Christos Kurios*, is to confess his divinity, to declare that he exercises the same authority as God himself.

Just how far does this jurisdiction of Christ extend? First of all, to the church of which he is the Savior. The church is the New Israel of which Jesus is the King. In him all the Messianic promises are fulfilled, and the church is the place where his Lordship is recognized and confessed. But from the very earliest prophecies, this Lordship of God's Anointed One included the entire world (Isa. 49:5-6). His attributes are the very attributes of God:

> and his name will be called
> Wonderful Counselor, Mighty God,
> Everlasting Father, Prince of Peace.
>   (Isa. 9:6.)

The New Testament likewise proclaims that Jesus' sovereignty includes the whole universe: all authority has been given to him " *in heaven and on earth* " (Matt. 28:18; cf. Phil. 2:9-11) .

The Defeat of the " Principalities and Powers "

At this point we have reached to one of the deepest mysteries of faith: the salvation procured by Jesus Christ on the cross does not simply affect humanity. It has a *cosmic* meaning. In him, the whole of creation was condemned and redeemed. His resurrection is the first fruits of God's *new creation,* which will be revealed at the end of time.

Over and over again the New Testament tells us that God has conquered the " principalities and powers." It is hard to be sure of the exact meaning of terms like " authorities," " principalities," " powers." It is clear that they refer to angelic powers (who can be either good or demonic) , and to intermediary powers who inhabit the universe and intervene in the affairs of men. Hidden behind the human forces that are at work in Jesus' condemnation and death are all the enemy powers that are engaged in mortal combat with God. These powers succeeded in getting Jesus nailed to the cross, but he confounded them and triumphed over them so that they were brought into subjection. " He disarmed the principalities and powers and made a public example of them, triumphing over them in him," i.e., by the death of Christ upon the cross (Col. 2:15).

It is possible that the apostle Paul had looked upon the earthly authorities as instruments of these angelic powers, and that as a result the human authorities who condemned Jesus were themselves implicitly included in this passage from Colossians. At all events, the apostolic church believed that all authority derives from God, whether it is the authority of men or of angels. And *all these authorities* from now on are, by the will of the Father, placed under the Son who has conquered them: " Jesus Christ, who has gone into heaven, . . . is at the right hand of God, with angels, authorities, and powers subject to him " (I Peter 3:21-22). According to the letter to the Ephesians, God displayed his power in Christ,

> when he raised him from the dead and made him sit at his right hand in the heavenly places, far above all rule and authority and power and dominion, and above every name that is named, not only in this age but also in that which is to come; and he has put all things under his feet, and has made him the head over all things for the church, which is his body, the fullness of him who fills all in all. (Eph. 1:20-23.)

We must be very clear about the *inclusive* character of Christ's redemptive work, for we often find the gospel being reduced to a message of individual salvation and individual resurrection. But God's unfolding purpose of salvation, as we find it revealed to us in the Bible, has a much wider scope. The ultimate goal of history is the *new creation,* a creation filled with all the fullness of God. And the agent of this new creation, He in whom and by whom it comes into being, is the well-beloved Son, " the image of the invisible God " (Col. 1:15), in whom the love of God becomes incarnate so that he may come to redeem and free a lost world. The first man mysteriously involves the whole of creation in his fall. This means that not only humanity but the whole created world is under the sign of death. Jesus Christ lives a life of perfect obedience in this world of death. He himself voluntarily submits to this death to which the world is subject, and thus destroys its power. For God, by raising him from the dead, makes him the first fruits of the new creation (Col. 1:18; cf. I Cor. 15:20-23, 35-49; Rom. 5:12-17).

What are these first fruits? The Jews always dedicated the first sheaves of the harvest to the Lord; they represented the entire harvest. Now in Jesus Christ the harvest of the whole world is being offered and consecrated to the

Living God. He is its "first fruits." The world itself was made so that there could be this final reconciliation, this new creation in Christ. Jesus is the predestined Son from before the foundation of the world, in order that he may take upon himself the world's condemnation and call into being the new creation (I Cor. 15:45; Eph. 1:4-10). God allowed humanity to run this terrible and mortal risk of freedom only because one day his well-beloved Son would give himself freely, snatch mankind from bondage to death, and lead it to true liberty: "He has delivered us from the dominion of darkness and transferred us to the kingdom of his beloved Son" (Col. 1:13). Thus, from the very beginning, God is with us in his Son, working out our redemption, reconciling the world to himself (II Cor. 5: 8-19; cf. Rom. 5:8-11; Col. 1:15-20).

The supreme glory of the Son in his exaltation to the throne of God on Ascension Day is in direct relation to his sacrifice:

> He humbled himself and became obedient unto death, even death on a cross. Therefore God has highly exalted him and bestowed on him the name which is above every name, that at the name of Jesus every knee should bow, in heaven and on earth and under the earth, and every tongue confess that Jesus Christ is Lord, to the glory of God the Father. (Phil. 2:8-11.)

The exaltation of the Son is not so much a "reward" for his voluntary humiliation as it is the *manifestation* of his true Sonship, which he revealed *in and by his humiliation*. For it is in and by this humiliation that Jesus "glorifies" God, namely, shows us what God is really like, and also shows us the true nature of the Kingdom that he came to establish. God is love. The incarnation is the amazing mystery of love. This is why being "lifted up" on the cross and being "lifted up" in glory both describe one and the same reality, and are simply two aspects of a single deed:

THE BIRTH OF THE CHURCH

" And I, when I am lifted up from the earth, will draw all men to myself " (John 12:32; cf. 3:13-15). Jesus glorifies his Father by his death, and the Father in turn glorifies Jesus by raising him from the dead and lifting him up to his right hand (John 12:27-28; 17:1-5).

Jesus as Priest and King

The letter to the Hebrews is saying much the same thing in other words, when it shows us how the honor of the Son surpasses that of the angels. The angels are no more than servants and they worship before the only Son. (Heb., chs. 1; 2.) In him the Messianic promises of the psalms are fulfilled:

> Thy throne, O God, is for ever and ever,
> the righteous scepter is the scepter of thy kingdom.
> Thou hast loved righteousness and hated lawlessness;
> therefore God, thy God, has anointed thee
> with the oil of gladness beyond thy comrades.
> (Heb. 1:8-9; cf. Ps. 45:6-7; Ps. 110:1.)

Here again the Kingship of the Son is placed in direct relationship to his obedience. (Heb. 2:5-18.) The offering that he made to his Father is the offering of his very life:

Sacrifices and offerings thou hast not desired,
but a body hast thou prepared for me;
in burnt offerings and sin offerings thou hast taken no pleasure.
Then I said, " Lo, I have come to do thy will, O God."
(Heb. 10:5-7; cf. Ps. 40:6-8.)

By taking a body, by learning " obedience through what he suffered," the Son glorified the Father and was " made perfect." Ever since then faith has acknowledged him as King and Priest of the New Covenant, which he sealed with his blood (Heb. 1:1-4; 5:7-10; 8:1-12; 10:12-13).

Under the Old Covenant, the entrance to the Holy of Holies was closed even to the faithful. A veil separated it from the Holy Place, and only the high priest went in

once a year to offer the sacrifice of expiation. (Lev., ch. 16.)
The Gospel tells us that the veil of the Temple was torn at
the moment when Jesus died. (Mark 15:38.) On the day
of the ascension, Jesus goes into the heavenly sanctuary, of
which the Temple was only an earthly and transitory image. And not only does *he* go in, but he opens it up to us
as well. By his voluntary expiation he becomes our almighty intercessor before the throne of God. (Heb., chs. 8
to 10.)

Christ's role as intercessor is an essential part of his function as Priestly-King. For by his incarnation he became a
brother to those for whom he intercedes:

> For we have not a high priest who is unable to sympa-
> thize with our weaknesses, but one who in every respect
> has been tempted as we are, yet without sinning. Let us
> then with confidence draw near to the throne of grace.
> (Heb. 4:15-16.)

Jesus alone has power to understand all things, for he has
experienced all things. He alone has power to remove all
condemnation, for he has atoned for all condemnation.
The Christian lives in the light of the victorious assurance
of Paul:

> Who shall lay anything to the charge of God's elect? It
> is God that justifieth. Who is he that condemneth? It is
> Christ that died, yea rather, that is risen again, who is
> even at the right hand of God, who also maketh interces-
> sion for us. (Rom. 8:33-34.)

Thus the assurance of the believer rests totally on the
fact that he has a Lord and Savior who stands in his name
before God.

Jesus as Judge of Mankind

The One who has taken our place before God will also
be our Judge on the Last Day. The message of the ascension concludes with the announcement of the *return* of

Jesus Christ (Acts 1:11). At present his sovereignty is hidden from the eyes of the world and is known only within the church. But before long it will be revealed so that all can see it, and this will be the hour of the Last Judgment (Rev. 1:4-7). How should we understand this judgment?

The Fourth Gospel, indeed, stresses the fact that Jesus has not come to " judge " the world but to save it. He is the light from above who reveals things as they are. To turn to this light means to see God as he is and ourselves as we are; it means faith in God's grace and mercy; it means salvation. But to turn away from this light means deliberately to choose darkness; by this choice we judge ourselves. (John 3:16-21; 12:44-48.)

To turn to God means to be born to the life of love. Therefore The First Letter of John insists relentlessly on the fact that he whose heart is closed to love both is and walks " in darkness " (I John 2:9-11; 3:14-18; 4:7-12).

Jesus illustrates this in the parable of the Last Judgment. (Matt. 25:31-45.) The Son of Man appears in his might and glory to judge the world. The nations (i.e., the whole pagan world) stand before him. He pronounces " blessed " those who have fed the hungry, welcomed the stranger, visited the prisoner. . . . He declares that everything done to them has been done *to him.*

In becoming man, Jesus has taken upon himself the plight of every man. Therefore he can say in all truth, and not just as a figure of speech, " What you have done or not done to your brother you have done or not done to *me.*" Some will have served him without knowing it. Others who have paid lip service to him will find that they have rejected him as an unwelcome visitor, perhaps in the person of a refugee, a man out of work, someone with a different colored skin.

The New Testament is full of stern reminders that God will be merciful to those who have shown mercy (Matt. 5:7), and that by the way we judge others we shall ourselves be judged (Matt. 7:1-5). No Christian, on these terms, can contemplate lightly his ultimate encounter with God — when all his thoughts, words, and deeds will be laid bare. The more we know ourselves, in fact, the more we shall adore the mystery of divine grace by which the Judge of the world is the same One who gave his life to save the world and took responsibility for it before his Father.

Our hope and faith rest on this certainty alone.

2. PENTECOST: THE CHURCH AS THE CREATION OF THE HOLY SPIRIT

Waiting for the Holy Spirit

The disciples who are assembled in the upper room on the day after the ascension are not yet the church in the full meaning of the word. Truly to become the church they must receive the outpouring of the Holy Spirit. The church is created from on high. The Spirit is the seal placed upon its existence and on its witness by the Lord himself. The baptism of the Spirit is a baptism of power, which alone is able to make the church on earth an effectual witness to the invisible Lord who reigns in the heavens.

Ten days elapse between the ascension and Pentecost. During that time the disciples wait in prayer for the baptism of the Spirit. This is a unique moment in the life of the church, but a moment that, like all the other important moments in the history of salvation, tells us something we must always remember. The church will never " possess " the Spirit. It can only keep praying that God will give it the gift of the Spirit; it can only wait for the Spirit in faith, knowing that without the Spirit its preaching and its works are in vain; it can receive the Spirit only as it relies upon the explicit promise of the Lord himself (Luke 11:13; John 14:16-20, 25-26; 16:12-15).

The Creation of the Church by the Holy Spirit

The church is created by the descent of the Holy Spirit on the Day of Pentecost. The Holy Spirit belongs to God's world; he is the one who breathes life into the new creation. Through him the church has a foretaste of the reign to come. (II Cor. 1:22; 5:1-5.) Its specific task is to proclaim the Kingship of its Lord and to " hasten " the day of his coming by its missionary activity. For before he comes, his salvation must be proclaimed to all the nations (Matt. 24:14; Acts 1:8; II Peter 3:8-13). The church is already, by its very existence, *a manifestation of " the last times."* Peter recognized this very clearly: " This is what was spoken by the prophet Joel: ' And in the last days it shall be, God declares, that I will pour out my Spirit upon all flesh ' " (Acts 2:16-17; cf. Joel 2:28-32). The ability to speak in many languages, by means of which men of all races can hear the gospel, is a kind of description of what the reign of God will be like on that wonderful day when all the barriers that separate men are broken down and mankind again finds its lost unity in God. Pentecost marks the beginning of the vast reassembling of the scattered children of God, which the prophets had hoped for and foretold (Isa. 2:2-3; 11:10-12; 43:5-7; Jer. 31:10; Ezek. 34:11-13, 23; cf. John 11:49-52). Pentecost is God's answer to the Tower of Babel. The Tower of Babel symbolizes unity created from below, on the basis of human pride that tries to lift itself up to heaven, and leads only to chaos. (Gen., ch. 11.) The church's unity, by contrast, is a gift from on high; it is the work of the Holy Spirit. Men do not create this unity; all they can do is receive it, manifest it clearly, and rely upon it.

Peter's sermon on the Day of Pentecost is the first Christian sermon. It is based on the joint witness of Scripture and the Holy Spirit. Peter reasons on the basis of the psalms: David is dead, therefore, when he speaks of Him who conquered death (Ps. 16:10), of him who was exalted into heaven and is seated at the right hand of God (Ps. 110), he is certainly not speaking about himself. Rather, he is speaking figuratively, and is proclaiming the victory of the true successor to his throne, the Messiah. And this victorious Messiah is none other than Jesus of Nazareth.

Who is this Jesus of Nazareth? He is a man who was put to death on the outskirts of Jerusalem fifty-three days before, and whose execution everyone still remembers. Let us not forget that in the eyes of a strict monotheistic Jew it was a frightful piece of blasphemy to proclaim that the one who was crucified on Golgotha was the *Messiah*. However, Peter's sermon is a " demonstration of the Spirit and power " (cf. I Cor. 2:4). Those in the crowd are " cut to the heart " by his testimony, and they say to Peter and the apostles, " Brethren, what shall we do? " And Peter proclaims what is henceforth the wonderful message of salvation:

Repent, and be baptized every one of you in the name of Jesus Christ for the forgiveness of your sins; and you shall receive the gift of the Holy Spirit. For the promise is to you and to your children and to all that are far off, every one whom the Lord our God calls to him. (Acts 2:38-39.)

The church is no longer a future hope, it is a present reality.

The Church and " the Signs of the Kingdom "

The baptism of the Spirit gives the church a foretaste of Christ's reign, and we presently see " the signs of the Kingdom " that had marked Jesus' ministry being reproduced in the apostolic ministry: the authority to preach (Acts 2:37-41; 4:33), the forgiveness of sins (Acts 2:38), the healing of the sick (Acts 3:1-11), and a sovereign freedom from the powers of this world (Acts, chs. 4; 5). The name of Jesus has power to liberate bodies and souls from those things which hold them in bondage. (Acts 3:6, 16; 4:7, 12.) A new world has come into being, a world of men who are truly free because they are subject to God alone.

The thing that is most characteristic of this new freedom is that it involves the whole man, both as a physical and a spiritual being. Furthermore, it immediately brings him out of his isolation and creates true community (Acts 2:37-47; 4:23-37). No one looks upon his possessions, for example, as belonging solely to himself. (Acts 4:32 ff.; cf. 2:44-45.) The sharing of material goods is just as natural as the sharing of spiritual goods, for all believers are devoted to serving the same cause, and that is all that counts. Here is a fellowship, in other words, that is *different* from all other kinds of human fellowship. Its beginning and its ending receive their meaning from Jesus, and its members are no longer living to themselves but to the Lord who died and rose on their behalf.

The sign of this break with the past and entrance into the Christian life is *baptism*. In Christ, the believer knows that he is dead to his former way of life and raised up to newness of life. He knows that he is pardoned, forgiven, and endowed with the Spirit. (Acts 2:38; cf. Rom. 6:3-7; Gal. 3:26-27.) The breaking of the bread, the *Eucharist*, unites the believer both to Christ whose body was broken for him, and also to his brethren, who are recipients of the same forgiveness (cf. I Cor. 11:23-29). When everyone shares in the same benefits in this way, how can they avoid sharing everything else as well? What is often called the " communism " of the first Christians is neither the fruit of logic nor of some curious vision. Rather, it is the spontaneous fruit of the Spirit, who opens men's pockets because he opens their hearts. The one who truly gives himself to God discovers that the distinction between " mine " and " thine " is relatively unimportant. Everything is seen from the perspective of God's reign, and is measured by the standard of things eternal.

Thus the community of believers is founded and ratified by the Word which draws it together, and by the Holy Spirit who convicts it of sin and assures it of forgiveness. The book of The Acts puts it, " Now the company of these who believed were of one heart and soul." (Acts 4:32.) The church will not experience this unclouded joy for long (cf. Acts 5:1-11) , but it is permitted to enjoy it for a moment, and in this first hour of grace, the church has a foretaste of the perfect unity that will be one of the characteristics of the Kingdom. The church is called into being to realize this unity (John 17:20-26) , and sins every time that its life denies this unity.

3. THE FIRST STRUGGLES

The descent of the Holy Spirit on the Day of Pentecost creates the church militant. It transforms a little group of disciples shut up in a guestchamber into a community with a mandate to evangelize the world (cf. Acts 1:6-8) , a community that will not retreat in the face of defeats or threats. This missionary character of the church, as we have seen, belongs to its very essence, for its task here below is to proclaim God's word until he comes. But this proclamation of the reign arouses the opposition of the world in the midst of the church's life, just as was the case in the life of its Lord.

Attack and Counterattack

Every time God attacks, the adversary must counterattack. We have seen how Jesus' reign and Satan's reign were pitted against each other on every page of the Gospels. As soon as the Holy Spirit breathes life into the church, and the signs of God's reign become manifest in it, the resistance of the opposing powers begins to operate. Any church that is truly alive must expect to be *attacked* from within and from without. And any church that the world ignores must ask itself whether it is really fulfilling its divine calling or whether it has not compromised too much with a world that tolerates it so easily.

Jesus warned his disciples of what lay in store for them:

> Remember the word that I said to you, "A servant is not greater than his master." If they persecuted me, they will persecute you; if they kept my word, they will keep yours also. (John 15:20; cf. Luke 12:49-53.)

The struggles of the church date from the very Day of Pentecost. Those within it are immediately confronted by the taunt, "They are filled with new wine" (Acts 2:13).

Besides, even in his first sermon, Peter himself takes the initiative and makes some accusations of his own. He holds not only the leaders of his people, but the whole of Israel, responsible for Jesus' murder: "Let all the house of Israel therefore know assuredly that God has made him both Lord and Christ, this Jesus whom you crucified" (Acts 2:36). The accusation is even stronger in the second sermon:

> The God of Abraham and of Isaac and of Jacob, the God of our fathers, glorified his servant Jesus, whom you delivered up and denied in the presence of Pilate, when he had decided to release him. But you denied the Holy and Righteous One, and asked for a murderer to be granted to you, and killed the Author of Life. (Acts 3:13-15.)

This attack is so direct that it places the Jewish authorities in danger (Acts 5:26), and the high priest exclaims, "You have filled Jerusalem with your teaching and you intend to bring this man's blood upon us" (Acts 5:28).

In reality, Peter places the full responsibility for Jesus' crucifixion upon Israel; he exonerates the Roman authority (Acts 3:13). But this very judgment is a call to repentance and to salvation. In the name of the God of Abraham, Isaac, and Jacob, Peter confronts the people with a final decision: they acted in ignorance (Acts 3:17), and now they must repent and be converted. Only then can all the promises made to their fathers come to fulfillment in them (Acts 3:19-26).

Preaching that is not translated into action remains relatively inoffensive. In Jesus' ministry, it was the healings he effected that provoked the initial hostility of the scribes and Pharisees. The same thing happens in this case. It is the healing of the cripple that serves as the pretext for the intervention of the Jewish authorities: " By what power or by what name did you do this? " (Acts 4:7). The authorities are bitterly resentful. They thought they had gotten rid of Jesus — and now everything is starting all over again! The people are being won over! Conversions are proceeding at a great rate! The name of Jesus is enough to work miracles! At whatever cost, the authorities must make sure that his name will not be heard any more. (Acts 3:6; cf. 4:7, 17; 5:28.)

But the men who appear before the Sanhedrin are no longer the cowardly disciples they had previously been. They are now men whom the Holy Spirit leads and empowers, men whose assurance is very disconcerting to their judges. In them, Jesus' statement is fulfilled to the letter:

> For they will deliver you up to councils. . . . And when they bring you to trial and deliver you up, do not be anxious beforehand what you are to say; but say whatever is given you in that hour, for it is not you who will speak, but the Holy Spirit. (Mark 13:9, 11.)

The disciples say, quite unpretentiously, to the Sanhedrin:

> Whether it is right in the sight of God to listen to you rather than to God, you must judge; for we cannot but speak of what we have seen and heard. (Acts 4:19-20; cf. 5:29.)

It is said of the apostles, after their second imprisonment, that they left rejoicing that they had been counted worthy to suffer dishonor for the name of Jesus (Acts 5:41). To suffer for the Lord has *become a privilege.*

Stephen, the First Martyr of the Church

Stephen's sermon in Acts, ch. 7, returns even more forcefully to the theme of Israel's guilt. Retracing the history of the chosen people, Stephen shows that they have always resisted the Holy Spirit (Acts 7:51). Stephen is the first martyr of the church, i.e., he is the first " witness " who ratifies his profession of faith with his own blood. At the moment of his death, filled with the Holy Spirit, he sees " the heavens opened, and the Son of man standing at the right hand of God " (Acts 7:56). This statement is an almost exact reproduction of Jesus' statement before the Sanhedrin (Mark 14:62), and leads to the immediate stoning of Stephen. His last words likewise recall the words of Jesus, with the important difference that he commits his spirit to the Lord Jesus. (Acts 7:59; cf. Luke 23:46; Acts 7:60; cf. Luke 23:34.)

It is worth noticing that the first Christian to die for his faith is neither an apostle, nor an Israelite of Judea. He is a deacon appointed to serve tables (Acts 6:2-3), a Hellenistic Jew who was an Israelite of the Dispersion. The Jews who practiced strict observance of the law were quite prepared to regard them as second-rate believers. Stephen seems to have been the first to understand the full consequences of the new faith. He is the embodiment of the church militant, in which those who come last are sometimes first in their faithfulness to the gospel (Matt. 20:16).

4. THE MISSION TO THE PAGAN WORLD

a. For quite a while, the Judean Christians continued to be practicing Israelites, faithful in their attendance at the Temple (Acts 3:1), and strict in their observance of the law. They recognized that Jesus was the Messiah who had been foretold in Scripture, and they proclaimed his resurrection and his coming again. But the mission of the chosen people was limited to themselves; all their efforts were bent to the conversion of Israel.

Breaking the Bonds of Judaism

And it was just here that God himself overruled the plans of Israel according to the flesh. Persecution had the unlooked-for consequence of enlarging the church's field of activity (Acts 8:1-8). Jesus' prophecy came to pass: the heretics and the pagans surpassed the sons of the Kingdom in their faith. (Matt. 8:11-13; Luke 14:15-24; Acts, chs. 8; 10; 11.) This new situation seems to have caused more anxiety than joy in Jerusalem. The Judaeo-Christians rebuked Peter in the same terms that the Pharisees had previously rebuked Jesus: " Why did you go to uncircumcised men and eat with them? " (Acts 11:2; cf. Mark 2:15-17). On this matter, as on so many others, the disciples were slow to understand their Master's thought, and they limited him by their own narrow standards. The book of The Acts is very careful to emphasize that it is under the constraint of the Holy Spirit that Peter consented to baptize the pagan Cornelius. (Acts, chs. 10; 11.) Peter himself, so strong before the Sanhedrin, becomes timid and fearful over the matter of breaking with Jewish traditions (Gal. 2:11-14). And this is precisely the heart of the problem. The church in Jerusalem would have received converts, provided that the new converts were willing to fulfill all the demands of the law. Unconsciously, just as the Pharisees had previously done, it was repudiating the *undeserved* character of God's gift.

Judging these events from the perspective of the twentieth century, we realize that the whole future of Christianity was at stake in this initial crisis of the church. Humanly speaking, it might have remained no more than a Jewish sect.

But we can also understand the alarm of the Judaeo-

Christians, for the boundaries of ancient Israel were being broken forever. The " Vineyard of God " was passing into other hands (Matt. 21:33-43; cf. Ps. 80:14-19; Isa. 5:1-7) .

Persecution and Scattering Leads to Mission

Stephen seems to have had a presentiment that the coming of Jesus Christ marked the end of the Temple and of the law (Acts 6:13-14) . By an act of sheer grace, which God alone can explain, God transforms Stephen's persecutor, Saul of Tarsus, into the apostle to the Gentiles, the stanch witness to justification by faith. (Acts 7:58; 8:1; 9:1-30; cf. Gal. 1:15-17; 2:8.)

We have seen that under the pressure of events the church in Jerusalem extends its mission to those on the outside. Sometimes God allows persecution in order to force the church to go outside its own walls; he stirs up Christian diasporas, or scatterings, as he had previously stirred up a Jewish diaspora and established the communities of the Dispersion. The first church that understands the missionary task as a real part of the church's job is the new community at Antioch. (Acts 13:1-3.) Under the command of the Holy Spirit, we are told, this church set apart its two best leaders, Barnabas and Saul of Tarsus, to engage in " foreign missions."

This decision marks the beginning of the apostolic activity that, in conformity with Christ's command, carries the gospel to the ends of the earth. The mere account of Paul's missionary journeys fills more than half the book of The Acts (chs. 13 to 28) . We see him traveling to Asia Minor, then to Greece. As soon as churches are established, he sets out again, for his particular vocation is to carry the gospel to those places where it has not yet been proclaimed (Rom. 15:15-29) . Nothing but captivity and death can finally put a stop to his activity.

However, it is important to observe that Paul, faithful to the example of his Master, begins by proclaiming the gos-

pel in the synagogue. Jesus first of all appealed to the chosen people (Matt. 10:5-6), for in God's unfolding purpose
of salvation the latter had a priority in terms of their special calling. The apostles maintained this priority and only
when they were driven out of the synagogue did they deliberately turn toward the pagan world (Acts 13:13-48;
14:1-7; etc.) .

Actually, the first initiates into the new faith often turn
out to be the so-called " proselytes," the pagans who fre-
quented the synagogue without observing all the Jewish
rites. These mixed communities, which include those of
Jewish origin and also many pagans, immediately raise in
the clearest possible fashion a problem that had already
been raised in the church in Jerusalem: What is to be the
status of the new converts? Shall the Jewish practice of circumcision and the whole Mosaic law be imposed on them?
The Jews who practice strict observance say yes. Paul says
no. Out of this disagreement a conflict arises that goes on
for several years and threatens the unity of the newborn
church. A conference is assembled in Jerusalem — the first
synod of the Christian church! (Acts, ch. 15; cf. Gal., ch.
2.) A satisfactory decision seems to have been reached. But
scarcely has Paul turned his back when an underhanded
campaign is launched against him in the young churches of
Asia Minor, a campaign that soon threatens to spread elsewhere. At this point, the apostle to the Gentiles takes up
his pen. He is filled with righteous indignation. He refuses
to see the young church imprisoned again under the yoke
of the law, when he has just revealed the full joy of salvation in Jesus Christ to them.

The stirring polemics of the letters to the Galatians, the
Romans, and the Corinthians, are not the work of a theol-
ogy professor but of an apostle. He speaks as a missionary
who waxes indignant in order to save his churches in a per-
ilous situation. This is the reason for the amazing vigor
that is such an offense to our indifferent attitude: " If we.

or an angel from heaven, should preach to you a gospel contrary to that which we preached to you, let him be accursed " (Gal. 1:8). Contrast with that his cries of distress and tenderness: " I am afraid I have labored over you in vain." (Gal. 4:11.) " My little children, with whom I am again in travail until Christ be formed in you! " (Gal. 4:19.) " Who is weak, and I am not weak? Who is made to fall, and I am not indignant? " (II Cor. 11:29.)

Anyone who speaks this way confronts those close to him with the " all or nothing " character of the gospel: either we commit ourselves to Jesus Christ or we commit ourselves to someone other than Jesus Christ. There is no third alternative.

This is not a matter of adherence to this or that practice, but concerns the very nature of salvation and of the catholicity (i.e., the universality) of the church.

The heresy of the Judaizers leads the apostle to set forth his doctrine of justification by faith. Other heresies will soon take form in the midst of the newborn church. In the Hellenistic environment, for example, attempts will be made to transform Christianity into a human philosophy, a kind of wisdom (gnōsis). In the face of these attempts, Paul continues to preach the cross, a scandal to the Jews and foolishness to the Greeks, but the power of God and the wisdom of God to all those who believe (I Cor. 1:22-23; Col. 2:8-15).

In the apostolic church, life precedes doctrine. Doctrine is only the intellectual translation of the great certainties that are the very life of the church. When these certainties are challenged or questioned, doctrine is worked out and stated with precision. The apostolic letters witness to this living development of a faith that is continually enlarged and deepened until it finally includes all the fullness of Christ and his redemptive work.

CHAPTER IX

THE MYSTERY OF THE CHURCH
(The New Testament Letters)

SUMMARY

The mystery of the church is that Christ loved it and gave himself up for it (Eph. 5:25-32). This love is the basis of its unity, its faith, and its hope. But the church's life here below remains a life of humiliation.

1. THE GOSPEL OF SALVATION BY GRACE (Eph. 2:1-10)

Paul's gospel is Jesus Christ and him crucified (I Cor. 1:17 to 2:16). The apostle's personal experience (Gal. 1:13-16; Phil. 3:4-11). Paul's faith as set forth in Scripture (Rom. 1:16 to 8:39; Gal. 2:15 to 4:7). Christians as men " dead " and " raised from the dead " in Christ (Col. 3:1-4; Gal. 2:20; Rom. 6:3-11; 8:1-17).

ISRAEL ACCORDING TO THE PROMISE AND ISRAEL ACCORDING TO THE FLESH

The cross of Christ as the foundation of Christian universalism:

a. The true Israel is the Israel of the promise. One becomes a child of Abraham by faith (Rom., ch. 4; Gal., ch. 3). The mystery of the reconciliation of the Jewish and pagan world (Eph., chs. 2; 3).

b. Israel's destiny: the mystery of its election and rejection. Even the rejection has a place in God's unfolding pur-

pose of salvation (Rom., chs. 9 to 11). The key to the
mystery found in Rom. 11:32.

3. THE CHURCH, THE BODY OF CHRIST

The character of the life of the church is such that it is
totally dependent on its head, it is a living community, and
it prolongs and incarnates the life of its Lord in the midst
of the present world:

a. The image of the church as a " structure ": Jesus Christ
the chief cornerstone; the "foundation" of the apostles
and prophets; the believers as "living stones." The new
temple as a temple of flesh (Eph. 2:20-22; I Peter 2:4-10;
I Cor. 3:9-17; Heb. 3:2-6; cf. also John 2:18-22).

b. The image of the church as a " body ": the church as the
visible body on earth of the Lord who reigns in the heavens. The indissoluble connection of body, head, and
members one with another (Eph. 1:20-22; 4:4-16; 5:22-
33; I Cor. 12:4-31; Rom. 12:3-8).

The " sharing of suffering " (Phil. 3:10; cf. 1:29; II
Cor. 4:7-12; 6:4-10; 11:18 to 12:10; Col. 1:24; Heb. 12:3-
11; Rom. 5:3; I Peter 1:3-9; 4:12-14; James 1:2-4).

c. The church's ethic consists in its call to be conformed to
the Lord who has died and been raised for it. In the reality of its existence it is to become what it already is in
faith (Phil. 2:1-16; Rom. 12:1-16; I Cor., chs. 12 to 14;
Col., ch. 3; Eph. 1:20; I John 2:7-11; 3:11-24; 4:7-21; cf.
Matt., ch. 5). But it is saved only in " hope," and its pilgrimage remains a pilgrimage by faith (Rom. 8:18-39;
Eph. 6:10-20).

4. THE CHURCH AND HUMAN SOCIETY

The church affirms the sovereignty of Jesus Christ over
the world; human authorities can never be anything but his
representatives (Rom. 13:1; Eph. 1:20-23; Col. 1:15-20).

a. The exercise of authority in the family is an image and
reflection of the exercise of the divine authority (Eph.
3:15; 5:21-33; I Cor. 11:3; cf. Gen. 1:27). The believer is
called to command and to obey "in the Lord" (Eph.
6:1-9; Col. 3:18 to 4:1; I Peter 2:18 to 3:12). Limits to
this obedience (Matt. 10:35-37).

   b. The civil authority instituted by God. Its basis (Rom.
      13:1-7; I Tim. 2:1-4; I Peter 2:13-17; John 19:11) and its
      limits (Mark 12:13-17; 13:9; Acts 4:19; 5:29; Rev., ch.
      13; 14:9-12; 20:4).
   c. The church's involvement and freedom in the affairs of
      this world (I Cor. 6:12; cf. Mark 13:31).

The mystery of the church, as described in Eph. 5:21-33,
is that Christ loved it and gave himself up for it. He suffered on the cross in order to call it to life and freedom.
This life and freedom are the free gift of his love.

This is the basis for a second mystery of grace, for the
blood of Christ ratifies the unity of the Jewish and pagan
worlds. Henceforth, pagans and Jews are members of the
same body. (Eph. 3:6.) Together they constitute the New
Israel, the Israel according to faith, born not of the flesh
but of the Holy Spirit.

The church, the body of Christ, makes the life of its
Lord visible in the world. It proclaims salvation through
him, and witnesses to his Lordship over all the created
world.

1. THE GOSPEL OF SALVATION BY GRACE

The entire Biblical revelation affirms that salvation is
by grace. We have seen this in the course of our study of
the Old Testament and of the gospel. But this revelation
is so utterly contrary to the natural heart of man that it
must be emphasized again and again, for man always keeps
trying to achieve salvation on his own resources. Nothing
is so humiliating to his pride as to owe everything to the
grace of God alone, and to be able to live only on the basis
of his pardon. Little by little, postexilic Judaism had
erected a legalistic religion of salvation by works. Jesus had
denounced it. The first apostles clearly understood that
they owed their salvation to the Lord who was crucified
and risen for them; they preached the remission of sins,
but they dared not break the chains of Jewish legalism.

The Gospel of Christ Crucified

A Pharisee named Saul, who had been trained in all the subtleties of rabbinic dialectic, was given the task of showing that legalism was a dead-end street, and of developing the doctrine of justification by faith in its full logic and power.

Paul's gospel grows out of his own personal experience. (Phil. 3:3-11.) But the revelation that God gave to him (Gal. 1:15-16) is confirmed and corroborated by the unanimity of the apostolic witness (I Cor. 15:1-11), and, indeed, by the whole of Scripture (Rom. 1:1-6). The apostle makes a great deal of this point. His testimony is not at all subjective. His gospel possesses indisputable authority, precisely because he is not the author of it, but is rather the recipient of a revelation, and knows that he can scarcely deny a part of it without denying it all. (Gal. 1:6-12.) What is this gospel? It is the gospel of Christ crucified. The apostle can do nothing but " portray " and preach him. (Gal. 3:1; I Cor. 1:17-31.) " For I decided to know nothing among you except Jesus Christ and him crucified," is how he puts it in writing to the Corinthians (I Cor. 2:2).

Why is this central and unique place given to the cross? The apostle knows better than anyone else that the gospel of the cross is " a stumbling-block to Jews and folly to Gentiles " (I Cor. 1:23), for this same cross had previously been a stumbling block and folly to Paul himself. God had to vanquish and disarm him on the road to Damascus in order to enlist him in the service of his Son. But, having come to understand all this, Paul cannot henceforth preach anything else than Christ crucified. For it was precisely in the acceptance of the scandal of the cross that he found salvation. If God had to give his Son for the salvation of the world, then without him we would be truly lost, and in him we are truly saved. The vision of the Crucified One destroys all our human righteousness. It says to each individual directly, " Here is what *you* have done to God, and here is what *he* has done for you."

And the apostle knew all about this destruction of his own righteousness. He, the zealous upholder of the law, a Hebrew born of a Hebrew, knew that he was *lost* on the day when the Lord of glory spoke to him on the way to Damascus, and said, " I am Jesus, whom you are persecuting " (Acts 9:5; cf. I Cor. 15:9). This law, in which Paul had placed his full trust, far from saving him, now became his condemnation. For the sake of Christ, he says, " I have suffered the loss of all things " (cf. Phil. 3:4-11). All things — this means all his security and all his status as an influential Pharisee. But most of all it means the loss of all his spiritual confidence and his own righteousness.[29] Naked and laid bare, he is henceforth reclothed only in the righteousness of Christ.

What does all this mean, anyway? What is this " righteousness of Christ " which saves the apostle from himself? What is he really saying when he claims that his only concern henceforth is to " know [Christ] and the power of his resurrection " (Phil. 3:10), or again when he identifies himself with Jesus Christ to the point of saying, " I have been crucified with Christ; it is no longer I who live, but Christ who lives in me " (Gal. 2:19-20) ?

Christians as Men " Dead " and " Raised from the Dead "

We must do our best to understand the meaning of these phrases, for they contain the whole mystery of salvation. Paul regards himself, and indeed all Christians, as *dead persons raised to life*. Why " dead," and in what sense " raised to life "?

God is the Living God who is the author and giver of life. This world, as cut off from God and in rebellion against him, is a condemned world. Physical death, which is in store for everyone, is the sign of this end which awaits the whole world (cf. Rom. 5:12). From God's perspective, from the perspective of eternal life, we are simply dead persons walking around, as long as the Spirit has not given us life. The prodigal son was " dead " (Luke 15:32) and he returned to life when he re-entered the house of his father — and this parable is not just the story of a juvenile delinquent, but actually the story of all mankind. Paul is trying to express the same thing in more abstract language, when he shows that *all* men, whether pagans or Jews, are under the sign of condemnation (Rom. 1:18 to 3:20). It is clear that a law, no matter how perfect, cannot bring dead persons to life; all it can do is to make plain that they are dead, by exposing their inability to live up to the law's demands. Paul points out that this is why the law, far from saving man, merely completes his condemnation. For before the law was given to man, he sinned through ignorance. Now he knows that evil is evil, but he does it just the same, and for this reason he is even more guilty than he was before (Rom. 5:13; 7:7-23). It goes without saying that man's situation under the law is therefore hopeless! This is why God, in accordance with his steadfast love, has done something about the situation. In place of the law, which simply judges us, God has appointed a person who gives *to* us what he commands *of* us.

Let us amplify this point by looking from a different perspective at the parable we referred to a moment ago. The father of the prodigal son (who is mankind) was not willing just to send his son a list of all his mistakes and then command him to return to him. Instead, this father sent his own beloved Son, so that he might deliver the younger son, pay his debts, and suffer punishment in his place. And this is the wonderful miracle of love, the miracle of the coming of Jesus Christ into the world:

> Why, one will hardly die for a righteous man — though perhaps for a good man one will dare even to die. But God shows his love for us in that while we were yet sinners Christ died for us. (Rom. 5:7-8.)

Jesus Christ " died for our sins." By a mysterious act of substitution, he agreed to represent the whole of mankind all by himself, to fight our fight, and to take the sin of his people and of all peoples upon himself. Paul did not hesitate to put it in its bluntest form: " Christ redeemed us from the curse of the law, *having become a curse for us* " (Gal. 3:13, italics added). But by submitting voluntarily to the assault of all the powers of sin and death, he conquered them. God made the fact of this victory crystal-clear by raising Christ from the dead.

Jesus made our condition his own; he makes his victory our own. Our sin is nailed to the wood of the cross, really condemned and really taken away. Our old self is dead, crucified with him and in him. And the life that we now live is the life of the resurrected Lord, the life of the Spirit. " To know the power of his resurrection " is to believe in his victory and to know that this victory is *our* victory, to know that by him and in him we are promised life with God, free from the power of death (cf. Rom., chs. 6 to 8).

" Consider yourselves dead to sin." (Rom. 6:11.) Paul knows very well that we haven't arrived at this stage yet, and that the struggle with sin will continue as long as we live. But from now on, our *true self* is no longer a divided and disunited self, which carries the indelible marks of sin. Our true self is actually the risen Jesus, our true life is the life that we have with him, and that at the time of his coming again will be fully evident and will become wholly ours. To know Jesus Christ and the power of his resurrection means that we look no more to the past, to our dead self, but that we look ahead, to the risen Lord whose victory guarantees our own. It means that we look only to him (cf. Heb. 12:2), and that we look in such a way that we are " changed into his likeness, from one degree of glory to another " by the activity of " the Lord who is the Spirit " (II Cor. 3:18).

If then you have been raised with Christ, seek the
things that are above, where Christ is, seated at the right
hand of God. Set your mind on things that are above, not
on things that are on earth. *For you have died, and your
life is hid with Christ in God.* When Christ who is our
life appears, then you also will appear with him in glory.
(Col. 3:1-4, italics added.)

Christian living means a " being conformed unto Christ "
by the active power of the Holy Spirit. We are under " the
law of the Spirit," which is not a set of rules but a life-
giving Person (Rom. 8:2).

This is what the mystery of salvation is all about. In the
light of this, we can understand Paul's vehemence against
those who try to cancel the unique power of the cross of
Christ by their own teaching, and try to re-establish a religion of works under the pretext of being faithful to the
law. To do that is to " nullify the grace of God " and render the sacrifice of the Son of God futile (Gal. 2:21). And
this sacrifice is something so great and at the same time so
shocking that if God has agreed to it, it means that he alone
is able to save us and enable us to pass from death to life.
The apostle bursts forth with the same vehemence against
those who deny the resurrection of the dead. For him, the
resurrection is the manifestation of Christ's victory over
sin and death: " If Christ has not been raised, your faith is
futile and you are still in your sins " (I Cor. 15:17).

But Christ *did* die, and he *was* raised up from the dead,
and one who lives by his grace has nothing more to fear
from any of the powers of earth or hell (Rom. 8:32-39).
He knows that the resurrection of the Lord is only the first
fruits of his own resurrection and of the resurrection of
the world (I Cor. 15:20-28).

2. ISRAEL ACCORDING TO THE PROMISE AND ISRAEL ACCORDING TO THE FLESH

Salvation by grace is the foundation of Christian universalism, and it comes from a single cross raised up for the salvation of all men. But if this is true, then what happens to the Old Covenant and the mission of the chosen people?

Israel According to the Promise

Paul's whole case rests on the distinction that he makes between Israel according to the flesh and Israel according to the promise: " Abraham believed God, and it was reckoned to him as righteousness " (Rom. 4:3; cf. Gen. 15:6). One is a child of Abraham *by faith*. (Rom. 4:16-25; cf. Gal. 3:6-7.) The law doesn't appear until after the time of Abraham, and it acts as a custodian (Gal. 3:24-25). The promise made to Abraham is fulfilled in Jesus Christ. " In thee shall all the nations be blessed." (Gal. 3:8; cf. Gen. 12:3.) Pagans and Jews are joined together once again: " in Christ Jesus you are all sons of God through faith " (Gal. 3:26).

The sign of the Old Covenant was circumcision, reserved for one race and one sex. The sign of the New Covenant is baptism, conferred on all those who repent and believe, without distinction of race or sex. In this action, immersion in water symbolizes the penitent's death to self, and his resurrection in Christ, while the baptism of the Spirit endows him with the new life that the risen Christ shares with those who belong to him (cf. Rom. 5:11; 6:4; 8:9-11, 14). Jews and pagans are on an equal footing in the face of this verdict of death and this promise of salvation.

> For as many of you as were baptized into Christ have put on Christ. There is neither Jew nor Greek, there is neither slave nor free, there is neither male nor female; for you are all one in Christ Jesus. And if you are Christ's,

then you are Abraham's offspring, heirs according to promise. (Gal. 3:27-29; cf. I Cor. 12:13.)

Today, after twenty centuries of Christianity, it may be very difficult for us to understand the full meaning of this " neither Jew nor Greek." In order to do so we must remember the racial exclusivism of postexilic Judaism, which forbade all contact with the pagan world. Paul does not take this historical development lightly. He takes much more seriously than we are inclined to, the " wall of separation " that separates the Jewish world from the pagan world (Eph. 2:11-22).

It is precisely for this reason that nothing less than the blood of the cross is necessary to reconcile these two worlds. Paul considers this reunion of Jews and pagans in a single body one of the most amazing mysteries of the faith (Eph. 3:1-6).

We should try to understand the full meaning of the apostle's position, for we live in a time when the Jews have undergone the most terrible persecutions of their whole history. To explain away the conflict between Jew and Gentile as a sheer racial problem, or in terms of economic competition, is not enough. Another tragic factor has played its part: the church for centuries has used the Jews as a scapegoat and made them responsible for the death of Jesus, instead of acknowledging that this responsibility belongs to mankind as a whole. But we need to go even deeper than that, for the destiny of the Jews as the " chosen people of God " has forever set them apart. No secular civilization can assimilate them fully — when it does, they lose their soul. It is significant that the totalitarian state turns its hatred against both the Jews and the Christians, for they are the hard core of God's elect that dictators cannot conquer but can only destroy.

In a mysterious way, Israel goes on being the Suffering Servant exposed to the world's rejection.

We Christians cannot therefore approach the Jews as we would those who stand outside God's revelation. They bear the marks of God's election. And the fact that they have undergone centuries of persecution at the hands of Christians (or so-called Christians) should make us very humble in our approach to them. But when all this has been said, the fact remains that there is only one Savior, whose blood was shed for both Jews and Gentiles. A Christian knows that only in him can all " walls of hostility " be broken, whether it be the wall between Jew and Gentile, or all the other walls that racial, social, or national prejudice create between men. Only through our reconciliation to God in Christ, through the shared experience of God's gracious forgiveness, can the road be open for a genuine and lasting reconciliation between those whom a deep-rooted hostility divides.

The mission of the church to the Jews remains; for the apostolic church this task was always a primary concern. But the rejection of Christ as its Messiah by a large portion of the Jewish nation set the apostle Paul wrestling with the question: How did God allow this to happen? His answer is to be found in Rom., chs. 9 to 11.

Israel's Election and Rejection (Rom., chs. 9 to 11)

The problem seems to have haunted the apostle. He goes as far as to say that he could wish himself accursed for the sake of his brethren according to the flesh (Rom. 9:3). What is the place of Israel according to the flesh in God's unfolding purpose of salvation?

The part played by Israel, as a people, is tremendous. For it is to Israel that " the sonship, the glory, the covenants, the giving of the law, the worship and the promises " pertain; it is " of their race according to the flesh " that the Christ, the Lord, is born (Rom. 9:4-5). Salvation is from the Jews. (John 4:22.)

But the very history of this people shows us that not all the Children of Israel are true Israelites. The authentic Israel is the Israel of the promise: it is *by faith* that one is a child of Abraham (Rom. 9:6-8; cf. Rom., ch. 4). God chooses instruments of his salvation from wherever it pleases him to do so, and his purposes remain unfathomable. (Rom. 9:6-29.) Israel's election remains a mystery of grace throughout the length of its history: " I will have mercy on whom I have mercy, and I will have compassion on whom I have compassion " (Rom. 9:15; cf. Ex. 33:19). Did not Scripture proclaim that " only a *remnant* of them will be saved "? (Rom. 9:27; cf. Isa. 10:22.) And from this remnant God raised up a " shoot " who, by himself, now gives birth to a new people (Rom. 9:29; cf. Isa. 11:1). Most of the Israelites placed their confidence in works; the message of salvation by grace was for them an occasion of stumbling (Rom. 9:30-33).

But the pagans who accepted the message of the cross entered into the covenant of grace. Thus the hardness of heart of a part of Israel opens the way of salvation to the pagans. Without desiring it, without even being aware of it, Israel in this case again was the instrument of God's unchangeable purposes, the instrument of the world's conversion.

God's final word concerning Israel is not his condemnation but his steadfast love. In dealing with this problem, Paul is conscious of revealing a new *mystery of the church* to his readers (Rom. 11:25). It is this: the rejection of Israel, of a part of Israel, is *only temporary*. When once the multitude of pagans has entered the church, it will be Israel's turn to be converted. For " the gifts and call of God are irrevocable." (Rom. 11:29.) God wanted no one to be able to glorify himself before God: " For God has consigned all men to disobedience, that he may have mercy upon all " (Rom. 11:32).

This passage is quite basic. It throws a unique light on God's purpose of salvation as it unfolds throughout the history of men.

The anguish expressed by the apostle at the beginning

of this whole section (Rom. 9:1-4) gives place to a cry of adoration before the inconceivable grandeur of the divine mercy: " O the depths of the riches and wisdom and knowledge of God! How unsearchable are his judgments and how inscrutable his ways! " (Rom. 11:33).

We have seen many times in the course of this book how in the ineffable divine mystery deserved punishment can become an occasion for the gift of grace, far beyond what could have been anticipated. This is what we see happening in the present case. When the pagan world has found its way to the Father's house, Israel will find its way back home, and its return will be " a resurrection from the dead " (cf. Rom. 11:15, 25). In the apostle's thought, Israel's return to faith will mark the end of time.

3. THE CHURCH, THE BODY OF CHRIST

The church is the New Israel to whom the torch of faith has been given until the final resurrection.

There are certain images drawn from the New Testament that convey the reality of the church's life in a helpful way. They all stress, on the one hand, the church's close dependence on its Lord, and on the other hand its character as a community.

The Church as a Structure

The church is frequently compared to a *structure*. The chief cornerstone of this structure is Jesus Christ (Eph. 2: 20-22; I Peter 2:4-10; cf. I Cor. 3:9-15; Heb. 3:2-6), and the believers within it are its " living stones." The divine architect has laid down the foundation of the structure, which is the witness of the apostles and prophets (Eph. 2:20). Jesus Christ is " the chief cornerstone, in whom the whole structure is joined together and grows into a holy temple in the Lord " (Eph. 2:20-21).

A structure only fulfills its function if all its parts are " joined together," i.e., if each stone is in its proper place, if each hidden tiny stone is content with its modest task, and if all the parts of the structure are subordinated to the harmony of the whole.

In ancient Israel, we recall that the Temple was the place where " the glory of God " dwelt. In place of this temple of stone God has henceforth substituted temples of flesh. Jesus Christ regards himself as the new temple, the place where God encounters his people (John 2:18-22). Paul calls upon every believer to look upon his body as " a temple of the Holy Spirit " (I Cor. 6:19). Thus it is the whole company of believers who comprise the " temple " or the " house of God " (Eph. 2:20; cf. Heb. 3:6).

In English, the word " house " can mean a structure or a building, but it can also designate the family who lives in it; it can even stand for a dynasty (as when we refer to the " House of Savoy"). The church is likewise the " house " of God in this threefold sense: it is the *structure* that God has built to live in, the place where he makes his glory shine; it is the *family* of God (Eph. 3:14-19; cf. Rom. 8:14-16) ; and finally it is the *heir* of all the promises that have found their fulfillment in Jesus Christ (Rom. 8:17). The church is associated with his reign: " To him who loves us . . . and made us a kingdom, priests to his God and Father . . ." (Rev. 1:5-6). It is " the holy nation," the " royal priesthood," set apart for the service of God, just as Israel had formerly been set apart. (I Peter 2:9; cf. Ex. 19:6.)

The Church as a Body

More frequent than the image of the structure are images taken from the world of living things, for they express even better the vital and necessary character of the bonds that unite Jesus Christ to his church. These are the images of the vine and the branches (John, ch. 15) , and the image of the *body*.

Jesus Christ is the head of the body and fills the whole

GOD'S UNFOLDING PURPOSE

body with his fullness (Rom. 12:5; I Cor. 12:12-27; Eph. 1:23; 4:4, 11-16; 5:30; Col. 1:18; 2:9). The Holy Spirit is the quickening principle that gives it life.

Just what is a body? First of all, it is an organic unity, all parts of which are essential to one another and to the whole. No single member can be curtailed or become ill without upsetting the functioning of the whole body. But the body is something more than this, for as we make use of the senses the body is our means of communication with the outside world. If the senses are damaged, we are closed off from the outside world, and we become dumb, unconscious, blind, or deaf.

To describe the church as the body of Christ is therefore to say, first of all, that the only life possible for it is in a unity of faith, obedience, and love with its Lord, and that it is functioning normally only if all of its parts are healthy and living, and recognize their mutual interdependence. A body where the head is no longer in control of things is a paralyzed body, which is to say that it is already partially dead.

To describe the church as the body of Christ is to say, in the second place, that the existence of the church is the means by which Jesus Christ manifests himself to the world. In order for him to be known in the world, there must be mouths that proclaim the Word (Rom. 10:14-17), eyes that see, ears that hear, feet that travel across the world, hands that bind up the world's wounds.

The church is the visible witness on earth of the invisible Lord who reigns in the heavens; it is his mouth and his hands. If the church does not speak, the world dies in ignorance of the salvation that is offered to it. If the church ignores its responsibility to even the least of its members, the effect is felt in the full scope of its witness.

The Church and the " Sharing of Suffering "

While he was on earth, Jesus Christ, the Lord of the church, suffered from the attacks of the world. The church, which is his body, will necessarily suffer from the same attacks — attacks from within and from without. " ' A servant is not greater than his master.' If they persecuted me," Jesus says to his followers, " they will persecute you; if they kept my word, they will keep yours also." (John 15:20.) But much worse than the attacks from outside are those which will come from inside. Has not Satan claimed the right to sift the church like wheat? (Luke 22:31.) He will never stop trying to separate what God unites, to divide the house, to tear the body to pieces. The faith of the church is tested and purified, just as gold is tested by fire (I Peter 1:6-8) . Since the church exists in human form it walks by faith and not by sight, and as long as the present world lasts, the church will remain fallible and vulnerable to attack.

We saw earlier that the " mystery of the kingdom " consisted in the fact that it was none other than the coming of Christ in the humiliation of the incarnation. It is also a " mystery of the church " that it possesses a double nature: to the degree that Jesus Christ is its Lord, it has a foretaste of the Spirit and the promises of his reign, while to the degree that it is involved in the present world, it is a congregation of sinful men. That is the church — a curious mixture of grandeur and misery.

The Christian who knows what it means to be a member of the body of Christ will never be surprised if he is called upon to experience in his own spirit and flesh the kind of assaults that his Lord suffered. Even more, he will look upon this opportunity to " share [Christ's] sufferings " as a *favor* God has granted him (Phil. 3:10) , for to participate in his struggles is both the sign and the condition of intimate union with him. Paul writes to the Philippians:

> For it has been granted to you that for the sake of Christ you should not only believe in him but also suffer for his sake, engaged in the same conflict which you saw and now hear to be mine. (Phil. 1:29-30.)

This must be clearly understood. What is being described is not a morbid interest in suffering for its own sake. It is, rather, a willingness to take part in the great battle that the Lord wages ceaselessly against the powers of this world until the day when he will have " placed all enemies under his feet." The apostle Paul gives us a magnificent description of this battle which he waged on his Master's behalf during his entire ministry. Speaking of the gospel of salvation, he says:

> But we have this treasure in earthen vessels, to show that the transcendent power belongs to God and not to us. We are afflicted in every way, but not crushed; perplexed, but not driven to despair; persecuted, but not forsaken; struck down, but not destroyed; always carrying in the body the death of Jesus, so that the life of Jesus may also be manifested in our bodies. For while we live we are always being given up to death for Jesus' sake, so that the life of Jesus may be manifested in our mortal flesh. So death is at work in us, but life in you. (II Cor. 4:7-12; cf. 6:4-10; 11:18 to 12:10.)

The recital of Israel's history, particularly that of the faithful remnant, has shown us that in their bodily existence the servants of the Lord in the time of the Old Covenant suffered ahead of time something of the disgrace that would come to the Son of God. In like manner, in its own day-to-day life, the church, the New Israel, shares in the sufferings of him who gave himself for the church. This is how we must understand the words of Paul: " Now I rejoice in my sufferings for your sake, and in my flesh I complete what is lacking of Christ's afflictions for the sake of his body, that is, the church " (Col. 1:24) .

The Church and Ethics

We have seen that the life of the believer is a life lived by faith, under the sign of the risen Lord. By faith the believer is already free, already raised up, for his real life

is " hid with Christ in God " (Col. 3:3) . And what is true
of the members of the body is true of the whole body. The
church is called to a life lived by faith in its Lord. All the
apostolic preaching can be summed up in the words, " Live
as one in whom Christ dwells," which means, quite simply,
Behave *in fact* as men and women who know that they
have been uprooted from the present world and are living
with God (Col. 3:1-4) .

In the New Testament Letters, ethics is always understood as a response to what God has already done (Rom.
12:1-2) . The apostles address themselves to a redeemed
community, whose faith and hope rest in Christ. We have
to do with the *ethics of the church*. It is no more possible
to make a code of morals out of them than it would be possible (as we saw earlier) to make a code of morals out of
the Sermon on the Mount. The type of conduct that the
apostles set forth for the Christian community is directed
to men and women who have " died " and been " raised "
in Christ, and whose corporate life as a community should
bear witness to this fact. For them, what counts is living in
a manner worthy of their high calling. " You also must
consider yourselves dead to sin and alive to God in Christ
Jesus," Paul writes to the Romans (Rom. 6:11; cf. ch. 8) .
The Christian is grafted onto the tree that is Christ, and
to be grafted means to bear fruit (Matt. 7:16-20; John 15:
1-4; Gal. 5:22) . His freedom comes out of his absolute dependence on the Lord who commands him and the Spirit
who leads him. " Those who belong to Christ Jesus have
crucified the flesh, with its passions and desires. If we live
by the Spirit, let us also walk by the Spirit." (Gal. 5:
24-25.)

Here we must digress for a moment. The word " flesh,"
as Paul uses it, is often badly misunderstood. It is occasionally interpreted as though it implied a condemnation
of the life of the body, as though sexual life, for example,
were wrong in and of itself. Paul seems, on these terms, to

be demanding something impossible and contrary to nature, namely, that we behave as pure spirits! As a matter of fact, in the New Testament the word "flesh" really stands for the old creation, the "old" man, everything, in other words, that has not been remade and given new life by the Spirit (cf. I John 2:15-17). The apostle Paul, like Jesus himself, puts what we call the "sins of the flesh" and the "sins of the spirit" on precisely the same level. Enmity, strife, and dissension are fruits of the flesh just as much as unchastity. (Cf. Gal. 5:19-21.)

The life "in Christ" rules out any pride, any feeling of one's own righteousness, any concern for self. But since pride and a feeling of one's own righteousness and concern for self are the basic sin of the human race, they tend to reappear and corrupt the whole life of the church all the time. This is why the apostles always keep talking about the inseparability of humility and love in the life of the church. They set before the church the figure of him who, being God, humbled himself and took the form of a servant; the glory that God gave to him is the divine response to his voluntary humiliation. How can those who belong to him henceforth take pride in their talents, and look for ways to exalt themselves one above the other? Rather, they must humble themselves voluntarily, not only before God but also among themselves. (Phil. 2:1-16; cf. Rom. 12: 1-16; I Cor., ch. 13; Eph. 5:21.)

The church is called upon to distinguish itself from the pagan world that surrounds it by the extraordinary quality of its love and humility (Matt., ch. 5; cf. Luke 6:27-40; John 13:34-35; 17:22-23; I John 2:7-11; 3:11-24; 4:7-21). The thing that differentiates the church from all human societies is that its beginning and end is Jesus Christ, and that it is his Spirit that sets the tone for everything it does. Only the church can show the world what true community is — an association of persons opening out in freedom and mutual respect, where the individual serves the group and the group serves the individual.

To say this is to say that the church betrays its mission every time factions or frictions divide it, and every time its members succumb to the temptation to seek glory for themselves rather than seeking the sole glory of Christ. Internal bickerings in the church tear the body of Christ to pieces, but even more they are a stumbling block, an occasion of falling, for the world that sees them taking place.

We must admit that history bears tragic witness to the frequency of these failings. By its unfaithfulness, the church of Jesus Christ is always trying God's patience. Is this reason enough for us to doubt the church, or refuse to involve ourselves in its life?

The amazing mystery of the divine wisdom, as we have seen several times already, is that God's plan of salvation is always unfolded by means of feeble instruments — through the poverty of words, through the dense veil of the flesh, and the stammering witness of a faithless people. God wanted it this way! He desires that his power be made known through weakness. He placed the torch of faith in our weak human hands, to make it quite evident to everyone that salvation does not come from us, but from him. This body, the church — divided, stained, bruised, responsible through the course of twenty centuries for many crimes — is nevertheless *his* body, the body of the Lord in glory, the body for whose life he let himself be crucified. Who, therefore, knowing that, will dare to repudiate the church or to separate himself from it? For this sick and bruised church is also the glorious and triumphant church that will reign with him in eternity!

We are not called to serve an imaginary, ideal church. It is on the church-as-it-is that through our baptism we have been grafted. We are required to be involved in the *visible* church, with all of its grandeur and all of its misery — holy and catholic because of the Spirit that dwells in it, yet made up of sinners! Its misery belongs to us, just as our misery belongs to it, and this is the misery of a world that is as yet saved only in hope, and that lives, struggles, suffers, and hopes under the sign of God's patience.

4. THE CHURCH AND HUMAN SOCIETY

If the church considers the present world as " dead " and condemned, and if, among men, it proclaims God's new creation, should it set itself up here on earth as a closed society, shut off from the problems and struggles of the vast world that surrounds it? Can it refuse to be concerned about the destiny of human society?

The answer is a clear " no." For the church believes and proclaims that its Lord is the Lord of heaven *and earth,* an earth that belongs to him both because he created it and because he redeemed it. This is the world in which Jesus Christ's victory over " the principalities and powers " took place. He has placed " all authorities under his feet." The latter can, to be sure, ignore this sovereignty, but they are not, for all that, less dependent upon it. They shall still have to render account, on the Last Day, for the way in which they have carried out their tasks and the way in which they have managed their possessions.

To assert that Jesus Christ is the sovereign Lord of the whole created world is to assert that there can be no other authority besides his, and that there is no authority that is not either *derived* from his or in *revolt* against it. This is why, as the Christian sees it, all human rules (whether they be those of the family, or the city, or the state, or anything else) have their foundation in the sovereign authority of Christ himself. The authority that they wield is never more than a delegated power. The believer who obeys a human authority is to obey " in the Lord," which means as though obeying the Lord himself. On the other hand, when this human authority usurps a right that does not belong to it, and instead of being an instrument of the divine purposes sets itself against those purposes and thwarts them, then the Christian's duty is to *resist openly.*

Authority in the Family

The pattern of authority within the family has been ordained by God. More than that, it is a reflection of the
pattern of the divine authority: " I bow my knees before
the Father," Paul writes, " from whom every family in
heaven and on earth is named " (Eph. 3:15; note that the
word for " family " is derived in Greek from the word for
" father ") . And again, " The head of every man is Christ,
the head of a woman is her husband, and the head of
Christ is God." (I Cor. 11:3.) When authority is claimed,
its aim must be the welfare of the recipient; the husband
must be ready to give his life for his wife's sake, just as
Christ gave his life for the church's sake. And correspond-
ingly the wife's submission is her response to the love that
is given to her, just as the church's obedience is its response
to Christ's love. So there is a pattern of authority in the
bosom of the family, but it is based upon the obedience
that all members of the family give to the same Lord, and
upon the fact that each one of the partners gives himself
fully to the other. They do not belong to themselves any
more; they are one body, just as Christ and the church are
one body (Eph. 5:28-30; cf. I Cor. 7:4) . In Jesus Christ,
a husband and wife regain the possibility of the kind of
unity that was destroyed by the Fall, in terms of which
the first human couple could be described as made " in the
image of God " (Gen. 1:27; 2:23-24; Mark 10:6-8) . From
this point of view, every family is a " cell " of the church,
a church in miniature. Every family is called upon to reflect, in its own inner life, something of the unity of the
Father and the Son, and the unity of Christ and the church
(cf. John 17:22-23) . In a Christian family, the parents command " in the Lord," and the children obey " in the
Lord," that is, at the Lord's command and for his glory
(Eph. 6:1-4; Col. 3:20-21) . But if it comes to the point of
having to choose between Christ and an authority within

the family, the child is released from his human obliga-
tions. On this point we must remember the explicit statement of Jesus: " He who loves father or mother more than
me is not worthy of me; and he who loves son or daughter
more than me is not worthy of me " (Matt. 10:37; cf. Matt.
10:34-39).

Similarly, in the relationship between a master and a
servant, he who commands, commands " in the Lord,"
and he who obeys, obeys " in the Lord." Both recognize
that there is one who is greater than either, and it is this
realization that in the last analysis both of them are dependent upon God alone, which gives the slave just as
much dignity and freedom as the free man himself possesses
(Gal. 3:28; Eph. 6:5-9; Col. 3:22-24; 4:1; Philemon 8-21;
I Peter 2:18-25).

Thus all human relationships are brought into relationship with Christ.

Civil Authority

We find the same thing to be true of the governing authorities of the city and the state — the magistrates,
princes, and governors. The power that they wield is given
to them from above. (John 19:11; Rom. 13:1.) They are
among the " principalities " that Jesus Christ conquered
once for all on the cross. One of the results of the wisdom
and goodness of God, and the grace of our Lord Jesus
Christ, is that the world in which we live does not go
down in total chaos, but that a certain degree of order is
maintained in human society, an order that makes it possible for citizens to " lead a quiet and peaceable life "
(I Tim. 2:1-4). At the time that Paul wrote his letter to
the Romans, he certainly considered the Roman Empire
as a force for *order,* even though it was a pagan empire. He
felt that one could give thanks to God for its existence,
and even view the Roman magistrates as " ministers of
God " (Rom. 13:6). We have a right to expect that the

magistrate do his duty faithfully, fulfilling the requirements that correspond to his specific responsibility (cf. Deut. 1:16-17). The duty of the church is to pray for those in authority and to submit to their jurisdiction in those areas where they rightly exercise authority, remembering that their power is given to them by God.

But this is not the last word. The time may come when the civil authority oversteps its power, misunderstands its real job, and becomes despotic. The natural inclination of any human authority, when it no longer recognizes a sovereign and divine authority over it, is to become autonomous, or, in other words, to deify itself. It becomes, finally, a power in the hands of antichrist, the " beast " of the book of Revelation. In this case the duty of the church is to resist such authority, even to the shedding of its blood, which means even to the point of martyrdom, if necessary (Rev., chs. 13; 14:9-12; 20:4).

Proper Christian Concern for the World

Can we say, then, that aside from this final qualification, the apostolic teaching is not very revolutionary, and actually tends to be uncritical of the established order? Such a conclusion would be both true and false. The New Testament does not spend much time denouncing the collective forms of sin in the way that the great prophets of the eighth century B.C. did. But the reason for this is not to be sought in some kind of social conservatism. It is rather to be sought in the fact that the apostolic church is conscious of living at the dawn of a new world. And this makes it so radically revolutionary that it is not concerned with partial and temporary reforms. It confesses and proclaims something much more basic — the death and resurrection of the world and its *re-creation* in Christ.

We say quite advisedly the resurrection and re-creation *of the world*. For the church was not concerned with an individual flight into a hereafter, but with the coming of the reign of Christ, with an entirely new order of things that will direct all things, institutions and men, to the one Lord.

Nothing could be farther removed from the thinking of the apostolic church than the type of modern individualism that insists that "religion is a private affair," or a single compartment of life. This was the notion that, in the nineteenth century, led to autonomy in philosophy, economics, politics, art, and science. Ever since then man has constructed his world on his own terms, and since this world is no longer in submission to any transcendent principle, and no longer has any universal foundation, it is faced with chaos.

The only way we can possibly emerge from this chaos is by reminding the world, which has been diverted from its course, that God is the Lord of heaven *and earth*. The gospel stresses the cosmic significance of the redemptive act. It deals with nothing less than the resurrection of the world. The Christian awaits this resurrection and in the meantime he knows that anything he may concern himself with here below will bear the stamp of human relativity. But this does not mean that he can be unconcerned with this world. He must struggle all the time to raise up signs of the world to come in the midst of the present world. He knows that the secret of all wisdom, all truth, all righteousness, all beauty, and all love is to be found in Jesus Christ, and that everything that is thought, created, or constructed apart from him is destined for death. He will try to express in words and deeds the conviction that gives meaning to his life. He will do this within the concrete situation, and in terms of the customs and institutions, where he is called upon to live. He will do this with a conviction stripped of illusions, knowing that it is not in his power to build heaven on earth, but only to proclaim by word and deed this renewal of all things which God alone will bring to pass. For a while the enemy forces still exercise their power on earth. But the church, which possesses a foretaste of the Kingdom, *knows* that they have been condemned and conquered; it no longer trembles before them; it refuses to give over to them this world for which Christ died; it knows that their power is passing away and that the words of life that were given to it will never pass away. The church, in other words, does not cease to claim this world for its Lord, as being promised to him and belonging to him in a twofold way, by reason of creation and redemption (Col. 1:16-20).

" All things are yours . . . and you are Christ's; and Christ is God's." (I Cor. 3:21, 23.) The whole Christian ethic is contained in this affirmation: in Christ, all things are ours, all things are *given back* to us, for in him all things — men, society, the world, life itself — rediscover their true destination. In him we can make use of all things, as he himself made use of all things in the freedom of Sonship. We can do this, so far as we are his, just as he is God's, for our total submission to God is the absolute prerequisite of our freedom in relation to men and the world.

We cannot open the Gospels without being astonished at the perfect freedom with which Jesus moves in the world of men. It is the freedom of a son who knows that all things are his Father's. If the church, the body of Christ, does not show forth in the midst of the world this glorious freedom of the sons of God, how can the world really take its message of liberation seriously? We breathe the air of this freedom in the first witnesses of the apostolic church. We breathe it anew every time the church rediscovers that the secret of true freedom lies in exclusive devotion to its Lord. And we also breathe it every time the astonished world stops long enough to listen to the church; for in this freedom, not only affirmed but actually lived, the church asks the world a question from which the world finds it more and more difficult to escape.

CHAPTER X

THE END OF TIME
(The Book of Revelation)

SUMMARY

1. THE CHURCH LIVES EXPECTANTLY

The first generation of Christians believed in the imminence of the return of the Lord (I Thess. 4:13 to 5:3; II Thess. 2:1-12; I Cor. 15:51-57; cf. Mark 13:28-30).

The place that the expectation of his coming holds in the faith of the church (Phil. 1:10-11; 2:14-18; 3:20-21; Col. 3:4; I Cor. 15:22-23; II Cor. 4:16 to 5:10; etc.). The church's attempts to explain the delay in this coming (II Peter 3:3-15). The battle will become intensified (Matt. 24:4-13; Luke 18:8).

2. THE FINAL BATTLES: "CHRISTUS VICTOR" (The Book of Revelation)

The visions of the book of Revelation must be understood as "signs" of things to come: a message of warning and comfort to the persecuted churches.

The glory of the Lamb: Christ, the Lord of the church, holds all the powers of this world and the other under his sway; no trial can harm the church without his permission. The time of the Last Judgment draws near; enemy forces ravage the earth; they will finally be wiped out forever.

After this, the glorious final victory of God and the Lamb will break forth (Rev., chs. 20 to 22; cf. I Cor. 15:24-28).

1. THE CHURCH LIVES EXPECTANTLY

The first generation of Christians, perhaps basing their hopes on certain words of Jesus himself, believed in his imminent return. We see the apostle Paul restraining the impatience of believers, and urging them to keep on working at their daily tasks. But for a long time he himself shared their conviction. (I Thess. 4:13 to 5:3; II Thess. 2: 1-12; 3:1-15; I Cor. 15:51-57; cf. Mark 13:28-30.)

Christ Has Won the Victory

Even when Paul was confronted by the possibility of his own death, the things in which he most surely believed were not threatened. The expectation of the reign of Christ remains the great hope of his life, and it is in the light of this reign that he does battle, and in the light of this wonderful " day of Christ " that he pleads with the churches to remain faithful (Phil. 1:10-11, 20-21; 2:14-18; 3:20-21; Col. 3:4; I Cor. 15:22; II Cor. 4:16 to 5:10) . The other apostolic letters reflect this same burning expectation. The fervor of this expectation makes it possible for Christians to bear up victoriously in the face of every kind of trial (I Peter 1:3-21; 2:20-25; 4:1-19; 5:8-11; II Peter 3:8; I John 3:2; Heb. 10:37-39; 12:22-29) . The more intense the battle becomes and the more the forces of antichrist are made manifest, the more also the church anchors its faith and hope in the victory of its Lord, a victory that it knows has already been won on the cross and that will soon be clearly evident to all. It is the assurance of this final victory that gives the apostolic message its objectivity, strength, and serenity, for infinitely more is involved here than personal salvation. What is involved is the triumph of the church's cause — the cause for which it suffers and struggles. What kind of violence can be done by an enemy that has been destroyed and that knows that it has been destroyed? The enemy may be able to win some apparent victories, but these will not change the final outcome of the battle one whit. In this situation, the important thing is to avoid being taken in by these tricks, and dazzled by these short-lived successes. In more positive terms, the important thing is to " hold fast," and to remain faithful to the end, come what may.

The Problem of Delay

Why does the Lord wait so long to manifest his glory, and deliver his church? Why is this coming, which was foretold by the prophets and then by Jesus himself and finally by his apostles, so long in appearing? Isn't it really just a delusion, like the great dream of a golden age that has always haunted humanity? The Bible anticipates the irony that the world exhibits before this always unfulfilled hope:

> First of all you must understand this, that scoffers will come in the last days with scoffing, following their own passions and saying, " Where is the promise of his coming? For ever since the fathers fell asleep, all things have continued as they were from the beginning of creation." (II Peter 3:3-4.)

We are all familiar with this line of reasoning. When confronted by evil that seems to be all-powerful, there are plenty of skeptics who no longer believe in the reality of God's intervention in the world, and occasionally even the hearts of believers are plagued with doubt when they are asked, " Where is your God? " (Ps. 42:10). Why does the Lord wait so long?

Second Peter answers this question by contrasting human impatience with the patience and long-suffering of God. Unbelievers choose to ignore the fact that God's judgment is a reality written into history, that he who created the world by his Word and has destroyed it once already [30] actually sustains the world by the power of this same Word — and that if he does this, it is a mark of his patience toward us.

The believers, on the other hand, forget the fact that God's times are not our times, that " with the Lord one day is as a thousand years and a thousand years as one day " (II Peter 3:8). The times of testing are short compared to the glory by which they will be followed, and if they last a long time, it is in order that all may come to repentance and salvation (II Peter 3:3-10). By the ardor of their faith and witness, believers can *hasten the day* of the coming of their Lord (II Peter 3:11-13).

Jesus had clearly indicated that the last battles would be the most terrible of all, and that these trials would be so exacting that many would succumb. His teaching has nothing in common with that easy optimism which believes in inevitable progress and the gradual transformation of this world. In the church's history, as in Israel's history, only a *remnant* may stand at the time of the great final battles. Jesus himself asks the disturbing question, " When the Son of man comes, will he find faith on earth? " (Luke 18:8). And the Gospel of Matthew, describing these battles, says:

> And then many will fall away, and betray one another, and hate one another. And many false prophets will arise and lead many astray. And because wickedness is multiplied, most men's love will grow cold. But he who endures to the end will be saved. (Matt. 24:10-13.)

In the second half of the first century, the apostolic church endured terrible persecutions, and came to know the full import of this warning from its Master. In a time of ease, our Western world had almost forgotten such things. It had trusted that the Kingdom of God would be established in this world by means of material " progress." Today we are beginning to take more seriously the stern warnings of the New Testament. But at the same time, the certainty of God's ultimate victory takes on deeper meaning.

2. THE FINAL BATTLES: "CHRISTUS VICTOR"
(The Book of Revelation)

The book of Revelation, one of the strangest and most powerful books of the Bible, was written during a time of persecution.

Warning and Comfort

This book is quite baffling to the modern reader, because its symbolism, inspired by Jewish apocalypticism, is not immediately understandable to the uninitiated. It has given rise to the dangerous speculations of the sect groups, who were eager to do exactly what their Lord had forbidden them to do, namely, to calculate the time and place of his coming. This book is strangely wonderful, however, when one fathoms its true meaning, which is both *warning* and *comfort*.

Perhaps the dangerous literalism that has plagued the history of its interpretation could have been avoided if the very first words of the seer had been taken more seriously:

> The revelation of Jesus Christ, which God gave him to show to his servants what must soon take place; and he made it known *by signs,* by sending his angel to his servant John, who bore witness to the word of God and to the testimony of Jesus Christ, even to all that he saw. (Rev. 1:1-2.) [31]

The visions of the seer of Patmos are therefore " signs " of things to come. A " sign " contains part of the reality to which it is pointing, but it does not pretend to express the fullness of that reality, and it never completely unveils the mystery to which it is pointing.

Now such things as the will of God, the world to come, the last things, and what we call " the beyond," remain

veiled in mystery to our mortal gaze. The seer of the book
of Revelation raises the veil just enough for us to be truly
comforted and also clearly warned. And then he lets the
veil fall again, for our pilgrimage here below must remain
a pilgrimage by faith and not by sight.

The Unfolding of the Visions

The book is written by an exile who suffers for his faith,
and its message is addressed to those churches which are
likewise suffering for their faith and are in danger of
abandoning the love they had at first (Rev. 2:4).

It is the Lord's Day — a Sunday. John is standing by
the seaside; he cannot worship with his fellow Christians,
and he is cut off from his brethren. And then he is trans-
ported in spirit to the threshold of heaven. A magnificent
heavenly liturgy unfolds before him. He sees the throne
of the Lord of Lords, before which all the glory of every
kingdom on earth is no more than fleeting pomp. He is
present at the enthronement of the Lamb. (Rev., chs. 4; 5.)

For the rest of the book, the visions of judgment and
grace follow one another in an ordered pattern. It is revealed to John that war, famine, and pestilence will ravage
the earth. Power is temporarily given to the forces of
death, but only temporarily. John hears the wails of the
martyrs, and they are promised that their deliverance will
come soon. The angel of God marks the 144,000 righteous
of Israel with a seal,[82] and the multitudes of all tongues
and all races sing to the glory of the Lamb. (Rev., chs. 6; 7.)

New visions of judgment unfold, interrupted by a new
song of praise to the triumphant Christ. (Rev., chs. 8 to
11.) Chapter 12 symbolically describes Christ's victory
over Satan (the dragon) and the trials that the church
(the woman) must still undergo for a while. During this
time the world is subjected to the reign of the beast. The
beast governs the people, and it has such control over com-
merce that no one can buy or sell unless he has the mark

of the beast on his hand (Rev., ch. 13). But at the very
moment when the power of the beast seems to have reached
a paroxysm, the Lamb appears on Mt. Zion and gathers in
all the redeemed (Rev. 14:1-5). The eternal gospel is proclaimed once more to all the inhabitants of the earth
(Rev. 14:6-7) before the final harvest (Rev. 14:14-20).
The song of Moses and the song of the Lamb burst forth
from heaven. (Rev. 15:1-4.) Then seven angels pour out
on the earth the seven bowls of the wrath of God, and
Babylon, the city that symbolizes the idolatrous worship
of the state and the reign of antichrist, is finally destroyed.
(Rev., chs. 15 to 18.) We are present at the marriage supper of the Lamb. (Rev. 19:6-10.) The dragon is chained
for a thousand years. Christ shares this " reign of a thousand years " with the faithful church. At the end of a
thousand years, Satan is unbound and conquered in a final
and decisive battle. It is the Last Judgment. Death and the
Abode of the Dead are swallowed up forever.

God's reign is now under way: " Then I saw a new
heaven and a new earth; for the first heaven and the first
earth had passed away, and the sea was no more " (Rev.
21:1). The City of God appears in all its glorious splendor:
the Lord is its temple and the Lamb is its torch. The River
of Life flows there freely, and the leaves of the Tree of Life
serve " for the healing of the nations " (Rev. 22:2; cf. Gen.
3:22).

The book concludes with the church's cry of expectation and hope: " Come, Lord Jesus! " (Rev. 22:20).

The Assurance of God's Victory

What does it all mean? The basic affirmation that stands
out in this book is the assurance of *God's final and absolute
victory.*

At a time when bloody persecutions endanger the very
existence of the church, the seer of Patmos reminds the
church that the Lord is he " who *is* and who *was* and who

is to come " (Rev. 1:4) , and that all the evil forces of this world, no matter how strong they may seem to be, are doomed.

God's total victory presupposes either the submission of the opposing forces or their final destruction. The forces of death still retain a certain power, even after the victory of the cross. But the seer of the book of Revelation emphasizes the fact that this power is not autonomous: it exists because God permits it to exist. Even more strongly, it is on God's order that the plagues burst forth on the earth. The Lamb presides at the opening of the seven seals. The calamities unfold in accordance with God's will. Angels carry out his commands. They are also the ones who mark the elect so that no evil will befall them, and who see to it that the eternal gospel of grace is proclaimed to all the earth before the Final Judgment. Thus these times of testing are conceived as a final call to a rebellious world. Everyone will have a chance to declare himself for or against God, to accept or to reject his salvation (Rev. 14: 6-7) . And this time Christ's reign will not come in a secret and hidden manner; his sovereignty will manifest itself before all men: " Every eye will see [the Lord], every one who pierced him " (Rev. 1:7) . And, as he promised, those who have suffered with him will take part in his reign and in his judgment (Dan. 12:1-3; Luke 22:28-30; II Tim. 2:11-12; Rev., chs. 7; 14:1-5; 20:1-6) .

This is surely the real meaning of the intermediate " reign of a thousand years " that has given rise to so many different interpretations. It marks the culmination of the long Messianic expectation, and in it the Lord shares his glory with the church that served and loved him.

But the " reign of a thousand years " is still not the end of the matter. For in God's eternal purposes the work of salvation results in *the resurrection of the world*. And this is why the last chapter of the book of Revelation shows us a picture of the new heavens and the new earth foretold by the prophets (Isa. 65:17). The description of the City of God is clearly full of symbolism, for God's world cannot 'be described in human language. But it must be emphasized that this Kingdom has nothing abstract or unreal about it. It is not some pale paradise peopled by pure spirits, but a world watered by the great River of Life, which flows forth from the throne of God and the Lamb.

Until the very end, however, the book of Revelation sets darkness and light against each other. Death will be swallowed up (Rev. 20:14; cf. Isa. 25:8; I Cor. 15:26, 54-56) in man's destruction, but Satan will carry along all who belong to him (Rev. 20:11-15; 21:8; 22:12).

Judgment and Grace

The terror of judgment echoes and re-echoes like a formidable warning through the entire book of Revelation, and indeed through the entire Bible. When confronted by this, there is one question that unfailingly comes to our lips: Are some persons eternally *lost?* The Bible will not permit us to give a clear and precise answer to this question, for the Bible itself does not give that kind of answer.

The Bible does say, however, that divine justice is real, and that it is a fearful thing to fall into the hands of the Living God. God is not mocked. His judgment seat is a reality. We will have to stand before it.

But the Bible also says that it is God's will that all men be saved and come to the knowledge of the Truth (I Tim. 2:3-4). It is in order to accomplish this eternal purpose that God has called us into being and has sent his Son so that, by the power of his grace, he might draw all men to himself (John 12:32). In him we are *all predestined to life, to receive the gift of salvation.*

The whole meaning of the Christian life is found in the tension between these two affirmations just stated. It is a life of serious, but also joyful, tremulousness before the

wonder of God's gift. To fall outside the activity of the
grace in which Christ has placed us is always a frightening
possibility, since our pilgrimage is not finished (Phil. 3:
12-16; I Cor. 9:24-27). There is a sin against the Holy
Spirit (Mark 3:28-30), but it is never a sin done in ignorance. It is rather a deliberate rejection of the grace we
have received. (Heb. 6:4-8.) And precisely because it is
not we who possess God but God who possesses us, to the
very degree that we live by his grace alone, we can trust
ourselves to him in full and joyful confidence, knowing
that he will bring to completion that which he has already
started. His eternal love is our peace and our security.
(Rom. 8:31-39; cf. Phil. 1:3-6; I Thess. 5:23-24; etc.)

Henceforth, the attitude of the believer toward those
who do not know God will be before all else a sense of responsibility. He must proclaim God's unfolding purpose of
salvation to them. This is precisely the task of the whole
church militant. Anyone who keeps the message of grace
just for himself shows by that very action that he does not
really love, and that he is still dead. The gospel is most explicit about this. (I John 3:16-17; 4:7-21.)

But secondly, the attitude of the believer will be a calm,
firm conviction that God loves the souls of those for whom
he is concerned infinitely more than the believer is able to
love them. Anyone who has been the object of the miraculous grace of God waits for the *fullness* of that grace, knowing that his God is the God who raises from the dead. He
knows that the last can be first at the heavenly banquet. He
looks forward with prayer and faith to the day when the
glory of the Lamb will convert the hardest hearts and will
take them subdued and conquered before the very throne
of God. He lives in the faith that the last word about the
world in which he lives will be that of victorious love.

Strong in this assurance, the believer can submit without
wavering to the assaults of the enemy, for the dragon has
already been dealt a mortal blow. He may indeed continue

to ravage the earth, but he is in his final death throes, lashing his vicious tail for the last time, and doing it the more furiously since he knows that he is defeated.

To be aware of all this does not mean being less concerned about the immediate conflicts of the present. But it means seeing beyond these conflicts and putting them in their proper perspective. For the great crises of history are like forerunners of the final struggle. Their rhythm is the same: wars, famines, persecutions. The church must again and again be sifted like wheat, and — to change the figure — purified and tempered in the fire of testing. For the "world" is not just a power outside the church. It is at work in the church as well, attempting to destroy it from within, to rend it asunder. The events of history must always remind the church of something that can easily be forgotten when things are "going well," namely, that its calling remains that of the Suffering Servant, exposed to the assaults of the enemy. It is the calling to be "in" the world and not "of" it (John 17:15-16), with all the tensions that this implies.

All through this ongoing battle against the powers of evil, the church lives under the sign of the resurrection of its Lord and in the expectation of his final manifestation: "Heaven and earth *will pass away,* but *my words will not pass away*" (Matt. 24:35).

The depth of the faith and hope by which the church lives is measured by the degree of conviction with which it waits for its Lord, the joyful assurance with which it believes in and proclaims his reign, and the constancy with which it prays for his coming and testifies to the present reality of his redeeming power (Matt. 6:10; Rev. 22:17).

EPILOGUE

"NEW HEAVENS AND A NEW EARTH"

HE who has an ear, let him hear what the Spirit says to the churches. To him who conquers I will grant to eat of the tree of life, which is in the paradise of God. — Rev. 2:7.

CHAPTER XI

EPILOGUE

"New Heavens and a New Earth"

The history of salvation, as was pointed out in the Preface, takes place between two visions that constitute the prologue and the epilogue to the human drama. These visions were described as the vision of paradise lost and the vision of the City of God, or as the vision of what could have been and the vision of what will be when the redemptive work of God has been finished. But we immediately went on to add that these two visions are like two beacons that illuminate everything that lies in between them.

We have seen, indeed, in the course of our pilgrimage through what tradition rightly calls "salvation-history," that the expectation of God's reign is what gives this history its real meaning from beginning to end. Patriarchs and prophets have "seen it and greeted it from afar" (Heb. 11:13). In Jesus, the Kingdom has drawn near to men, and the church has received a foretaste of it. Henceforth, it waits with unshaken confidence for "new heavens and a new earth in which righteousness dwells" (II Peter 3:13; cf. also Isa. 65:17).

The final pages of the Bible try to describe this coming glory. The word "try" is used advisedly, for human language is no more than stammering when one is trying to describe eternal realities. All sorts of images are employed. The New Jerusalem has the splendor of precious stones. It is pure and transcendent gold. Darkness has been swallowed up by light. There is no more night. " And the city has no need of sun or moon to shine upon it, for the glory of God is its light, and its lamp is the Lamb." (Rev. 21:23.) The nations bring their glory to it (Rev. 21:24), and the entrance to the Tree of Life is reopened for them (Rev. 22:1-2; cf. Gen. 3:22).

What does this " glory of the Lamb " mean?

The mystery of the Lamb is the mystery of self-giving love, the mystery of God himself. This is the love that governs every moment of world history. It is the love that inspires God's creative act of calling the world into being. It is the love that inspires all of his subsequent gracious acts throughout the course of history, until the final act that will destroy the last manifestations of death and inaugurate the reign of victorious love.

Jesus Christ is the Lamb without blemish and spot, " destined *before the foundation of the world* " (I Peter 1:19-20) to reveal to men, by his voluntary sacrifice, God's unfolding purpose of salvation on their behalf, and the infinite love with which they have been loved.

Thus the great drama of human freedom is completed by God's victory. His love, which gives itself without limit, succeeds in creating the response that it seeks, but that it could never force without betraying itself. God's love calls into being a new humanity, free and freely offering itself, a humanity made " *in the image of God.*"

This humanity will at last be able to see its Lord face to face, to understand fully even as it has been fully understood. (I Cor. 13:12.)

" WE SHALL BE LIKE HIM, FOR WE SHALL SEE HIM AS HE IS."
(I John 3:2.)

NOTES

PREFACE

1. Readers who are interested in these problems may be referred to such works as the following:

    a. For Old Testament historical background in the light of recent archaeological discoveries, one may consult:

        W. F. Albright, "The Biblical Period," in Finkelstein, ed., *The Jews: Their History, Culture and Religion*. Harper & Brothers, 1949.

        G. Ernest Wright and Floyd V. Filson, *The Westminster Historical Atlas to the Bible* (Revised Edition). The Westminster Press, 1956.

        The Interpreter's Bible, Vol. 1. Abingdon Press, 1952.

        D. Baly, *Multitudes in the Valley*. The Seabury Press, Inc.

        B. Anderson, *Understanding the Old Testament*. Prentice-Hall, Inc., 1957.

    b. On the New Testament:

        A. M. Hunter, *The Message of the New Testament*. The Westminster Press, 1944.

        C. H. Dodd, *The Apostolic Preaching*.

        E. Hoskyns, *The Riddle of the New Testament*. Faber & Faber, Ltd., London.

        H. Kee and F. Young, *Understanding the New Testament*. Prentice-Hall, Inc., 1957.

c. On the message of the whole Bible:

John Bright, *The Kingdom of God*. Abingdon Press, 1953.

Oscar Cullmann, *Christ and Time*. The Westminster Press, 1950.

C. H. Dodd, *The Bible Today*. The Macmillan Company, 1947.

J. Marsh, *The Fulness of Time*. Harper & Brothers, 1953.

Pierson Parker, *Inherit the Promise*. The Seabury Press, Inc., 1957.

W. Vischer, *The Witness of the Old Testament to Christ*. Lutterworth Press, London, 1949.

d. Commentaries for laymen:

The " Torch " series. S.C.M. Press, Ltd., London.

The Layman's Bible Commentary (ed. Kelly and Miller). John Knox Press.

PROLOGUE

Chapter I. The Creation and the Fall

2. The Hebraic Old Testament is divided into three main parts:

a. *The Torah or Law:* Genesis, Exodus, Leviticus, Numbers, Deuteronomy (the Pentateuch).

b. *The Prophets,* which contain two parts: the Former Prophets (Joshua, Judges, I and II Samuel, I and II Kings), and the Latter Prophets (Isaiah, Jeremiah, Ezekiel, and the twelve Minor Prophets, i.e., from Hosea through Malachi).

c. *The Writings:* Psalms (in five parts), Proverbs, Job, Song of Solomon, Ruth, Lamentations, Ecclesiastes, Esther, Daniel, Ezra, Nehemiah, I and II Chronicles.

It is obvious that the order of the books is different from that adopted in our English versions (which follow the order of the Greek version of the Septuagint, produced by a group of Jewish scholars in Alexandria). The order of books in the Hebraic Old Testament is much more logical than ours.

The Law (Torah) came to have a unique authority in Judaism. Jewish tradition in the time of Jesus considered it as dictated by Moses. Actually it contains many ancient sources. Some cycles of tales were probably written down for the first time by the prophetic schools of the ninth and eight centuries B.C. Others were written down much later, but contained ancient material (Deuteronomy and the " Holiness Code "), and the final editing probably dates from the time of Ezra, i.e., the fifth century B.C.

The first *historical books* are the work of the prophetic schools of the eighth to the sixth century B.C. (Judges, I and II Samuel, I and II Kings). They are included among the prophetic writings because they give us a prophetic interpretation of history.

The Writings are more clearly works of piety. The Psalms are the five books of Israel's songs, and tradition attributes them in large part to King David himself. The Song of Solomon, Ruth, Lamentations, Ecclesiastes, and Esther were read at the five great Jewish festival days in the church year. The collection of these Writings dates from a much later time — the fifth to the third century, or perhaps even the second century B.C.

When there are references in the New Testament to " the law and the prophets " (Matt. 5:17) or to " the law of Moses and the prophets and the psalms " (Luke 24:44), these terms stand for the whole of Scripture, i.e., what we today call the Old Testament.

3. The *name* plays a very important role in the Biblical tradition, as well as in all antiquity. It tells us what the person is like. To know the name of a person or a thing is to have authority over it. This is why God's name is hidden, and why " a new name . . . which no one knows " (Rev. 2:17) will be given to the elect at the time of the new creation.

4. " God created man . . ." " Man " is here understood in its generic sense, as when, for example, we talk about " man's destiny on earth." For a further treatment of the image of God as the human couple, see Bonhoeffer, *Creation and Fall* (The Macmillan Company, 1959) , especially pp. 33–38. Barth, *Kirchliche Dogmatik,* III, 2, develops the point in great detail.

PART ONE

Chapter II. The Promise

5. How should we understand these ancient stories? They were handed down from generation to generation for centuries before being written down. Their historical accuracy is of secondary importance: they express *more* than the experiences of just one or a few individuals, namely, Israel's soul, the basic realities of its life, its faith, and its struggles. The ancestors embody the faith by which Israel lives but also the temptations to which again and again it succumbs.

Thus the ancestral stories become the medium through which Israel is reminded of its high calling, of God's gracious promises and stern demands. They are charged with theological meaning.

6. W. Vischer, *The Witness of the Old Testament to Christ*, p. 141.

7. The word "righteousness" is of utmost importance in both Testaments. The root of the Hebrew word is a concept of relationship. God's "righteousness" is revealed in his faithfulness to the covenant he has initiated with his people. He freely restores and maintains the relationship that man's revolt has broken. Man can only accept the outstretched hand and enter trustfully into the graciously offered relationship. And this trust is reckoned by God as righteousness. Of course, it implies obedience.

Israel's story (and ours) is a sad story of repeated breaks in this God-given relationship. When this happens, God's righteousness reveals itself in judgment. But the ultimate goal of judgment itself is the restoration of the right relationship.

Only in Christ is the full requirement of this relationship met, and this is why he is "our righteousness" (I Cor. 1:30).

The so-called "righteous" in the Old Testament (see The Psalms) are not morally perfect people, but men who trust God and stand in a relationship of faith and humility to him.

It should be noted that in this perspective God's "justice" is a manifestation of his Holy Love.

Chapter III. The Covenant at Sinai

8. Perhaps a few historical observations are called for here. The history of the people of God is set beside that of the great empires that, from about 3000 B.C., struggled for control of the East. Because of its geographical location Palestine was destined to be the scene of many invasions. But such is God's way of doing things that the vicissitudes of history actually contribute to the strengthening of his people, and give them the delays necessary for the fulfillment of their destiny.

From 3000 to 1926 B.C., the Babylonian civilization dominated the East and extended its influence as far as Syria. Abraham, it will be remembered, originally came from Ur of the Chaldees. The Code of Hammurabi (2000 B.C.) may have influenced certain points of Mosaic legislation, and in any case has certain similarities with it. In 1926 B.C., Babylonia was destroyed by the Hittites, and went into eclipse for thirteen hundred years. (We shall see it play a major role once more at the end of the seventh century B.C.)

Soon the Egyptian civilization was supreme throughout the East. The nomadic tribes of Israel, forced into Egypt by famine, seem to have lived there, free and protected under the Semitic Hyksos dynasty. But in 1600 B.C. the Hyksos dynasty was defeated and the Israelites experienced much more difficult conditions. Then the exodus took place. Invasions from the north drove the Egyptians out of Palestine and Syria in the twelfth century B.C., and among these Northern tribes were the Philistines, born enemies of Israel. The weakening of Egypt gave the smaller nations of Palestine and Syria four centuries of respite (marked, of course, by constant internal warfare) until the time when the massive Assyrian invasions began. It is during these four centuries that the history of Israel is described as that of a free people, from its arrival in the Promised Land to the conquest of the Northern Kingdom by the Assyrian Empire in 722 B.C. (cf. A. Lods, *Israel from Its Beginnings to the Middle of the Eighth Century* B.C.; Alfred A. Knopf., Inc., 1932).

The four books that are the basis for the present chapter tell us how Moses delivered Israel from Egyptian slavery and led

it through the wilderness to the threshold of the Promised
Land. The central event of this period is the covenant at Sinai
and the giving of the law. This law is given to us as though it
had been fully formulated in the time of Moses. Moses remains
in Israel's memory as the one who established Israel's existence
as a people and gave it the law. We see him proclaiming God's
justice (Ex. 18:13-16), we see him engrave the law of God on
two tablets of stone, and this in itself proves that the commandments must have been quite brief! It is incontestably Moses
who established the foundations of law and order in Israel and
promulgated the law in God's name. On the other hand, it
would be an anachronism to attribute to him the whole of a
legislative code, which took centuries to grow and which reflects radically differing social conditions in various of its parts.
Most critics today agree in recognizing that Deuteronomy is a
work of the seventh century B.C., and some would date it even
later, while Leviticus and Numbers in their present form are
believed to be the work of the postexilic priestly school (fifth
to fourth centuries B.C.). All these books contain ancient material, the editing of which took place at a later time.

In a strictly chronological study of the history of salvation,
the study of the priestly laws ought to be postponed until the
postexilic period, in which they were fully developed (cf.
Ezra). We have preferred to approach the problem of the law
in its totality at the point where the Bible itself raises the
issue, i.e., in direct relation to the covenant at Sinai.

9. Calvin, John, Commentaries on the Four Last Books of
Moses, Arranged in the Form of a Harmony, translated by
Charles William Bingham (Wm. B. Eerdmans Publishing
Company, 1950), p. 44.

10. In the Bible, numbers often have a symbolic meaning.
For example, seven is the perfect number: the creation was
completed in seven days, the number seven plays a considerable part in the cultic regulations, and we find it again in the
book of Revelation. The number forty seems to correspond to
a period of testing in which God both proves his elect and reveals himself to them. The downpour of the Flood lasts forty
days. Moses is exiled in Midian for forty years. Moses struggles " forty days and forty nights " to obtain God's pardon for

his guilty people (Deut. 9:18-25). Israel walks forty years through the wilderness. (Deut. 8:2.) Elijah's journey in the wilderness lasts forty days. (I Kings 19:8.) Jesus' temptation in the wilderness also lasts forty days (Matt. 4:2) ; etc.

11. A. Lods, *op. cit.,* p. 323.

12. W. Vischer, *op. cit.,* p. 170.

13. For a full treatment of the mystery of election, particularly as it is related to Jesus Christ, see K. Barth, *Church Dogmatics,* II, 2 (Charles Scribner's Sons, 1958).

14. The number seven, and its multiples, represents a perfect number, just as the number twelve does. The Jewish tradition thought that there were seventy nations on earth. The number twelve usually stands for *all* Israel — the twelve tribes, the twelve apostles, cf. the twelve pillars (Ex. 24:4). The number seventy usually stands for *all* the nations (cf. the mission of the Twelve and of the Seventy, Luke 9:1-6; 10:1-20). See further note 10.

15. The worship of the Israelites in the desert apparently did not include the fast described in Ex., chs. 35 to 40, which reflects a much later situation.

16. W. Vischer, *op. cit.,* p. 218.

Chapter IV. The Promised Land

17. Under the title " Former Prophets " we find the following books: Joshua, Judges, I and II Samuel, I and II Kings (cf. note 2). A good many historians think that on account of its form and content The Book of Joshua was not originally a part of the cycle of prophetic books, but was part of the Law (Torah). It makes use of the same sources as the five books of the Law. It is a logical conclusion to the books of the Law, since in it the Israelites are brought into the Promised Land. The covenant at Sinai is renewed at Shechem. Those scholars who suggest that the books of the Law were drafted by Ezra and sent by him to the king of Persia have put forth the hypothesis that in doing this Ezra omitted The Book of Joshua for reasons of political expediency.

The Book of Judges describes the settlement of the Israelite tribes in Palestine, and the struggles they went through to maintain the freedom they had gained. Except for Abimalek, who crowned himself king on his own authority at Shechem and does not seem to have counted among the judges, there remains a total of twelve judges up to, but not including, Samuel. The two books of Samuel (which originally were only one) describe the establishment of the monarchy. The cycle of stories dealing with Saul and David has wonderful precision and brilliance, and is certainly the work of a contemporary witness. The exact dates within it are extremely difficult to ascertain. If we begin with the date of the division of the ten tribes (ca. 935 B.C.), we can establish the date of David's reign at about 1000 B.C., for his reign and Solomon's are said to have lasted forty years each.

The first eleven chapters of Kings are devoted solely to Solomon's glorious (and also vainglorious) reign. Then the division of the ten tribes creates a fatal break. The books of I and II Kings tell the story of the two kingdoms side by side until the disappearance of the Northern Kingdom in 722 B.C., and then tell the history of the Kingdom of Judah until its disappearance in 586 B.C.

18. The tribe of Benjamin has a special place in the Biblical revelation. Benjamin is the favorite son of Jacob, and the only one who was born in the Promised Land. It is said of his tribe:

> Benjamin is a ravenous wolf,
> in the morning devouring the prey,
> and at even dividing the spoil.
>
> (Gen. 49:27.)

The Book of Judges (chs. 19 to 21) describes the frightful war of extermination that the tribe of Benjamin incited by violating the laws of hospitality. The victim is a Bethlehemite, and the guilty ones are inhabitants of Gibeah. The first king of Israel is a Benjaminite of Gibeah, but he is rejected in favor of the Bethlehemite, David, and the strife between these two houses is intense. After the division of the tribes, the territory of Benjamin becomes part of the Kingdom of Judah, and its descendants boast that they represent the purest Israelite tradition. Saul of Tarsus, for example, is proud of the fact that he is " of the tribe of Benjamin " (Phil. 3:5).

19. We are told in II Kings, chs. 22; 23, that *the book of the Law* was discovered in the Temple and read to King Josiah,

and that when he had heard the words of the book he rent his clothes (II Kings 22:11). He had the book read to all the people of Jerusalem, and renewed the covenant. Then he had all the idols and all the other objects dedicated to pagan worship cleaned out of the Temple. He also abolished the " high places," i.e., all the sanctuaries in the country.

What was this book, the reading of which led to such radical reforms? Most historians today agree that it must have been Deuteronomy. Jeremiah, who was present at the event under discussion, supported the reform, but was quickly forced to recognize that its influence was not very great and that it did not change the course of history. He makes only a brief reference to it (Jer., ch. 11).

Chapter V. The Exile

20. The section of the Hebraic Bible entitled " Latter Prophets " contains the works of three " Major " and twelve " Minor " Prophets. The terms " Major " and "Minor " refer only to the length of the books.

The preaching of the prophets takes the form of predictions or " oracles." The language is rhythmic, and must frequently have originated in songs of lamentation. Historical material is often interpolated into the writings of the prophets, material that is generally the work of a later redactor, and occasionally does no more than repeat the ideas found in I and II Kings.

Are all the poems in a given book by the same person? Here again the critics have come to the conclusion that there are many instances of composite authorship. For example, The Book of Isaiah can be divided into two distinct parts: chs. 1 to 39 are by Isaiah, the son of Amoz, a prophet of the eighth century B.C., while chs. 40 to 55, in a very different style, proclaim the restoration of Judah by Cyrus, and must have been written during the exile, i.e., toward the middle of the sixth century B.C. Certain portions of the book are probably even later (e.g., Isa., chs. 55 to 66, and chs. 24 to 27).

Why have all these poems been attributed to one person? The author of what is called " Second Isaiah " or " Deutero-Isaiah " is unknown. Was it the inspiration of his work, the stress placed upon the holiness of God, or the Messianic element in his prophecies that caused his work to be attached to that of his illustrious predecessor? We cannot be sure. However, the unity of the *message* of The Book of Isaiah is much more significant than the centuries that divide its various parts.

We have already noted the fact (cf. note 2) that in the Hebrew Bible The Book of Daniel is not classified among the prophetic books. It is from a much later period and is an example of apocalyptic writing. We will discuss it in the next chapter.

The following chronology will make it possible to place the activity of the prophets in their historical setting:

Eighth Century B.C.

783–743 — Reign of Jeroboam II, King of Israel. Preaching of *Amos* and *Hosea* in the Northern Kingdom

740 — Death of Uzziah, King of Judah. Beginning of the ministry of *Isaiah* (ca. 740–700 B.C.) and *Micah,* in the Kingdom of Judah

738 — Syro-Ephraimitic war against Judah

734 — Assyrian invasion. Israel and Judah under Assyrian control

724–722 — Siege of Samaria. End of the Kingdom of Israel

720 — Hezekiah succeeds Ahaz on the throne of Judah

701 — Siege of Jerusalem by Sennacherib. Isaiah promises deliverance, and the siege is lifted

Seventh Century B.C.

692–638 — Reign of Manassah and Amon. Judah remains under Assyrian control

638 — Josiah's succession to the throne

627 — Beginning of *Jeremiah's* ministry. Preaching of *Zephaniah*

625 — Scythian invasion. Weakening of Assyria

621 — Josiah's reforms (Deuteronomy). *Nahum* (ca. 612?)

609 — Death of Josiah at Megiddo. Judah comes under Egyptian control

605 — The king of Babylon defeats Egypt at Carchemish

604 — Jeremiah dictates his prophecies to Baruch

Sixth Century B.C.

597 — Capture of Jerusalem by Nebuchadnezzar. First deportation

593 — Beginning of *Ezekiel's* ministry (593–571)

586 — Second deportation. End of *Jeremiah's* ministry. *Habakkuk* (?)

550–538 — Editing of Isaiah, chs. 40 to 55

538 — Edict of Cyrus, authorizing the return of the exiles. Beginning of Persian domination

520 — Prophecies of *Haggai* and *Zechariah,* chs. 1 to 8 (and probably Isaiah, chs. 55 to 66)

Fifth Century B.C.

Obadiah
Malachi
Joel (?)

Fourth or Third Century B.C.

Isaiah, chs. 24 to 27 (?)
Zechariah, chs. 9 to 14 (?)

Question marks indicate that dates are uncertain and controversial. Cf. A. Lods, *The Prophets and the Rise of Judaism* (Kegan Paul, London, 1937), pp. xii-xiii, for a convenient summary of the chronology of the period, which is developed in detail in the main body of the book.

21. See further on this, note 7.

Chapter VI. The Remnant of Israel

22. Flavius Josephus, *Antiquities of the Jews,* translated by Whiston (Henry G. Bohn, London, 1862), p. 441.

23. The period of the exile and the centuries that follow it are times of intense literary activity, but now we have *priestly* literature instead of prophetic. The priests endeavor to reconstitute the history of the rites and customs of Israel. In all probability, what we call the " Holiness Code " (Lev., chs. 17 to 26) dates from the end of the exile. It is closely related to the work of Ezekiel. A little later what the critics call the " Priestly document " is worked out; it picks up and supplements the traditional ideas about the origins of Israel, and the

Mosaic legislation, by emphasizing the ritualistic element. The present Pentateuch results from the fusion of the Priestly document with the older documents of the prophetic school and the book of Deuteronomy (cf. note 2). Some scholars think that the law that Ezra read publicly was the " Holiness Code," while others believe that it was the Pentateuch in its present form.

The same priestly influence can be seen in the editing of the books of I and II Chronicles, which retrace the history of the Kingdom of Judah, i.e., the house of David. These books retell, and expand at certain points, the materials in I and II Samuel and I and II Kings. The books of Ezra and Nehemiah describe the history of the restoration.

We have already noted that the other writings contained in the third part of the Hebraic Bible date from this postexilic epoch (cf. note 2). We can only mention them briefly.

We have already seen that tradition attributed a major portion of The Psalms to David, but that they date for the most part from the postexilic period. They seem originally to have been songs that were meant to be sung or recited in the temple ceremonies and adapted to many kinds of situations: songs of thanksgiving, supplication, and grief, as well as pilgrim songs, which the pilgrims sang on their journeys. These songs expressed the faith of the community, but they left a large place for individual piety, and expressed its hopes, struggles, and assurances.

The book of Proverbs, attributed to Solomon, is a collection of aphorisms. In it, the book of creation opens before our eyes. We see Wisdom presiding at the creation of the world, and the very mention of Wisdom reminds the Christian of the prologue to the Fourth Gospel (compare Prov., ch. 8, and John, ch. 1). Jesus Christ is " our wisdom " as well as our righteousness (I Cor. 1:24-30; 2:6-8).

The Book of Job probably originates in an ancient tradition that makes Job a representation of righteousness (cf. Ezek. 14:14), who resists every attempt of the adversary (signified by Satan) to turn him away from God. This legend becomes the basis for a powerful poem in which the true nature of faith is portrayed.

People today often wonder why the five books listed below are in the Bible at all. The answer is that they had an important place in *the liturgy of the great Jewish festivals:*

The Song of Solomon is a wedding song; it was read during the Passover festival (Deut. 16:1-8, cf. Ex., ch. 13).

The Book of Ruth was read at the Feast of Weeks, i.e., the festival of the first fruits of the harvest — Pentecost (Ex. 34:22; Num. 28:26; Deut. 16:9-12).

The Lamentations of Jeremiah was read at the time of the commemoration of the destruction of Jerusalem.

Ecclesiastes, which tradition attributes to Solomon, was read at the Feast of Tabernacles, or the festival of the harvest (Deut. 16:13-15; Lev. 23:39-43; Neh. 9:13-18), a recalling of the time when Israel lived in tents. Ought not this book to remind them of the vanity of worldly goods?

The Book of Esther, written in a time of persecution, was read at the Feast of Purim, instituted in the second century B.C. by the Jews of the Dispersion.

The Book of Daniel dates from the Maccabean period. Daniel's name is mentioned in Ezek. 14:14, and except for this we have no information about him. Was he a real or a fictitious person? We are not sure, but it doesn't really matter. The account makes him a hero of the Babylonian captivity; he and his friends symbolize the faithful church in time of persecution.

24. The books of I and II Maccabees are not included in the canon of the Hebrew Bible. They are among the books sometimes referred to as the Apocrypha. These were introduced in the Greek translation of the Jews of Alexandria (the Septuagint), and from there they made their way into the Latin translation. Today they are found in certain Lutheran versions and in all Roman Catholic Bibles.

PART TWO

Introduction

25. The witness of the apostolic church was above all the *preaching* of the " good news," and this good news or " gospel '

is that Jesus of Nazareth, crucified under Pontius Pilate, is the Christ of God, the Messiah proclaimed throughout Scripture, the true King of Israel. The oral preaching is supplemented by letters, by means of which the apostles continue the instruction of the newly organized communities. The church lives in the expectation of the Lord's return. Only when the first generation of Christians begins to die is much attention paid to getting the words of the Lord down in written form, and bringing together the recollections of those who had been eyewitnesses of Jesus' earthly ministry, death, and resurrection. This is the way the Gospels came into being.

In the order in which they appear in the Bible, the New Testament writings can be grouped in three categories: (1) The witnesses dealing with the historic facts that are at the foundation of the apostolic faith, i.e., the four Gospels and The Acts of the Apostles. (2) Instruction dealing with various matters of doctrine and conduct, i.e., the Letters, some of which are real theological treatises (Romans and Hebrews), while others are merely brief notes. (3) The book of Revelation must be put in a third category. This is a prophetic book that occupies a place in the New Testament similar to that of Daniel in the Old Testament. It is a vision of the " last days," which will precede the inauguration of God's reign.

Chronologically, the earliest *written* documents that we possess are the letters of Paul. The two letters to the Thessalonians date from about the year A.D. 50, and the rest of the Pauline letters were written during the next eight to twelve years.

It is generally conceded that the Gospel of Mark, in its present form, was written before the year A.D. 70, that the Gospels of Matthew and Luke were written several years later, and that the Gospel of John was written toward the end of the first century.

Matthew and Luke both follow the historical outline of Mark, which they both reproduce nearly in its entirety, but they introduce certain other material into their accounts. They probably made use of a collection of Sayings of Jesus, which had been in circulation for some time in the churches. Moreover, each one had private sources available to him, either oral or written, such as infancy narratives, resurrection narratives, and accounts of the journey of Jesus to Jerusalem (see, for example, Luke, chs. 10 to 18, in which there are a great number of parables found only in Luke) .

The purpose of the Evangelists is to witness to the fact that Jesus is the Christ, the Son of God. They do not try to say everything that could be said, but to bring together the facts and the most important witnesses. Their choice of material is influenced by the purpose that they set for themselves and the readers to whom their writings are addressed.

The Gospel of Matthew is written to appeal to the Jewish mentality. It makes constant use of the Old Testament to show that Jesus came to fulfill all that was predicted about the Messiah. Its version of the Sermon on the Mount stresses the fact that Jesus fulfilled the Law and the Prophets. It alone mentions the fact that the Twelve are first of all sent exclusively to Israel (Matt. 10:5). But it also states Israel's guilt more strongly than the other Gospels. (Matt., chs. 23; 27:6-25.)

The Gospel of Luke, written to appeal to the Greek mentality, gives less attention to the things that are related to Jewish customs and traditions, and stresses the universalistic note of the Gospel.

The Gospel of John, written later, shows great independence of earlier sources; on certain points it seems to have wished to fill in missing details and even to correct them. The earlier Biblical criticism called its historical accuracy into question, but contemporary historians of note have corrected this hasty judgment. The Fourth Gospel is a theological work of notable power, and shows the marks of the style and thought of its author much more clearly than the three Synoptic Gospels do.

We shall not attempt in this present study to deal with the matter of the " sources," i.e., an attempt to disengage the words of Jesus from their context. This kind of attempt is never more than a hypothesis. Our faith is based on the witness of the whole apostolic church. It is in the basic unity of this witness, under its apparent diversity, that we recognize the work of the Holy Spirit. For all New Testament writings have but one purpose, which is to attest that Jesus is indeed the Messiah proclaimed throughout Scripture, the Prophet, the King and the Priest of the New Covenant, the Son of God, and to show that in him God's eternal purpose for the salvation of the world is fulfilled.

Chapter VII. The Incarnation

26. Alan Richardson points out in *The Miracle-Stories of the Gospels* (Harper & Brothers, n.d.), pp. 81–90, that there is a deliberate parallelism in Mark, chs. 6 to 8, between the actual blindness and deafness of the ill whom Jesus heals and the blindness and deafness of the disciples. The disciples also have to have their blindness cured, and this is what happens at the moment when Peter confesses his Master (Mark 8:29-30).

The Gospel of John sees the miracles of healing as living parables of the spiritual deliverance that, within its pages, is always a passage from death to life, from darkness to light (cf. John 1:4-9; 3:19-21; 9:5; I John 1:5-7).

27. The Biblical word translated in our versions as "fox" seems, in certain cases at least, to refer rather to the jackal (Ps. 63:10; Ezek. 13:4). The two animals have in common the fact that they feed on corpses. The characteristic of the fox is slyness. The moral significance of the two words is practically the same.

28. Pascal, *Pensées*, No. 792.

PART THREE

Chapter IX. The Mystery of the Church

29. See further in this connection footnote 7.

Chapter X. The End of Time

30. In II Peter, ch. 2, there seems to be a deliberate opposition between destruction by water (v. 5) and destruction by fire (vs. 7, 10, 12). The sea, the great abyss, is the symbol of the forces of evil; it is from the sea that evil power comes forth (Rev. 13:1). God, on the contrary, is represented throughout the Bible in the guise of *fire* (Gen. 15:17; Ex. 3:3; 19:18; Luke 12:49; Acts 2:3). The forces of evil would have swallowed humanity entirely if God had not, by an act of grace, saved Noah from the Flood (Noah's ark is a symbol of the church and of baptism, cf. I Peter 3:20).

After the Flood, God promised Noah that he would never again destroy humanity by water. (Gen. 9:15.) However, on the last day the fire of divine holiness will consume all that is impure; testing is the fire that purifies the church before the last days, thus sparing it at the final consummation (I Cor. 3:12-15; II Peter 3:7).

31. The Revised Standard Version omits the italicized words " by signs," which are found in the Greek text (cf. Ch. Brutsch, *L'Apocalypse de Jesus-Christ,* p. 19, and the note on p. 34).

32. The number twelve, and its multiples (Rev. 7:4-8), stands for " fullness " in Biblical language, and these 144,000 stand for all Israel. Does this refer to a promise of salvation addressed to the people of Israel in terms of Rom. 11:25-26 (" all Israel will be saved ") or to Israel according to faith, i.e., to the church?

The opinions of the commentators differ on this point. The passage in Rev. 14:3 seems to favor the latter hypothesis, and would seem to refer to the first fruits of the church (Rev. 14:1-5; 20:1-6; cf. I Cor. 15:23), whose resurrection precedes the final call addressed to all people, and the Final Judgment (Rev. 14:6-13; 20:12; 7:9-12).